CAMPAIGN FOR PRESIDENT

CAMPAIGN FOR PRESIDENT

The Managers Look at 2012

**The Institute of Politics
John F. Kennedy School
of Government
Harvard University**

ROWMAN & LITTLEFIELD PUBLISHERS, INC.
Lanham • Boulder • New York • Toronto • Plymouth, UK

Published in partnership with the Institute of Politics, John F. Kennedy School of Government, Harvard University

Published by Rowman & Littlefield Publishers, Inc.
A wholly owned subsidiary of The Rowman & Littlefield Publishing Group, Inc.
4501 Forbes Boulevard, Suite 200, Lanham, Maryland 20706
www.rowman.com

10 Thornbury Road, Plymouth PL6 7PP, United Kingdom

British Library Cataloguing in Publication Information Available

Library of Congress Cataloging-in-Publication Data Available
ISBN 978-1-4422-2246-5 (cloth : alk. paper)—ISBN 978-1-4422-2247-2 (pbk. : alk. paper)—ISBN 978-1-4422-2248-9 (electronic)

∞™ The paper used in this publication meets the minimum requirements of American National Standard for Information Sciences Permanence of Paper for Printed Library Materials, ANSI/NISO Z39.48-1992.

Printed in the United States of America

CONTENTS

THE PARTICIPANTS

David Axelrod
Senior Advisor
Obama for America
Member
Institute of Politics Senior
Advisory Committee

Brian Baker
President and General
Counsel
Ending Spending Action
Fund

Dan Balz
Chief Political Correspondent
The Washington Post

Rich Beeson
Political Director
Romney for President, Inc.

Rick Berke
Member
Institute of Politics Senior
Advisory Committee
Assistant Managing Editor
The New York Times

Jeremy Bird
Field Director
Obama for America

Mark Block
Chief of Staff
Herman Cain

Gloria Borger
Chief Political Analyst
CNN

John Brabender
Senior Advisor
Rick Santorum

Ron Brownstein
Editorial Director
National Journal

Bill Burton
Senior Strategist
Priorities USA Action and
Priorities USA

Dave Carney
Strategist
Rick Perry

Jan Crawford
Political Correspondent
CBS News

Stephanie Cutter
Deputy Campaign Manager
Obama for America

Matt David
Campaign Manager
Jon Huntsman

Frank Fahrenkopf
Cochair
Commission on Presidential
Debates

Eric Fehrnstrom
Senior Advisor
Romney for President, Inc.

Peter Flaherty
Senior Advisor
Romney for President, Inc.

Carl Forti
Political Director
American Crossroads

Gail Gitcho
Communications Director
Romney for President, Inc.

Teddy Goff
Digital Director
Obama for America

Trey Grayson
Director
Institute of Politics

Vince Haley
Campaign Manager
Newt Gingrich

Linda Hansen
Deputy Chief of Staff
Herman Cain

Gwen Ifill
Moderator and Managing
Editor
Washington Week
Senior Correspondent
The PBS Newshour

Rob Johnson
Campaign Manager
Rick Perry

Jonathan Karl
Senior Political
Correspondent
ABC News

Ron Kaufman
Senior Advisor
Romney for President, Inc.

Steven Law
President and CEO
American Crossroads

Jim Margolis
Senior Advisor
Obama for America

Jonathan Martin
Senior Political Reporter
POLITICO

Morgan Martinez
Director of Digital Strategy
Buddy Roemer

Jim Messina
Campaign Manager
Obama for America

Zac Moffatt
Digital Director
Romney for President, Inc.

Phil Musser
Senior Advisor
Tim Pawlenty

Beth Myers
Senior Advisor
Romney for President, Inc.

Keith Nahigian
Campaign Manager
Michele Bachmann

Ana Navarro
Senior Strategist
Jon Huntsman

Neil Newhouse
Director of Polling
Romney for President, Inc.

Brett O'Donnell
Senior Policy Advisor
Michele Bachmann
Fall 2012 Fellow
Institute of Politics

Trygve Olson
Senior Advisor
Ron Paul

Matt Rhoades
Campaign Manager
Romney for President, Inc.

Lois Romano
Senior Political Writer
POLITICO

Nick Ryan
Founder
Red, White and Blue Fund

Russ Schriefer
Strategist
Romney for President, Inc.

Dan Senor
Senior Advisor to
Congressman Ryan
Romney for President, Inc.

Carlos Sierra
Campaign Manager
Buddy Roemer

David Simas
Director of Opinion Research
Obama for America

Charlie Spies
Treasurer
Restore our Future

Stuart Stevens
Strategist
Romney for President, Inc.

Bob White
Chairman
Romney for President, Inc.

THE OBSERVERS

Anne Aaron
John F. Kennedy Library
Foundation

Jill Abramson
The New York Times

Sam Adams
Harvard College

Jonathan Alter
Bloomberg

Eric Andersen
Institute of Politics

Andrew Antrobus
Pfizer

Megan Badasch
Republican National
Committee (RNC)

Christina Bain
Harvard Kennedy School

Robert Barber
New England Steering
Committee for Obama

Katie Biber
Romney for President, Inc.

Jim Bildner
Harvard Kennedy School

Meredith Blake
Institute of Politics

Kevin Bohn
CNN

Sheila Burke
Harvard Kennedy School

John Carr
Institute of Politics Fellows
Program

David Chalian
POLITICO

Elaine Chao
Institute of Politics Senior
Advisory Committee

Lanhee Chen
Romney for President, Inc.

Tom Cochran
U.S. Conference of Mayors

Kerri Collins
Institute of Politics

Darrell Crate
Romney for President, Inc.

Callie Crossley
Nieman Foundation for
Journalism

Amin Cyntje
University of Chicago
Institute of Politics

Carlos Rosillo Diaz
Harvard University

John Dickerson
Slate Magazine

Jim Doyle
Institute of Politics Fellows
Program

Nina Easton
Institute of Politics Fellows
Program

Sam Feist
CNN

William Feltus
National Media Research
Planning and Placement LLC

Mason Fink
Romney for President, Inc.

Christian Flynn
Institute of Politics

Amanda Fuchs Miller
Seventh Street Strategies

Katie Packer Gage
Romney for President, Inc.

Heather Gain
Institute of Politics

Marshall Ganz
Harvard Kennedy School

Taegan Goddard
Political Wire

David Gregory
Moderator
*Meet the Press with David
Gregory*
Political Wire

Charlie Haight
Harvard Kennedy School

Tony Halmos
City of London Corporation

Mark Halperin
Time Magazine

Peter Hamby
CNN

John Harwood
CNBC

John Heilemann
New York Magazine

Fred Hochberg
Export-Import Bank of the
United States

Edie Holway
Joan Shorenstein Center on
the Press, Politics and Public
Policy

Amy Howell
Institute of Politics

Sasha Issenberg
Slate Magazine

Jyoti Jasrasaria
Obama for America

Alex Jones
Harvard Kennedy School

Lee Kalema
Institute of Politics

Elaine Kamarck
Harvard Kennedy School

Caroline Kennedy
Institute of Politics Senior
Advisory Committee

John King
CNN

Kyle Kondik
University of Virginia

Michael Kranish
The Boston Globe

Jill Lawrence
National Journal

Mark Leibovich
The New York Times

Eric Lesser
Harvard Law School

Vivien Li
Boston Harbor Association

Ryan Lizza
The New Yorker

Kent Lucken
Citi Private Bank

Dotty Lynch
American University

Mark McKinnon
Institute of Politics Fellows
Program

Catherine McLaughlin
Institute of Politics

Eileen McMenamin
Bipartisan Policy Center

Ari Melber
The Nation

Zeke Miller
Buzzfeed

Susan Milligan
U.S.News & World Report

Nick Mitropoulos
Monitor Group

Christine Moore
The New York Times

Ashley O'Connor
Romney for President, Inc.

Casey O'Neill
Institute of Politics

Nancy Palmer
Harvard Kennedy School

Cathey Park
Institute of Politics

Ashley Parker
The New York Times

Mark Preston
CNN

Joe Roxe
Harvard Kennedy School
Dean's Council

Phil Rucker
The Washington Post

Jim Rutenberg
The New York Times

Kellie Ryan
Institute of Politics

Anthony Salvanto
CBS News

Michael Scherer
Time Magazine

Christian Scheucher
Christian Scheucher
Consulting

Karly Schledwitz
Harvard Kennedy School

Robert Schlesinger
U.S.News & World Report

Julie Schroeder
Institute of Politics

Sonal Shah
Institute of Politics Fellows
Program

Walter Shapiro
Yahoo! News

Harry Sherr
Harvard Kennedy School
Dean's Council

Laura Simolaris
Institute of Politics

Roger Simon
POLITICO

Jon Sisk
Rowman and Littlefield
Publishers

Jeff Solnet
Obama for America

Robin Sproul
ABC News

Richard Stevenson
The New York Times

John Sununu
New Hampshire Republican
Party

Lynn Sweet
Chicago Sun-Times

Annie Tomasini
Harvard University

Karen Tumulty
The Washington Post

Theresa Verbic
Institute of Politics

Sarah Wald
Harvard Kennedy School

Amy Walter
ABC News

Jon Ward
Huffington Post

Barbara Whalen
Harvard Kennedy School

Jeff Zeleny
The New York Times

Jason Zengerle
New York Magazine

Peter Zimmerman
Harvard Kennedy School

Spencer Zwick
Romney for President, Inc.

INTRODUCTION

This book documents the quadrennial campaign decision-makers con-ference hosted by the Institute of Politics at the Harvard Kennedy School after every presidential election since 1972. Forty years after that first gathering, much has changed, but the personal stories and insights into the decisions made by candidates and their campaigns still

Institute of Politics Director Trey Grayson kicks off the conference.

teach us a great deal about American politics and our presidential election system.

The 2012 election was unique in many ways. We saw record amounts of money spent on the election with major candidates rejecting public financing and the proliferation of super PACs and other independent groups, which led to TV airwaves being bombarded with ads for months leading up to Election Day. We also saw traditional polling outlets such as Gallup struggle to accurately sample an electorate that featured fewer traditional landline phones and more young and minority voters.

Technology played a role in a way that nobody could have imagined as campaigns utilized mobile phones and social media, like Twitter and Facebook, to communicate with supporters and potential supporters and to turn out the vote. (For example, we learned President Obama supporters were Facebook friends with 98 percent of U.S. voters). In addition, both campaigns, but especially the Obama campaign, used data and analytics in a more systematic and comprehensive way to more efficiently and effectively recruit volunteers, target and shape TV ads, craft e-mails and mailers, raise money, and, most importantly, identify new voters in the battleground states. Despite all of this technology, Barack Obama's campaign manager, Jim Messina, told us, "The single most surprising thing that we learned is that door-knocking matters more than anything."

The Republican primary was marked by numerous debates and a cycle of different candidates rising and falling seemingly every week to compete with former Massachusetts Governor Mitt Romney before Romney was able to secure the nomination. President Obama avoided a primary and overcame a struggling economy and a 2010 midterm election setback for his party to win a comfortable Electoral College victory.

In addition to looking back, these discussions are important for our next elections. Future campaign staff and candidates can use these conversations to learn what worked and what didn't. While we can't predict the new technologies or entities that may be in place when we call this conference together forty years from now, we, at the Institute of Politics (IOP), take pride in knowing that this book can serve as a resource for those involved and for those covering the campaigns.

The conference and this book could not have happened without the hard work of our staff at the Institute. Cathy McLaughlin and Christian Flynn managed the complex logistics of the conference and the production of this book with Casey O'Neill. Amanda Fuchs Miller edited the transcript. Harvard student Sam Adams (class of 2014) compiled the election timeline.

The actual conference was interrupted by a large power outage that impacted much of Cambridge. We continued talking in the dark for forty minutes with emergency generators providing only minimal power while Institute of Politics and Harvard Kennedy School staff worked to keep everyone informed and safe. Unfortunately, we had to cut short the discussion by about forty-five minutes, but thanks to the Voice Memo app on several iPhones, we were able to record the "dark" session for posterity.

In conclusion, I want to thank the campaign decision-makers and journalists who participated in this year's conference. Their openness and willingness to share insights and lessons learned will have a long-lasting impact on political campaigns. More importantly, their dedication to public service is what makes this country great.

Trey Grayson
Director, Institute of Politics
February 2013

EDITOR'S NOTE

On November 28 and 29, 2012, the Institute of Politics brought campaign managers, senior advisers, political analysts, and journalists to Harvard University to discuss the 2012 presidential campaign. The following is a transcript of the five sections of the conference. The transcript has been slightly edited to make it easier to follow, but for the most part, the text is a verbatim transcript so that readers can place themselves at the table of these conversations and hear about what happened in the voices of the campaign decision-makers. At the end of the book there is an abridged timeline of key events from the 2012 election cycle.

This year, the Institute of Politics, for the first time, released a podcast of the conference several weeks after the event so that the narrative of the campaigns could get out to a broader audience in a shorter amount of time. To listen to the recordings of the conference, please visit the Institute of Politics website at www.iop.harvard.edu.

One other note: In the midst of the last panel discussion on the general election, Cambridge, Massachusetts, experienced a citywide power outage that forced the conference to be cut short. Everyone did their best to wrap up the discussion—by the lights of their computers and smartphones—and the transcript was able to capture almost all of it in its entirety. However, there were several speakers who couldn't be identified and readers will see them noted by the campaign they were representing.

We hope that as you read the transcript of the conference, you get a true sense of what was unique about the 2012 elections and gain a better understanding of why what you witnessed happened the way it did.

Amanda Fuchs Miller

I

THE DECISION TO RUN FOR PRESIDENT

TREY GRAYSON: Good evening, everybody. I'm Trey Grayson. I'm the director of the Institute of Politics. And on behalf of the staff, the students, the Senior Advisory Committee of the Institute of Politics, and everybody else here at Harvard, we want to welcome you to our quadrennial campaign decision-makers conference. We've been doing this since 1972. A lot of people in this room weren't even born in 1972. We're really excited to bring everybody together to preserve for history, for scholars, and for future campaign folks the story of the 2012 election. I want to thank especially all the folks who were involved in those campaigns and in covering those campaigns for coming today. We're looking forward to a great conversation. I would like to introduce Rick Berke, a member of the Senior Advisory Committee of the Institute of Politics and the assistant managing editor of the *New York Times*, and Dan Balz, chief correspondent for the *Washington Post*. [*applause*]

RICK BERKE: Trey mentioned that this started in 1972. No one else has ever done anything like it. There have been imitators all over the place but no one like the IOP. That book that you get months later is a real historic record of these campaigns. And what I was wondering, when Trey mentioned 1972, is what was that like? Can you imagine the Nixon and McGovern group in this room? Now, what I want to know is, was anyone in this room? There are a lot of old-timers around here. Anyone in this room who was there then, raise your hand. All right, Frank Fahrenkopf, what was it like? Was Haldeman here? We have the book that would show '72 and the discussion but they probably missed out on the real drama, which was happening behind the scenes and that unfolded in the years hence. Let me just say that these events are wonderful, but also not so wonderful for people like me and many of the reporters here, because we all want to hear all these secrets from the campaign and we want you guys from the campaigns to spill your guts. But then if you do and we didn't have the story, then we look bad. So it's kind of a mixed thing. So we want to hear stories but we will be angry if you didn't tell us things that we needed to know in real time. So that's kind of our dilemma for reporters.

One person who loved coming to these things was our departed esteemed colleague, David Broder. My favorite quote from him after one of these was, after the '96 election, when he said, "Obviously, the 1996 campaign was not a classic." That was Dan's understated colleague. Now this one, I would say, while it wasn't historic like the one four years ago, I would call it a classic in terms of the surprises and the things that we didn't expect. Think about the speculation two or three years ago. How many of you in this room would have expected, if I had asked you two or three years ago, that someone representing the Sarah Palin campaign would be here tonight? So the world has changed from what we expected. [*laughter*]

I did some looking back to where things were two, three years ago. Romney was on the top of the list of all of the pundits. All of the political people were saying, everyone knew that he would be running. But there were more people we thought would run than actually ran. Remember Huckabee, Barbour, Jindal, Bush, Jeb Bush, Giuliani, Mitch Daniels, Condoleezza Rice? None of those people are represented here. And one of my favorites on the list that popped up was Paul Ryan. Can you imagine if he had run and the debates and what he and Mitt Romney would have been saying about each other in that debate? Think how the history of the whole campaign could have been different. Scott Brown was on that list; there was early speculation that he would run for president. And let me just say one other thing about Sarah Palin. We were so sure that she would be a factor in this campaign that a certain brilliant editor at the *New York Times*, that was me, went to the executive editor, Jill Abramson, and I said, "Shouldn't we get a full-time Sarah Palin reporter? And we'll be ahead of everyone." And you know what Jill said? "Great idea, Rick." [*laughter*] But the world changed so fast that we didn't end up doing that. Although I remember Jim Rutenberg[1] and a crew of other reporters flew to Alaska when they released her e-mails from her governorship because everyone took her very seriously. Now, my all-time favorite on the list of people who had been talked about, two, three years ago, that popped

---

1. Jim Rutenberg is a political correspondent for the *New York Times*.

up on this list was David Petraeus.[2] Just imagine that and imagine how much fun that would have been for all of us.

I want to say this campaign will be remembered for a lot of things, not just 9-9-9[3] or the Obama debate[4] or 47 percent[5] or Clint Eastwood,[6] and not only the surprises. This is one campaign that I remember where everyone who stayed in the race had their moment in the sun, it seemed like. Just about everyone was a front-runner for at least a day or two. I'd never seen that before. It was also the campaign of the super PACs.[7] Fact-checking proliferated in a way we've never seen before, truth-squadding the campaigns. More polling, if you could believe that that could ever happen. So now as we start launching into our examination of all this, I just want to advise all of the campaign people who so graciously decided to attend this event that we're all looking for candor and tight remarks, because we all see through campaign spin and this event has never been an event for bloviators or spinning. So just tell the truth. You can settle some scores, if you want. We like that. [*laughter*] But keep it tight. Tell the truth. Give us some secrets, but not secrets that will embarrass the reporters in the room. So if you could do all that, that would be great. Now, to lead us off is my colleague, Dan Balz, who is one of the most respected and fair-minded journalists in America today. Dan, take it away. [*applause*]

DAN BALZ: Thank you, Rick. I'm going to throw fair-mindedness to the winds tonight and be edgy and all the things that nobody thinks I really am or can be. [*laughter*] And as for secrets that embarrass us, we're prepared for that. You've spent most of the last year-and-a-half trying to embarrass us in one way or another and you think that we've tried to spend the last year-and-a-half trying to embarrass you guys in one way or another, so I would say we should all have at it. I'm pleased to be a part of this opening ceremony of this great tradition. I want to echo what others have said and just say thank you to everybody from the IOP

---

2. In November 2012 General Petraeus resigned from his position as director of the CIA when his extramarital affair was discovered in the course of an FBI investigation.

3. 9-9-9 was Herman Cain's tax reform plan based on a 9 percent corporate tax, a 9 percent personal income tax and a 9 percent national sales tax.

4. Obama had a poor debate performance in his first presidential debate against Romney in Denver on October 3, 2012.

5. In September 2012 a videotape was released from a Romney fundraiser in which Romney said, "There are 47 percent of the people who will vote for the president no matter what," and those are people who are "dependent upon government, who believe that they are victims, who believe the government has a responsibility to care for them, who believe that they are entitled to health care, to food, to housing, to you-name-it."

6. At his speech at the Republican convention, Clint Eastwood had a conversation with an empty chair, representing President Obama.

7. Super PACs are political committees whose primary purpose is to influence elections and that can take unlimited amounts of money, outside of federal contribution limits, from individuals, unions, and corporations, as long as they are independent and not coordinated with the candidate.

who has worked so hard to make this the event that it is. It's one of those events that everybody who's been involved in the campaign, on whatever side you're involved, wants to be at. It's both a homecoming and a moment to kind of relive everything. It's in large form what we often do at night at the end of the campaign day, which is to gather with people from the campaign and compare notes and talk a little bit off the record. And as, allegedly, Katharine Graham once said, "What does off the record mean? It means we don't do anything with it unless it's just too good." [laughter]

We have a lot of ground to cover tonight. We have eleven campaigns that we want to hear from. The rules of the road are that one person from each campaign will be asked to tell us a little bit about what the opening strategy was, where things were at the beginning of the campaign. We've asked people, as Rick said, to keep it brief. Rick will be the timekeeper. He looks like he's a very nice guy but for those of us who have competed against him over the years, we know he's got a mean streak, so don't cross him tonight on the running long. We want to get out of here by midnight, no later than that, so we'll go.

They say there are no do-overs in life. Tonight is do-over night. Tomorrow you'll all have to explain what went wrong, what didn't work out. Tonight we are interested in where things were at the beginning. In a sense, tonight you are all potential winners. This is where the campaign started. We are asking each person from the campaign to step back and recreate for us the thinking inside the operation as you sketched out your strategy. What was the rationale? What was the path to victory? We would like to get, if we can, a better sense of the analysis that ended with your particular candidate becoming the nominee of the Republican Party or perhaps taking the oath in January or, for others, perhaps a campaign that would end with somebody being the host of a new cable talk show. Or in the case of Mark Block, a pitch man for a tobacco company.[8] [laughter] To prod the conversation along, I am going to pose a question to each campaign that will work to complement the basic idea that we want to learn about their strategy. We are going in no particular order, other than that the Romney and Obama campaigns will be the last we will hear from tonight. They will bat clean-up in this. Other than that, I didn't have a particular sense of how we should do this but because Tim Pawlenty was the first out, Phil Musser from the Pawlenty campaign will be the first at bat tonight. Phil, the floor is yours. [applause]

---

8. Cain's campaign manager Mark Block appeared in a fifty-six-second ad in which he urges voters to support Cain and then takes a drag on a cigarette and blows smoke at the camera.

••• TIM PAWLENTY •••

PHIL MUSSER: I talked to Pawlenty this afternoon. I was driving across Massachusetts, and I said, "You know, Governor, I'm going to this thing you boldly nominated me for. What should I say?" He said, "Look, my campaign lasted for thirty seconds, so pack it into thirty seconds, Musser." So I'll be brief. But I'll try and frame a little bit of the thinking that you asked us to do, Dan, and talk about that. And thanks for having us here. Pawlenty started very early. If you think back to it, Tim started laying the groundwork to run for president in late 2009. And I think we essentially probably prodded Matt and the Romney team into a more proactive, forward-leading focus with their own PAC. Tim was a successful two-term governor from a blue state who had proven his ability to win with Independents. The Sam's Club message, I think, was attractive and appealing to a demographic that we thought we needed to win with and we could win with.

From a perspective of a policy accomplishment, we thought Pawlenty had a very strong record with respect to accomplishments in pension reform, health care, education, a lot of really good things to talk about. And he's just about the most likeable, nice, genuine, decent human

Phil Musser, Tim Pawlenty's campaign manager, talks about their "second-place" candidate strategy.

being that you could possibly find. We thought that would play well relative to the retail politics required in the early states of Iowa and New Hampshire. So we went about the business through 2009 and 2010, I think, of trying to build through the invisible primary phase, leveraging our role at the RGA,[9] leveraging our travel around the country to build relationships where we didn't have them. Tim's biggest challenge was he was largely unknown outside the state of Minnesota, but for the brief 2008 flirtation with vice president. We sought to build what we would call the Ford Taurus model presidential campaign, which was a modestly budgeted, appropriately scaled campaign that had the depths and scale to be able to grow when application of money and attention focused on it. And so, as we came into the early months of March and February of 2011, there are two things that I would highlight, one of which was touched on which was that the early going was extraordinarily difficult. Because in our view, the Romney campaign probably had about 30 percent of market share locked up that we figured they would have. And we figured that was roughly corollary, if not slightly greater, with the financial commitment. But what we had real trouble with, and what everybody who wasn't Romney had real trouble with, late in 2010 after the elections, was locking down major financial supporters. Romney moved quickly with a very aggressive, very focused, very well-led exercise to lock down big financial contributors. They looked down the road. They set up a super PAC very wisely and smartly. Laws allowed for that this go-round, but didn't four years ago, which I say from some experience. Competing for financial donors was a real challenge for us. But, nonetheless, we came to the starting blocks in this race thinking that we had some regional association. Tim was an Evangelical conservative. He had a record that was attractive and appealing to conservatives.

We thought we were the electable alternative to Romney and that, ultimately, when the party looked around, besides Mitt, that if we were standing and we were in a position to finance and grow, that that was the right place to be. I don't think we're supposed to go into what we did wrong until tomorrow. But Terry Branstad[10] is a wise man, and so is Nick Ryan.[11] Anyway, that was our mindset coming into the game, Dan.

DAN BALZ: Let me ask just one quick follow-up, Phil, and that is, was there any other option that you thought might be possible, other than

9.   Pawlenty served as vice chairman of the Republican Governors Association during the 2010 election cycle.
10.   Terry Branstad is the governor of Iowa.
11.   Nick Ryan is an Iowa Republican political consultant who headed the pro-Santorum super PAC, the Red, White and Blue Fund.

what I would call the slow and steady idea and the notion that if you could become everybody's second favorite candidate, then you could emerge? Was there any other alternative that you thought about that might have made sense?

PHIL MUSSER: We didn't want to say it. We didn't want to call ourselves the second-place strategy candidate, but we were the second-place strategy candidate. We just never gave that the time to play out. It isn't great to be going to your donors and say, "Hey, look, we're the second-place guy." [*laughter*] Get on board with this bus. And I had to do a lot of the pitching, so it was hard. But, no. Look, we believed that slow and steady would ultimately pay dividends and that the spadework in the grassroots effort in Iowa in particular, and subsequently, he had a great team in New Hampshire, could have provided us probably the platform for growth at the right time. And I think had we had an up elevator lift out of the June debate as opposed to a collapse.[12] After launching the campaign with what I thought was a good announcement, whether you agree with the policy or not, an ambitious growth policy agenda, the next plan was to ramp that up leading into that debate. And that debate was obviously a critical moment for our campaign. But then a funny thing happened along the way in the circus, and Nahigian and his bus and Michele Bachmann showed up. And that undercut the Iowa straw poll strategy, which for those of you who have done the Iowa straw poll, you just don't wake up and think about it and do it. I mean, Nahigian and the Michele Bachmann team put together a straw poll caucus with incredible speed and won it in an incredibly short period of time. The Ron Paul people and our people had been working on that since essentially February. It's not something that you can kind of get half pregnant on and then pull back on because you guys would have just killed us in the boom of expectations. We discussed the decisions going forward there. But, yeah, Dan, the quiet thinking was if we can be alive and then get the spotlight and have the architecture of a campaign that is the Ford Taurus to the Romney Mercedes, then we could grow.

DAN BALZ: Thank you. Next we'll do the Ron Paul campaign. Trygve, where are you? [*applause*]

---

12. In June 2011, at a New Hampshire Republican primary debate, Pawlenty failed to attack Romney on health care as he had done previously and he tried to back away from his past attack of calling Governor Romney's health care law "Obamneycare."

••• RON PAUL •••

TRYGVE OLSON: It's nice that we can all be friends here now. The Paul campaign started out as a continuation of what started in 2008. In some ways, it was a campaign about Ron Paul, but it was equally sort of movement politics in some ways. During the course of 2008 through 2012 the broader Ron Paul entities raised over a hundred million dollars, which probably surprises a lot of people. So as we were sitting looking at the campaign from the outset, we felt like raising money, unlike Phil's situation, was not really going to be an issue. And I, as sort of the establishment guy who was somewhat new to Ron Paul world, found it a little bit disturbing, because I would say to them, "We don't have any money in the bank." They'd be, "Oh don't worry. We're going to money bomb. We'll have a million dollars by Tuesday." One strategic assumption was that other than Mitt Romney's campaign we would have the second-most money to spend. We knew that we weren't going to be able to match Romney in terms of big-dollar donors, but we also knew that we had a lot of people that would give repeat donations based on ideas. Second strategic assumption that we had is that there were a lot of people in the early primary states, particularly Iowa, who were not

Trygve Olson, Ron Paul's campaign manager, lays out the four strategic goals of their campaign.

well informed with who Ron Paul was, even though Ron Paul is a national figure. When I first came on the campaign, which was in March of 2011, we went and did some polling, which wasn't something they had done a lot of in Iowa. We discovered 50 percent of Iowa Republicans assumed Ron Paul was pro-choice. And here he is, a doctor who's delivered 4,000 babies and is pro-life. So we looked at the campaign and we thought, there's some real opportunities to reinvent or educate people on Ron Paul. Hence, the importance of good advertising to the campaign, which was something that I think we really tried to do. We had a long debate about whether Iowa was going to be the place that we'd play, or New Hampshire. That obviously had strategic implications for us in terms of how we would interact with other candidates. Ultimately, when Pawlenty got out of the race, we decided that Iowa was the place where we really had a shot at winning. We thought we could get 20 to 25 percent, but in order for us to get there, we knew Romney was going to have an establishment percent. That meant when Newt Gingrich rises, Herman Cain rises, Rick Perry rises, Michele Bachmann rises, we felt like we had to take them down, because we had a ceiling of 25 percent.

We knew Romney was going to be somewhere in that range. We didn't really have the opportunity to let anybody get to 30. So we were constantly trying to take people down. But, and this was an assumption from the outset, we didn't play on the establishment field. The establishment Republicans weren't going to vote for Ron Paul. Tea Party Republicans, potentially. Social conservatives, potentially. Definitely Libertarians. We had four basic strategic goals.

RICK BERKE: I'm sorry to interrupt, because it's my role to interrupt. But I just want to know, you said he wasn't a mainstream candidate. Did you ever think internally that you could win the nomination?

TRYGVE OLSON: Well what I would say is from the outset and first conversations that we had with Ron, the goal was to get as many delegates as possible. They felt like if you could get to a position where it was a one-on-one race with somebody, you never know what was going to happen.

RICK BERKE: Did you or Ron Paul or any of the people say, "If we do this and this, we can win the nomination?" Or was that just a sort of dream?

TRYGVE OLSON: Well I think within the professional political class within Ron Paul's world, there was a realization that it was a long shot for Ron Paul to get the nomination.

RICK BERKE: So you never really expected to get the nomination? I mean, let's just be realistic here. [*laughter*] I mean, seriously.

TRYGVE OLSON: The strategic objective from the outset was to get as many votes as possible. What I would say is, did Ronald Reagan expect in 1968 to get the nomination?

FROM THE FLOOR: Yes. [*laughter*]

DAN BALZ: I do have a further follow-up, and that is to what extent, Trygve, was the goal of the campaign to, in essence, mainstream Ron Paul's ideas into the party, and what was the strategy of that? That obviously connected with your goal to get as many delegates as possible, I assume.

TRYGVE OLSON: So four strategic goals. One, get as many delegates as possible. Two, to create a platform where Ron Paul could talk about his ideas. Obviously, the professional and political class would have preferred he stick more to debt and deficit, devaluation of the dollar and defense of liberties. He decided that he would like to talk about defense policy and foreign intervention, which was more problematic because it was incongruent with the Republican primary electorate. Third, Ron believed, and this, I think, is important, that the young people who were coming out who were Libertarian belong in the Republican Party and that he needed to contest this campaign in part to say to the Republican Party, Libertarians are an important part of a winning coalition for you. You want 5,000 young people to show up at the University of Wisconsin. If your name isn't Barack Obama, Ron Paul can get that. I don't think there's any other Republican candidate here who can get that. He thinks that's important. But at the same time, he wanted to say to Libertarians, there's a home in the Republican Party for you. You can go to the convention. The last strategic goal was to create, and leave, his movement as part of a coalition in the Libertarian party with more leaders. That gets confused a lot with, Rand Paul 2016 or 2020, but it was not just about Rand Paul. Rand Paul clearly will be a leader of the Libertarian movement. It was also about electing people like Congressman Thomas Massie in Kentucky, another Libertarian, and Congressman Justin Amash, and really try to build a longer term effort of what should be an important part of a revamped Republican coalition. He didn't feel like he was anymore of a long shot, let's be quite frank, than anybody other than Mitt Romney, after Tim Pawlenty got out of the race. I mean, the truth is there's a 99 percent chance, and I don't mean to offend any of the other candidates. All the rest of this was semantics, from our perspective. Mitt Romney was likely to be the nominee. And so did Ron Paul have less of a chance, really, than Herman Cain, who got a lot more coverage? That would be my answer to your question.

••• HERMAN CAIN •••

DAN BALZ: We will turn now to Mark Block to answer that question. Mark, coming off of what Rick asked Trygve, it is hard to imagine that there was a sense within the Cain campaign that Herman Cain was going to become the Republican nominee.

MARK BLOCK: Bullshit. [*laughter*] And I say that in all due respect. [*laughter*]

DAN BALZ: Then explain to us what that path was.

Mark Block, Herman Cain's campaign manager, says it was the Tea Party movement that propelled Cain to run.

MARK BLOCK: We all got an e-mail from Dan earlier to keep this under five minutes and, Dan, do you know how long it takes to smoke a cigarette? About four and a half minutes. [*laughter*] We always felt that Cain could win the nomination. Cain's candidacy really came about on April 15, 2009. And I have to say hello to our governor from Wisconsin, Jim Doyle, because he actually helped the Cain campaign explode in Wisconsin. The Tea Party movement, really, was the gist of the Cain candidacy. On April 15, 2009, we saw this movement explode.[13] Cain was giving speeches across the country to Tea Party groups and to business groups, and those that have heard him talk, he's a very motivational speaker. He would always be asked, you should run for president. You should run for president. I had known Mr. Cain for eight years now and the deputy director, Linda Hansen, had been working with him for about three years. And we kept encouraging him to consider it, think about it. By the way, if anybody here tells you that they know what the Tea Party movement is, they're lying to you. Because I don't think anybody, including the media, has really got a handle on what that movement is. I still don't think we know what the Tea Party movement is. But it was that movement that propelled Mr. Cain, as he kept looking at whether he should run or not, to do it, because of the response he got.

DAN BALZ: Let me just briefly interject. If you didn't know what that movement was, how did you think you could, in some way, either capture it or give voice to it?

MARK BLOCK: When you have 15,000 people show up at the lakefront in Milwaukee for a rally, you know there is something out there. You really don't know what it is. A typical Tea Party person, I still don't think has been defined yet. It's the kind of crowds that would come to hear Herman Cain talk, the type of donors that would encourage him to do it. So as we walked through this process, and we had a six stage process before he made the final decision to run, every time we hit one of these it was positive, go forward. He, himself, would tell you that he wanted to become a candidate because, at that point in time when he made the decision over Christmas in 2010, he didn't think that the Republican Party really had a candidate that could win. And he felt that he could do it.

---

13.   When Mark Block was State Director of Americans for Prosperity in Wisconsin, on April 15, 2009, he organized the Madison Tea Party rally, the largest taxpayer rally in Wisconsin history, with over 8,800 people attending.

DAN BALZ: In that case, if you had that kind of confidence, what was the path that would get you to the nomination?

MARK BLOCK: I have to give credit to David Plouffe's[14] book *Audacity to Win*. That was standard reading for anybody who came onto the staff. And we followed their blueprint, just like in Wisconsin. We followed the Colorado blueprint and flipping the state of Wisconsin. We followed a lot of the stuff in *Audacity to Win*. People would ask me, what are you doing in Bismarck, North Dakota, in February when you should be in Iowa? I'm sure all the other campaigns would say, "You guys, you should be in Iowa." Our strategy was to work a lot of the back states, the back end, and get those locked down, then come into Iowa. We made a strategic decision not to compete in the Iowa Caucuses and to concentrate on Florida, which we'll get into tomorrow, and that strategy worked.

DAN BALZ: It worked in what sense? [*laughter*]

MARK BLOCK: We came out of Florida as a winner.

DAN BALZ: You mean in the straw poll?

MARK BLOCK: The straw poll, yeah.

DAN BALZ: Had you studied the Giuliani campaign's late state strategy from four years earlier? I mean, the notion that you can ignore the early states—

MARK BLOCK: We didn't ignore them, Dan. I didn't say we ignored them. We just spent a lot of time early on in a lot of the other states.

DAN BALZ: I guess the question I'm trying to get at, Mark, is you've got to win somewhere first. Where did you think your first win would be?

MARK BLOCK: We thought we would win Iowa and New Hampshire and Florida and South Carolina. And, I think if he would have stayed in the race we would have won those.

DAN BALZ: All right. Well we will find out more about that tomorrow. Thank you. Matt David from the Huntsman Campaign?

---

14. David Plouffe was senior advisor to the president in the White House and managed Obama's 2008 presidential campaign.

••• JOHN HUNTSMAN •••

MATT DAVID: Thank you, Dan. Unfortunately, there wasn't a big secret behind our strategy. It was New Hampshire or bust. And we experienced the latter. [*laughter*] We knew we needed two things to be successful in New Hampshire. First, we needed a decent media budget to improve our name ID, which was approximately zero in New Hampshire. And, number two, we needed someone to emerge to the right of Mitt Romney that posed a legitimate threat and would force him to defend his conservative credentials and effectively move him to the right. And if that happened it would open up even a narrow path for us in New Hampshire to his left. So we needed that to happen. We never felt like we could necessarily win New Hampshire because of Romney's lock on the state, but we felt like we could finish a strong second or a very close third, which would give us a little bit of momentum heading down into South Carolina. Now, we never really thought we could win South Carolina but we thought we could play defense. We thought we could fracture that moderate vote and prevent Romney from winning. And if we could do that, we could get down to Florida and it could be a wide open race. What we would need ultimately though would be for

Matt David, Jon Huntsman's campaign manager, discusses their need to be successful in New Hampshire.

conservatives to give us a second look, or a first look in reality. And to do that they would have to look past his service in the Obama Administration. But we felt like, given his conservative governing record in Utah, that we might be able to get over that hurdle.

RICK BERKE: Let me just ask, who besides Romney were you most fearful of?

MATT DAVID: Our focus was on Romney.

RICK BERKE: But was there one other person you were just eyeing?

MATT DAVID: We knew to get the nomination you had to go through Romney, period.

DAN BALZ: Matt, my question, and I think probably a lot of people who covered the campaign, is this: Was this always essentially a campaign in search of a candidate who never quite became that candidate? I mean that you guys did a lot of spadework before he ever came back from China. You had figured out kind of what you thought made the most sense based on what you thought Huntsman would be. He seemed like he was not always the most committed to the idea that you guys had. Can you give us any insight into the early stages, as you guys first laid it out to him, what was his level of enthusiasm, belief that it worked or reservations about what you guys had already put in place?

MATT DAVID: That's a really good question. There weren't any reservations initially. What I can say that we honestly struggled with was finding a message that he was comfortable delivering and one that resonated with the Republican electorate. And so we struggled with whether we were the truth teller, you know, for a couple of months in the middle of the summer. And then we kind of switched to the policy, Simpson-Bowles[15] and break up the banks, which are great policies, and you can put big red ribbons around them, but they weren't the tip of the sword that the electorate wanted in this cycle. So it's a very good question, and it's something we struggled with. I think at the end, we kind of caught our stride. The very last debate, literally three days before the New Hampshire election, was our best debate but it was frankly too late in the game.

---

15. Alan Simpson and Erskine Bowles served as cochairmen of the White House's 2010 deficit-reduction panel, which put together a bipartisan package of tax and spending changes.

DAN BALZ: Okay. Let me ask you just one more question on this. And that is, did you misjudge the state of the Republican Party?

MATT DAVID: Dan's got a lot of good questions. [*laughter*] Yeah, time. [*laughter*]

DAN BALZ: Touché.

MATT DAVID: Honestly, we may have. I think we believed that a moderate could make it through the Republican primary.

CARL FORTI: He did. [*laughter*]

MATT DAVID: Actually, it's a very fair point. But without sacrificing anything in the process, which would make them very competitive in a general election. That was our premise, and we tried to stick to that. Sometimes we were better at it than others, but that was our premise.

DAN BALZ: Good. Thank you, Matt. Vince Haley for the Gingrich campaign.

••• NEWT GINGRICH •••

VINCE HALEY: Thanks, Dan. In the case of the Gingrich campaign, we didn't tell the candidate what the deal was. He told us what his strategy was. [*laughter*] From the beginning what we wanted to do was run a change election against President Obama. That's where we wanted to end up. Therefore, we were going to run a change election in the primaries. It was not going to be a referendum election; it would be a change election. Therefore, the question was, what are the set of solutions that we were going to offer to the country to change the country. Obviously, analysts talk about this as a country ready for change. Clearly Newt was going to run a change election. So we offered a set of policy solutions. I was the policy director at the beginning of the campaign. Had our hands full. We talked about judges. We talked about brain research. The idea behind creating a broad framework of solutions was to try to enlarge the primary electorate. Gingrich didn't believe that he was going to have a better shot unless that primary electorate was enlarged and bringing in new voters into the Republican primary that had never voted before. So that was the design election from the beginning, all the way through the ups and downs of the summer. This strategy

Vince Haley, Gingrich's campaign manager, talks about their efforts to expand the Republican primary electorate.

also, right from the beginning, was always explicitly going to be a hundred percent positive. And through the debates and in a lot of gatherings—public gatherings, public debates, nonpresidential debates—especially in Iowa, Gingrich resorted to effectively a strategy of praising the other candidates, to great reception by the crowds in Iowa. You also saw this in the debates. While I don't think it was an explicit strategy in the debates, he also, many times, was very willing to aggressively challenge the bias of the debate questions.

DAN BALZ: I was going to say it was a hundred percent positive, except for debate moderators. [*laughter*]

VINCE HALEY: Yeah. And so, that in fact became a strategy, if you will, of the time. And did we think we could win? Yes, we thought we could win. It looked very bleak over the summer. In terms of the states we were focused on, clearly, Iowa and South Carolina, we knew we would always have a long haul winning New Hampshire. And slowly and steadily, he rose in the fall based upon this positive, solutions-oriented approach. And then also in the debates, he used the opportunity of things that were contemporary. For example, the super committee. He would aggressively challenge the super committee as an idea and offer practical solutions on how you come up with whatever the savings were that they were trying to find.

DAN BALZ: Let me ask a follow-up. Karen Tumulty, my colleague, who I think understands Gingrich better than anybody else in the room and who had endless conversations with him at various downs and ups, but usually after the downs. I remember after the departure of the first staff,[16] he had come up with ideas about how he was going to build a coalition that simply defied the logic of what we had seen in every previous campaign. Pet owners and things like that. Did you all accept that that was a viable path, or was this, as you said at the beginning, Newt designed the campaign he wanted to run and he was bound and determined to run it?

VINCE HALEY: Well you mentioned pet owners, so I might as well address that. [*laughter*] To get your newspapers sold and your media sold, you have to pick the most scintillating example. What he was trying to illustrate is that he wanted to have nontraditional conversations with the public. And to great critique by conservatives, the Obama campaign did this in spades. They were having President Obama in lots of different venues and talking lots in nontraditional ways that, for conservatives, we weren't comfortable with. So pets would be an outlandish example, but, for example, Newt often went to zoos and he talked to reporters at zoos. Well it turns out there are more people who go to zoos in this country than go to professional sporting events. So he wanted to carry on a conversation outside the context strictly of politics to enlarge the electorate. So that's what explains that.

DAN BALZ: Karen reminds us that another one was Chinese in Iowa.

VINCE HALEY: Sure. [*laughter*] Let me give you an example of that. In Iowa, there is a group called Strong America Now. And it had 50,000 people who signed a pledge that they would vote for a candidate who was in favor of reforming government. You may have heard Newt talk about Lean Six Sigma during the course of the debates, if you followed him closely.

DAN BALZ: Anyone here recall that? Yes.

---

16.   In June 2011 Gingrich's campaign staff resigned en masse.

VINCE HALEY: Our Gingrich guerilla team would be at someone's apartment, a more adolescent person on the team would say, "The first time he says 'Lean Six Sigma,' drink." Well the point of that was he was signaling to everybody who believed in modernizing government that he was going to be the champion. Well 50,000 primary voters in Iowa, that's pretty good if you can reach them because it's an electorate that's not that large. If you can get them to vote for him, that's a big payoff. I'll tell you a little story on that. Turns out if you go to LinkedIn, there is a group of 80,000 people who are in favor of Lean Six Sigma. From one day to the next, we organized a conference call to try to organize these folks and get them to support our campaign. We got 800 people in one day. So Gingrich was constantly thinking about how you appeal to different parts. For example, people who suffer from Alzheimer's. Now, he wanted to give speeches and talk about an initiative on brain research. Well everybody who's got somebody suffering from Alzheimer's or any kind of other brain degenerative disease were going to care about that. And that's going to be a Republican talking in nontraditionally Republican ways to try to grow an electorate.

DAN BALZ: Last question, Vince. And that is, why not just a campaign in which it's, I'm going to be the conservative candidate in this campaign? Just sort of focused on that as a way to defeat Romney.

VINCE HALEY: I think Newt communicated that in many ways, that he was the conservative candidate. Here is a guy who, in the mid-1990s, achieved enormous conservative accomplishments working with a Democratic president. Cut taxes, welfare reform, eleven million new jobs. So maybe he didn't emphasize that enough, but he had a record of conservative achievement. But he was also somebody who consistently, while he was Speaker and in enlarging the Republican majority ultimately to victory in '94, was also reaching out to moderates. Had them as a part of the coalition because he knew that you couldn't have a right-only majority. You had to have a center-right majority and that included, at times, moderates. So he was always looking to grow the party and that was part of the strategy.

RICK BERKE: Let me just throw in a thirty-second question, and that is, when you sat down with Newt at the beginning, I know he was friendly to everyone in the debates and put on a friendly front, but who was he most worried about?

VINCE HALEY: As I mentioned, in the course of the debate, he didn't really think too much about the other candidates.

RICK BERKE: But if he thought he was going to be the next nominee, he had to think, in some form at some point, about how he could do it.

VINCE HALEY: He was most worried about Romney's money. Romney's money attacking him.

RICK BERKE: Was there a second alternative to Romney that he was most worried about?

VINCE HALEY: Well I think you had to be worried about Rick Perry. Rick Perry, strong governor in Texas, big successful job creation record, Texas money, you know, he would be very, very formidable.

RICK BERKE: And he would talk about Perry?

VINCE HALEY: Not very much.

DAN BALZ: But he was also friends with Perry.

VINCE HALEY: Yeah, he was very good friends with Perry and people on Perry's team.

DAN BALZ: You've done the perfect segue because the next campaign we want to talk about is the Perry campaign. Rob Johnson, we will not ask you to talk about the first Gingrich campaign.[17]

ROB JOHNSON: Well that's good because we failed at the left-handed Chinese vote. [*laughter*]

••• RICK PERRY •••

DAN BALZ: Tell us about the Perry campaign. The rationale.

ROB JOHNSON: He was born a poor child on a farm. [*laughter*]

DAN BALZ: Paint Creek, Texas. I mean, here's the question I think that I would like to hear from you. Given the timing of his decision to think about it and get into it, what did he think was missing in the race that

---

17. Rob Johnson was Gingrich's campaign manager before he was Perry's.

Rob Johnson, Rick Perry's campaign manager, explains the challenges of entering the presidential race late in the game.

prompted him to say it's worth a very late start and, as it turned out, a reasonably ill-prepared candidacy?

ROB JOHNSON: We're supposed to talk about that part tomorrow.

DAN BALZ: But not at the beginning. The beginning is you have to cross that threshold. What was missing in the race at that point, in the field, that persuaded him he ought to get into it?

ROB JOHNSON: Well when he called and said, "I'm thinking about doing this, let's work on getting a plan together to make a decision," we had three questions. Is there an opening? Can we fill that opening? And, do we have the fire in the belly? And the answer to the first question, is there an opening, I mean, you just look at the public polls. And at that point, people in most public polls, with some of them by 37 to 40 percent, were voting for people who weren't even in the race. So, yes, there was an opening.

DAN BALZ: What did you conclude that opening was?

ROB JOHNSON: That opening was with a true fiscal conservative and a true social conservative with a proven record in both. The country was losing jobs by the millions. Texas was creating jobs by the millions. Iowa was still looking, in our opinion, for a true social conservative. And, ultimately, they picked a true social conservative. And then we thought South Carolina, with his military background, was the beginning of a southern wall. So we thought we could win Iowa or do very well in Iowa. We thought we could be a big enough distraction in New Hampshire because of our fiscal record, to make Romney spend money. We didn't think we could win. But then, we could go into South Carolina and we thought we could win South Carolina. And we had one of the best announcements of any of the campaigns out here. I mean, talk about the Iowa straw poll, what Iowa straw poll? We were in. Rick Perry announced in South Carolina and it was kaboom. And it was a big deal and we shot up in two weeks to frontrunner status and it was the most exhilarating three hours of my life. [*laughter*]

DAN BALZ: Here's another question. You guys had been enormously successful in Texas, and the team that started the campaign with Perry—including Dave Carney, who's here too—were very, very good in Texas. As you looked at a national race versus Texas, what were the things that were most daunting to you about trying to make that transition to go national?

ROB JOHNSON: Building out a true grassroots network of support in the constricted time frame. Governor Perry had been dogged and absolute in his comments publicly that he was not going to run for president and privately, behind closed doors. I mean, I walked into his office and told him about the Newt Gingrich offer and I said, "If there is a chance that you're going to run at all, I'm not going to do it." And he said, "I don't know how you say 'no,' Rob, I'm not running, go." He really was not running for president. So part of the daunting part was just getting everything together in weeks, a month, two months, a very short amount of time and building out a network. But the other exciting part of this was there was no shortage of people who wanted to help and, you talked about Giuliani, one thing that we learned from the Giuliani campaign, his campaign spent money in all states and paid these exorbitant salaries. We capped every salary. The ceiling was $10,000. So professionals that wanted to work for Rick Perry, $10,000 is not a lot of money, I get it. But we weren't going to pay above that. And people were coming out of the woodwork to work for us. But it was daunting to build that true grassroots network. That's what I'm saying.

RICK BERKE: Let me just ask a follow up on the daunting question.

ROB JOHNSON: We did raise $17.2 million in forty-eight days, I'm just saying.

DAN BALZ: Duly noted.

RICK BERKE: I understand the daunting on the grassroots level and building an organization, but how much discussion was there with the principal about how battle-tested he was to come in that late and run a national campaign? I mean, remember when George Bush ran from Texas, big state, he thought long and hard for a very long time about the psychic toll of what it would really take. Did that come up very much?

ROB JOHNSON: Absolutely. We had the grown-up discussions, the real discussions.

DAN BALZ: With him?

ROB JOHNSON: I would go to the mirror and be like, "Rob, this is going to be hard." [*laughter*] Yes, with Governor Perry.

DAN BALZ: How about when you would go to the mirror and then Carney would say "No, no, it's going to be fine, Rob. Don't worry about it."

ROB JOHNSON: It would turn into the evil Carney instead of my image. So, yeah, we had those discussions and we were prepared. But also, in that short amount of time, we had to learn and try to do a quick deep dive into a whole new set of issues, federal issues rather than the state issues.

RICK BERKE: But this is also, I think, very important in terms of how the campaign unfolded. How blunt were you about saying, "You're not that good on stage necessarily? You may think you were, but no." How blunt were you about what he had to overcome?

ROB JOHNSON: Well we didn't say that because we thought he was good on stage.

RICK BERKE: So the campaign didn't necessarily recognize it?

ROB JOHNSON: No, but we said—can you say the F-word at Harvard? We said this is going to be f—ing hard. This is going to be tough. We were blunt. We were very direct, and he listened and he asked real questions. This wasn't just a flip of a coin. I mean, he wasn't going to run, wasn't going to run, saw an opening, felt like his country was calling him. And he felt a true calling to go do this for his country. This wasn't about Rick Perry. This was about our country. And he did it with his feeling, with his being, and it just didn't work. Sometimes it doesn't.

DAN BALZ: Rob, last question for you. And that is, the role of Anita Perry. How important was her enthusiasm for him to run? What made her so enthusiastic and what role did she play in that formative stage?

ROB JOHNSON: She played a huge role, a very critical, important role. She also felt that they were being called to do this and they were doing this for their country. And, look, this is not a typical marriage. Rick and Anita Perry are best friends. They don't do things without doing it together. And she wanted him to run. She believed that he was the answer to the problems that our country was facing and she definitely talked very strongly to him about his need to do this. And, in her words, you say you have the greatest job in the world, you need to step outside of your comfort zone and go do this for your country and for your children and for your future grandchildren.

DAN BALZ: Thank you.

ROB JOHNSON: Thank you, Dan.

••• MICHELE BACHMANN •••

DAN BALZ: Now we will turn to the campaign that was eclipsed by Governor Perry. For anybody who was in Waterloo, Iowa, the night after the straw poll, we all remember that great scene,[18] and it will probably be relived tomorrow, but we turn now to Keith Nahigian for the Bachmann campaign.

KEITH NAHIGIAN: Thank you. Yeah, Waterloo, it was a blast. One thing that was different on this cycle than the other seven races I've worked on at the presidential level has been the fact that you saw the first couple of examples that there was organization. The Romney campaign

---

18. The day after Michele Bachmann won the Ames Straw Poll and Rick Perry announced his candidacy, Perry went to Bachmann's hometown of Waterloo, Iowa, and they both spoke to the Black Hawk County Republican Party's Lincoln Day dinner. Perry received praise for arriving early and for his performance, and Bachmann was criticized for her performance.

Keith Nahigian, Michele Bachmann's campaign manager, lays out their strategy to knock the other candidates out of the race one by one.

was going for years. The Pawlenty campaign was going for years. There was normally exploratory committees, you worked everything out. The Bachmann campaign was different. I had a meeting with her on May 15th, and she had nothing. And we had a kick-off of a campaign three weeks later. So imagine some of you trying to start a newspaper, start a television station in three weeks. It's a little interesting. But basically, as you know, I started the same day Ed Rollins did. Ed was the chairman of our campaign. Looking at Michele Bachmann started out of 2010, with the whole Tea Party movement and, really, the creation of the Obamacare Affordable Choice Act. That was the reason she got into the race. She thought that was kind of going over the line. Her strengths obviously are that she's a pretty good communicator, good on television, good at making news. Her coalition that we thought we'd want to put together is Christian conservatives, Tea Party, and then her national security background of being able to really work on foreign affairs. She just loved that particular area. She matched up really well with South Carolina. She matched up medium with New Hampshire because it had all those pieces. Iowa was a little bit of a stretch because it's not as strong in some of those areas—not as strong with the Tea Party, not as strong in national security. We started a campaign. We wanted to make some news right out of the gate so we announced on one of CNN's many awesome debates that she was going to sign papers.[19] And that makes news. We drew from a lot of different things that we have done in the past, like the old McCain years, when we tried to have access to the media, be responsible to the media and get as much earned media as we possibly could. We had no major donors and we did no fundraisers the entire campaign. We just had a lot of little donors that were giving to us all the time.

DAN BALZ: Why did you do no fundraisers? Because you didn't think you could raise?

KEITH NAHIGIAN: Really there weren't any because she came in so late. Every major donor was basically taken or courted.

DAN BALZ: Except the ones Rick Perry later got.

KEITH NAHIGIAN: Rick Perry, but he had them kind of frozen out. They were waiting for him and we were working on that.

DAN BALZ: She's not a big donor kind of candidate, right?

KEITH NAHIGIAN: She's not a big donor kind of candidate, but we didn't have a fundraiser. It's kind of amazing. When I was on Steve Forbes's campaign, we didn't have a fundraiser either. [*laughter*] So anyway, we kicked off, and we wanted to focus on a couple of different things. We wanted to get out of Iowa because we thought if we got out of Iowa, our organization in New Hampshire and South Carolina were very strong and we would be able to run.

DAN BALZ: When you say you wanted to get out of Iowa—I assume you're talking about the caucuses—you wanted to get out of Iowa in what kind of shape? I mean, what was your sense of what the minimum necessary in Iowa had to be at that point?

KEITH NAHIGIAN: We just heard the Huntsman strategy. We wanted to be the opposite. Michele Bachmann is unlike a lot of these other people. Normally, you get a candidate and it's like, ugh, they flipped on this issue, they were kind of wobbly on this issue, all these different things all the way around the road. You had to kind of deemphasize all those

---

19. In a June 2011 Republican primary debate in New Hampshire, Bachmann announced she had formally filed paperwork to run for president.

different areas. Well she was really the first completely pure candidate I'd ever worked for that hadn't had a move on anything. She hasn't moved on anything her entire career because she doesn't care. She really doesn't want to be a politician. She just believes what she believes, that's it.

DAN BALZ: Let me ask you, in a sense the flip of what I asked Matt, was there ever a point where you said, "She's too conservative"?

KEITH NAHIGIAN: No.

DAN BALZ: It's nice to be a conservative candidate, but she's too conservative?

KEITH NAHIGIAN: No. Our strategy was you have Romney over here; he's going to get what he's going to get. When you hold her against some of these other people running, our thought was to get in and then, we needed to shrink the stage. We needed to get rid of people as quickly as possible. So we used the debates, and Brett did a good job of this, of targeting each debate. So we ended Pawlenty. Then we went after Herman Cain. Then we went after capitalism with Perry. We were just going right down the line. Then we hit Newt Gingrich and the last ten days, we really hit Ron Paul a lot in Iowa. We wanted to just get Ron Paul out. And other things come to mind but that's what we were trying to do. We were just trying to be the number two or the conservative alternative to Mitt Romney.

DAN BALZ: Thank you. Buddy Roemer complained throughout the election that nobody gave him enough time to make his piece or to say his piece. So tonight, Carlos Sierra will do that for the campaign.

••• BUDDY ROEMER •••

CARLOS SIERRA: Early on, Buddy called, and I still remember the day he called me, and asked me to head up the campaign. I worked for Senator McCain for about ten years. And he's like, Carlos, you know, I'm sick of what's going on with this administration, and I just read the budget; I'm fed up with it. We need to change America. I'm like, all right, let's do it. Who are you going to support? He's like, no, I want to run. [*laughter*] And then it was, I want you to head up my campaign.

Carlos Sierra, Buddy Roemer's campaign manager, argues why his candidate should have been allowed to participate in the presidential debates.

DAN BALZ: And then what did you say?

CARLOS SIERRA: I was speechless. I was like, all right. Well give me a couple of days to think about it. I had a couple of kids, a mortgage, I had a cushy job with McCain, so give me a couple of days, Buddy. Before we hung up, he's like, by the way, Carlos, I want to have a hundred dollar cap on donations. I didn't have a chance to say anything. So, anyway, a couple of days later I had thought about it, talked to McCain about it. He told me to do it. The rest is history. I ended up being his campaign manager. I know a lot of people in the media thought that we were running just to prove a point but we weren't. Our big issue was campaign finance reform and he really wanted to be the reform candidate. I guess you'd compare it to Ross Perot in '92. But our big issue was campaign finance reform. We thought there was a lot of corruption going on. We thought the money in politics was out of hand. And that's what we were running on, the money. So we put a plan together, and with the hundred dollar limit, obviously that kind of changes things a little bit. But we did put a good team together. Our lawyer was Trevor Potter.[20] You guys know who Trevor Potter is. Mark McKinnon, who is in the room, was a good friend of Buddy's. I know he advised him early on. Becki Donatelli, before joining the Bachmann campaign did all of our online campaign. Mike Dennehy, who won New Hampshire for McCain in 2000 and 2008, was our advisor in New Hampshire. So I know a lot of people in the media thought we were running just to prove a point. But when you put that kind of team together, we were running to win. And unfortunately, I feel, and Buddy feels, that the people in the media just thought when you run with a hundred dollar limit that you're not being serious, you're just running to prove a point.

DAN BALZ: Let me interrupt for a second on that. Jerry Brown did that same sort of thing in 1992 and had a lot more success than Governor Roemer did. It's not as though Governor Roemer was somebody who had never held office, he had been in Congress and held the governorship. What's the difference?

CARLOS SIERRA: The difference is you, Dan, to be honest. I mean, you were one of the guys we e-mailed and asked, why didn't Buddy get invited to the *Washington Post* debate? And we never got an answer from you. I'll be honest, it was the media.

DAN BALZ: Just as an aside, there were a set of criteria for that debate, and he didn't meet them.

CARLOS SIERRA: So being a governor, being a four-term congressman, being a small business owner apparently doesn't qualify, but a pizza guy qualifies. I guess I'm missing something. I don't know what happened to our country but that's where we're going in our national politics.

RICK BERKE: Can we get a response from the pizza guy? [*laughter*]

CARLOS SIERRA: So it's scary. Buddy wanted to be the reform candidate. But with a hundred dollar limit, no Super PAC, no PAC money, and no lobbyist money, we had to have an awesome social media campaign. We had to focus on one state, which was New Hampshire. So me and him and the team moved to New Hampshire. We were there for seven to eight months. We literally went to every single county, city, town, met

---

20. Trevor Potter is a former FEC commissioner and served as general counsel to McCain's presidential campaigns.

with everybody. We were polling ahead of Rick Perry for two months. After what, 17.2 million in twenty-nine days you said?

So New Hampshire was a big strategy of ours. But our strategy was social media, earned media and public finance, which we accomplished. I still think we ran the best social media campaign. I think he tweeted every single person in this room. Again, the one thing that we did not accomplish was getting invited to any of the debates. And I think most of these people in the room know that Buddy is an awesome debater. I mean, two Harvard degrees, governor, four-term congressman, small business owner, he would have mopped the floor with any of these candidates here. You guys know that. And he was never given a chance, unfortunately. So our strategy all along was the debates. And unfortunately we never got that.

DAN BALZ: Given that you saw the resistance to having him in the debates, was there an alternative strategy?

CARLOS SIERRA: There was an alternative strategy and that was the third party, the Americans Elect.[21] And so we'll talk a little about that tomorrow but our strategy after we knew that the media was not going to let him participate was, all right, what's Plan B? So we met, we talked with a lot of people and we decided, let's explore this Americans Elect option. And we did that. And so, we're speaking candid and it's off the record, he came into my office one day in New Hampshire and we literally wrote it on a board in my office then. It was the Reform Party, the Whig Party, Americans Elect. We decided, why not build a coalition of the Whig Party, the Reform Party, Americans Elect, bring them all together and try to really have an impact in this election. And that's what we did. That was ultimately what we did after we knew we were not going to get into the debates.

DAN BALZ: Thank you. Rick Santorum started also as something of a dark horse. John Brabender will tell us the origins of the candidacy and what the strategy was.

••• RICK SANTORUM •••

JOHN BRABENDER: I think you almost have to look at our campaign, as far as strategy, in phases. We were there to announce the candidate, but

---

21.   Americans Elect was a nonpartisan organization that sought to nominate a legitimate third-party candidate for president in 2012.

John Brabender, Rick Santorum's campaign manager, describes the Santorum family meeting where the decision was made to run for president.

we weren't given credibility at the front end. And then, later on, we certainly were. The whole thing started when Rick Santorum lost his reelection, I think it was 16 points, 18, who's counting? And obviously when you lose a reelection by 18 points you sit around and say, what do I do next? And what popped into our mind was we run for president. [*laughter*] It seems perfectly logical. And the truth of the matter is, before Rick did get in the race, the final decision was his family. Those who know Rick know how he cares about his family. And we did have a meeting at his house with his children. It's a very densely populated household so it was a big meeting. And I remember, this is true, his kids said, we want you to run. It's important for our generation to run but, we ask two things. Do not embarrass us, and don't be the first one out. And so, Phil, where you may be disappointed about the Pawlenty campaign, forever you can hold your head high knowing that you helped a father keep a commitment to his kids. [*laughter*] In truth, I think the first thing I should do is maybe even remind people the success that Rick Santorum did have. He was involved in thirty different primaries. Out of those thirty primaries, he won eleven of them and tied two others in delegates.

DAN BALZ: John, don't leap too far ahead because we're going to get into some of that tomorrow.

JOHN BRABENDER: All right, then I won't even mention that he won more counties than the other Republican candidates combined. But our goal, quite frankly, before Iowa was not to get thrown off the island, for all practical purposes.

DAN BALZ: And what did that mean?

JOHN BRABENDER: That meant, first of all, we had a very small staff, and we were not going to have a lot of expenditures. I'll be honest, we thought one of our best days was when Herman Cain won the Florida straw poll because we thought he would be seen now as a credible candidate and go through the type of credibility check that you need to have. Rick Santorum, we realized, had gone through tough races, rose to the third highest spot in the U.S. Senate, twelve years in the Senate, four years in the House. So we knew we could survive as long as we could survive financially. And our goal was to get through the top tier in Iowa. If we could be in the top four in Iowa, we could go. And we really felt a big emphasis was going to be on debates and it was a much bigger challenge than we realized, because there were twelve candidates. And, often times, because of the poll numbers, we were on the end. In fact, it was really concerning the very first debate that Perry was in, we thought we must have really bad name ID because Santorum said something and Perry decided he was going to respond and said, "I want to respond to that fellow at the end." I kid you not. That's what he said. [*laughter*] In subsequent debates, we realized this had nothing to do with name ID. [*laughter*] But we did need to get through Iowa.

DAN BALZ: As Rick said, we are encouraging settling scores, and we appreciate that you're in the spirit of the evening.

JOHN BRABENDER: We did feel that we could own a big part of the social conservative platform by saying we not only have been a consistent vote, here are some of the things we did. And he could go into a lot of rooms, and those who have seen Rick Santorum give a speech on some of these issues, it matters in places like Iowa. He spent a lot of time in Iowa and that certainly was a go. We also thought that his early years as a reform-er would help him at least get his fair share of the Tea Party. So we ultimately, as you know, eventually, not on Iowa Caucus night but eventually, when we get to South Carolina, found out Rick Santorum was the winner. The next phase was really Iowa through Nevada. We knew we were not going to be particularly strong but, we wanted to keep our name ID, which actually our favorable rating was higher than any other candidate, very strong. We wanted to be the adult in the room at the debates.

DAN BALZ: Let me go back because, again, I don't want to get ahead of the morning panel. Everybody else has basically said, when they scoped this race out, Mitt Romney was the person that they felt they had to beat. If you're saying you hoped to get fourth in Iowa, who were the other candidates that you were worried about? Who did you feel that you also had to get around?

JOHN BRABENDER: The first thing is we were happy when Mike Pence decided not to run. That was very helpful we thought to us. We thought he would appeal to the exact same audience, would've had the same credibility, and would have split a lot of votes.

DAN BALZ: And hadn't lost a recent election.

JOHN BRABENDER: Exactly. So we were worried, frankly, about Mike Pence. Perry worried us a lot because he had money and we knew a lot of this was going to be about timing—who could ride the wave last. And we honestly probably thought that that was going to be harder for Cain to do. To some degree, we thought it was going to be harder for Gingrich to do in Iowa, especially because he was already being beat up. We thought Perry would have the money and the backing and, frankly, we were fighting for some of the same Evangelicals.

DAN BALZ: Were you ever, at any point, concerned about Michele Bachmann?

JOHN BRABENDER: Yeah, but not as much, because we just felt over time and debates that we could show a distinction. What we were finding, however, was we were running into an electability problem. We were finding people that wanted to support us but just felt we weren't going to be the nominee. At some point that changed, particularly when we won three states in one night—Minnesota, Colorado and Missouri. And we raised $1.5 million in the next twenty-four hours. We would have raised more, other than we had basically so much volume coming in, we couldn't handle it. But that let us move into now claiming we were the alternate to Mitt Romney that everybody was talking about. And that really was a big part of the race from that point on.

RICK BERKE: I just want to get back to the threshold question, the decision of Rick Santorum to run. And I'll raise what you raised, which is the whole question that he lost in a big way. He lost his Senate seat. I can't remember, were you in the room with his family, the crowded room?

JOHN BRABENDER: Yeah.

RICK BERKE: In that discussion, where they had this big fundamental moment of deciding to run for president, I'm trying to picture the scene with all the kids and everything. Did anyone ask about, how do you run for president of the United States when your own constituents turned you out?

JOHN BRABENDER: The reason for that is we knew the race that we lost well. It was 2006. Pennsylvania was the worst state in the nation. However, Rick Santorum did get 93 percent of the Republican vote in exit polls in Pennsylvania. So it was not a Republican problem. The other thing too is people said we lost because he was too conservative, which is a heck of a Republican primary message. So we were able to spin that. Look, everybody was telling us to become a moderate to win the Pennsylvania reelection; he refused to do that and lost. So he's a trusted conservative. Look, every time Rick ran it was against long odds. So that wasn't it. It was actually interesting because their kids were very engaged. In fact, I remember the daughter, Sarah Maria, was there, who was in seventh grade, I think, at the time, and she had this small file. I said, "Are you already keeping track of all the articles about your dad running for president?" That's why it was a small file at the time. And she said, "No. This is opposition research." And I thought, "That's great, they're engaged." They do stuff as a family. They spent two-and-a-half weeks right before the Iowa straw poll together, including their special-needs child, Bella, who was out there in Iowa with them.

RICK BERKE: So basically, it just wasn't a worry? It didn't come up at all in the early planning of, how do we overcome this perception issue? I mean, you can make all these explanations, but still, it's pretty striking when you lose your own state.

JOHN BRABENDER: It is, but I will tell you those weren't the questions we were being asked when we were out there. People weren't saying, geez, I love everything you stand for but you lost your last race. That really didn't become a factor, I don't believe, in the race.

DAN BALZ: Thank you. We are down to the last two campaigns. We're almost done. We'll start with Matt Rhoades from the Romney campaign. [*applause*] Matt, you brought a constituency with you.

••• MITT ROMNEY •••

MATT RHOADES: I guess so. Thank you. First off, I just want to congratulate the Obama campaign. I haven't had a chance to do so publicly. You guys ran a great campaign, and we have a lot of respect for your team. I also wanted to tip my hat to all the Republican candidates and everybody that worked on those campaigns. You guys were formidable opponents. Many of you helped out the Romney campaign in many ways after your candidates got out, and we thank you for everything that you did.

First off, on the primary side of things, we had three things that we were trying to achieve in the primary. The first was we wanted to run a lean campaign, because we knew that the calendar, the way it was, with allocated delegates, it was going to be a long process. And we never expected to win this early, never. I know some people have talked

Matt Rhoades, Mitt Romney's campaign manager, talks about their efforts to make the race about jobs and the economy.

tonight about how Mitt Romney was in their way and it was Mitt Romney, but we knew it was going to be a long fight, in part because we knew the calendar and, in part, because we had run before. And one of the most important things that we had to do as a campaign, and obviously as a candidate, was just stay relaxed and calm. And when you're third in the national polls, you've got to continue to execute on your plan. The second big part of the plan in the primary was to focus the campaign on the president's record on jobs and the economy. Everything we did, everything we said, we tried to talk about jobs and the economy, to the point where people like Phil Rucker and Ashley Parker[22] were probably getting sick to their stomachs about hearing about it, but that was our goal. And then the third step in our primary strategy, it seems pretty simple, we didn't want to chase shiny objects, things like straw polls, topics we didn't want to talk about. And it was always, always our goal to just keep it in Mitt's wheelhouse. And Mitt's wheelhouse was jobs and the economy and occasionally talk about cuts in spending. So those were our three simple steps, our three simple plans, our goals to win the nomination and we tried to stick to that throughout the primary process.

Then we got to the general. We had just spent $87 million in a primary, the long slog is what we called it internally in the campaign, and we realized we had to quickly build out our finance team, build out our digital team, and build out our political team so that we could compete with an incumbent president who had been working toward this general election race for a long, long time. So we quickly tried to do that. Then we made the decision to immediately lay out what Mitt Romney would do as president. That's why we did "day one, job one" ads, focused on how we would turn around the economy and cut spending. That was our goal coming out of the gate. We also, and this is always a big challenge and it's difficult to do, wanted this campaign to be about big issues and big ideas. Sometimes we failed at that but our goal was always to keep a positive information flow and give speeches on important topics that we thought voters cared about. This played into the governor's decision to pick Congressman Ryan as his running mate. It allowed us to talk about big issues. Sometimes people thought we were crazy to want to talk about spending and entitlement reform but that was the idea there. Then the fourth strategy, the fourth goal, was the debates. Governor Romney, more so than anybody else on the team, knew how important the debates were going to be and he insisted that we put more and more debate prep time on the calendar. He

---

22.   Phil Rucker is a reporter for the *Washington Post* and Ashley Parker is a reporter for the *New York Times*.

insisted that when we came to him in the early part of the summer with his first debate briefing books that it wasn't enough, he wanted more. He didn't care if people in the media were critical at times of like, where is Governor Romney, why isn't he campaigning four times a day? Why is he spending so much time in debate prep? He knew how important it was. In the end, I think he was very right. Finally, in the end, we didn't win. We came up short. But I'm very proud of the team we built. And I'm very proud of the man I worked for, and that was it. [*applause*]

DAN BALZ: Matt, let me ask you this. Go back to the early stage. To what extent did the change in the party, as the Tea Party became a real force, affect your analysis of what the primary campaign might be like, what it would take to win it? Did it make it look more daunting? Did it affect your thinking in any way about, this will be a harder race because of where the party is and where Governor Romney has been on some things?

MATT RHOADES: Well like I said, we always knew it would be long for a variety of reasons, and we always knew there would be an anti-Mitt candidate and whether they were blessed by the Tea Party or not, we knew that that was going to happen. I think where your question is going, and it might be your next question, is about Massachusetts health care and how that was going to impact Governor Romney in the primary. And I could tell you, when I was at his PAC, when I wasn't busy helping get Republican candidates elected across the country, occasionally people would call me about the presidency and whether Mitt should run and say, if he was going to run, he had to apologize for Massachusetts health care, he had to. And I knew, because I know Governor Romney and how he feels, he never was going to do that. It never crossed his mind.

So an important hurdle for Governor Romney, and we knew this from the very beginning in the very, very early stages, to your point, was that first debate when he finally went up there in the Republican primary. We knew he had to nail the health care answer. And I think that he did. It came up over and over in debates and he locked his answer down more and more during those debates. So I think that that was an important factor.

DAN BALZ: A lot of you have talked through the course of the campaign that, in a sense, he is an unlikely nominee for the Republican Party of 2012. Massachusetts in a party that is southern- based, a Mormon in a party where there are Evangelical Christians who are at the core, and obviously more moderate in some of his positions than some people in the party. How much did you talk about that at the beginning? How much did you think that was a potential problem? What did you do to deal with that?

MATT RHOADES: Well I think that that goes back to the second step that we had in our plan to win the primary, which was either we made the race about jobs and the economy or we didn't. Either we took the nomination or we didn't. We knew it was going to be a long fight. We knew there were going to be a lot of candidates that would have their moments. But if we talked about jobs and the economy as much as possible and made that the centerpiece of the entire campaign and what people were talking about, then Mitt Romney had a shot at winning the nomination.

RICK BERKE: Romney was running longer than any of the other candidates, any Republican candidates, and you look at the polls two or three years ago, and it's Palin-Romney. How much were you all really concerned about Palin, and did he talk about her as a threat?

MATT RHOADES: There were constantly candidates that were in the lead during the Republican primary process. And you just have to be patient. It didn't matter who it was. There certainly were times when Governor Palin was at the top of the list, but we just knew we had to stick to the plan we had.

RICK BERKE: I know that, but I want to know, when Romney would talk about the campaign and all these people coming at him, how much did he talk about Palin versus the others? I mean, he must have talked about the other candidates because that's what the primary is.

MATT RHOADES: Well I can tell you, for example, Governor Romney never was looking forward to debating Speaker Gingrich. And I think for the right reasons. The Speaker was very good in these debates.

RICK BERKE: Was it also their personal animus there?

MATT RHOADES: Speaker Gingrich and Governor Romney really didn't even know each other. Actually, we made an effort early on, at the very beginning of the primary, to introduce them and let them spend some time together. And they actually had a very, very, very nice meeting. They've grown to respect each other quite a bit. But there was no one particular candidate that the governor sat there pulling his hair out about. We just knew we had to be relaxed and patient.

RICK BERKE: In terms of campaign skills, Gingrich was the one who kind of was daunting for him, of all of them?

MATT RHOADES: Many of them were. I just used Speaker Gingrich as an example because of his debating skills.

DAN BALZ: As you look back on that early period, and I'm sure everybody who was involved in any of the campaigns looks back and says, we made certain assumptions at the beginning that just turned out to be wrong. If you look back on that, and you obviously were successful through the primaries, what were those assumptions? Or, were there any, as you look back, that you thought we were just wrong about that and had to adjust it, or that didn't unfold in the way you anticipated?

MATT RHOADES: In the primary? We knew we weren't going to win early for sure. We knew it would drag out. With that said, I don't think any of us realized that week in, week out, it was do or die for Mitt Romney, and that we had to have the resources to compete, week after week, to be up on TV usually for two straight weeks, going into states, whether it was Illinois was a must win, Wisconsin was a must win, Ohio was a must win. You know, they were all must wins. And, as much as we knew that this would be a long dragged out process, I don't think anybody on the team actually knew that everything would be relying on the Maine Caucus and competing with Trygve and Ron Paul up in Maine. There were adjustments that had to be made. We were wise to try to spend as little as possible in the beginning but that didn't mean that we didn't have to make more adjustments throughout the long slog because of that.

RICK BERKE: Related to that, Matt, when did you all anticipate you'd have it locked up, like roughly? How much earlier did you think?

MATT RHOADES: I actually don't remember. It's so long ago.

DAN BALZ: All right. There will be much more to tell of the Romney campaign tomorrow. Finally, President Obama's campaign. Jeremy Bird, the floor is yours, sir. [*applause*]

••• BARACK OBAMA •••

JEREMY BIRD: Thank you all for letting us be here. It's actually good to be back. I went to divinity school here about ten years ago, and I started in politics, in part, because of this building and the Kennedy School and Professor Ganz over there, who got me involved in working with kids here in Boston trying to get more money for their school. So it's good to be back. And, to the Romney folks and to all the Republican candidates and your campaigns here, you guys ran great races, and it's a pleasure to be up here following you, Matt. I'm sure there are going to be good conversations tomorrow. A lot of my colleagues on the Obama campaign couldn't be here so, I get the pleasure of talking a little bit about the campaign and what our strategy was. I remember meeting with Jim Messina and Jen O'Malley.[23] It was in December of 2010 and, if you remember back to that time, we had not had a good November of 2010. We were starting to put the pieces in place for the campaign and they asked me to come on to be the field director. And we were sitting there talking in D.C. about the strategy. One of the biggest pieces was that we

---

23. Jen O'Malley was a Deputy Campaign Manager on Obama's 2012 campaign.

Jeremy Bird, Barack Obama's national field director, explains how they built their grassroots organization.

could not let the Republican primary go on with us being a sort of back seat, letting 2011 be about the Republican primary and Republican candidates going across Iowa, New Hampshire, and all across the country, talking about the president's record without us fighting back and being a part of that conversation. At the same time, we knew that this was going to be a close race and that if we could have an electorate that looked anything like 2008, and not like 2010, we could win. But in order to do that, we had to not only be a part of the media debate, but a part of defining the candidates and being a part of that discussion. We also had to be building the grassroots campaign on the ground. And, we believed, if we started in 2011, and we had a lot of foundation already built through 2008, 2009, 2010, we could actually build a campaign where we treated every battleground state like a governor's race. That we could actually go into each one of these states, in Ohio and Florida, elsewhere, you know, states as massive as Florida, we could actually build a neighborhood team-based program where we had volunteers who actually covered their neighborhoods and could be ready when early vote started in 2012. So we believed, most importantly, that we had to start early and that we could not allow 2011 to go by without starting to build that foundation. We thought all along that Mitt Romney would be the nominee. There were obviously periods of time where that was in question, but we believed all along that we would be running against the Romney campaign and that, at times, when he wasn't being hit in the primary from his opponents, when other folks, as you have already talked about, were trying to position themselves to be the alternative, that we had to be a part of that conversation.

Then in 2012, as we were building up, we thought we have to build a grassroots campaign that has to do four things. We have to expand the electorate because the electorate cannot look like 2010. There are people who voted for us in 2008 that did not vote for us in 2010. Those were going to be a part of our persuasion universe. We also believed that there were new voters out there—that there were people out there that volunteered for us when they were in high school and they couldn't vote—so we needed to get them on the rolls. We needed to expand the electorate. So that organization would be focused and everything that we did, whether you're in the research department, in the field department or doing paid media, you would be focused at some point on registration, persuasion and then, ultimately, turnout in early voting turnout programs.

The fourth piece of that was building an organization. And that looked like the neighborhood team program that I talked about in all of our states, but it also looked like having the best research program, having the best paid media team, having the best analytics team, so that we could look at the electorate and figure out, how do we build a coalition that can look like the electorate looked like in 2008. It also meant building a fundraising team that could compete. We knew that Mitt Romney's campaign would be very formidable in terms of fundraising. And, we knew with *Citizens United*[24] and the super PAC money that we were going to be at a disadvantage. We had to build multiple revenue streams. Teddy is in the room somewhere. Teddy ran our digital program, an unbelievable program. We knew that early in 2011 we weren't going to have the kind of small dollar online fundraising that we would have in October of 2012, but we had to build the infrastructure, hire the right staff, test what did work in 2011 that we could then implement at a higher level in 2012. We knew that we had to have the big dollar fundraising coming in and Rufus[25] built out his team. And then we knew, with Jim Margolis and the paid media team, that we needed to make sure that the election in the general was not simply a referendum on the president, that it was a choice. We knew we needed to define our opponent and make that a choice for the voters we were trying to persuade early on. At the same time, we were trying to mobilize and excite the folks that were in our coalition in 2008. So we had to build a very, very good campaign because we knew it was going to be close. We had to take advantage of 2011 and use that time to build up something that's really hard to do in a presidential campaign. And, having worked the 2008 campaign for Obama, we knew what it was like to come out of a real primary and try to build a massive business, essentially, a grassroots organization across the country in such a short amount of time. We didn't want to let that happen. Our advantage was the grassroots that we could mobilize, the funding that we could get in from the grassroots, and also just the time that we had that we knew the Republican opponent would not have.

DAN BALZ: Jeremy, one question. And that is, there were certain things that you guys could control, and you've gone through some of those. The biggest problem that you couldn't control was the economy. How did that affect the thinking as you started the campaign? What were you going to do about it or not do about it or hope to do about it? And how much did that hang over everything else you were doing?

JEREMY BIRD: We never talked about it. [*laughter*] We thought we made this about the economy and the debates. No, I'm kidding. [*laughter*]

---

24. In *Citizens United v. FEC,* the U.S. Supreme Court in 2010 ruled that corporations, unions, and other special interests can spend as much as they like to advocate the election or defeat of political candidate.
25. Rufus Gifford was the Obama campaign's finance director.

Obviously, all of us know this as campaigners, we like to talk about all the great things that we can do as campaigners, but there are some things that you cannot control. And I didn't work in the White House. I didn't have control over what was happening there. We had a 9:00 a.m. meeting every day and the first Friday of the month was a big day for us to go in there and figure out what the jobs numbers were going to be and where we were with the unemployment numbers. We knew that we couldn't have a very complicated conversation about where we came in and make this about looking backwards and say, well, but when we came in in January of 2009, this is where things were, and it's gotten better. That's not a great argument for any of Jim's ads or for the conversations that we were trying to have with people at the door. So we needed to make it about forward-looking and, obviously, there were a lot of things—the economy, what was happening abroad, lots of things—that we couldn't control. Matt talked about this when he just presented, and I think this comes from the president, we had a great campaign leadership that was not about riding the highs and then getting down in the lows. We knew that we were going to be up and we were going to be down. Every time there was a good polling week, Jim Messina would come into the office and say, "Do not get excited about those numbers. They do not mean anything, especially national numbers. This is not a national race; this is about getting 270 electoral votes in the battleground states. Focus on that." And, when the polls were bad, we always had gotten people ready for that. So we tried to stay really focused and control those things that we could and not worry about the things that we couldn't control and just sort of manage them when we got there.

DAN BALZ: At the early stage of the campaign, there was a lot of stuff written by all of us about how strong or weak the coalition from '08 was and the different pieces of it. As you looked at that coalition, which were the groups that you were most worried about? Which were the groups where you had the most confidence that things were okay?

JEREMY BIRD: The most worrisome group was young people. And many of you wrote about that ad nauseam. We saw it in our polling early on. Part of this is about, how much are young people paying attention in mid-2011 when we did really start the campaign. But we always knew that that was the biggest thing that we had to address. And we did that on the ground. So I was in Ohio in 2008, and we had one or two organizers on OSU's campus. This time we had five to ten and we were ramping up the whole way. We knew we had to organize meticulously, doggedly, and be focused on these college campuses. We had to get something up early. We had to make sure that people were engaged. The first time in 2008, a lot of this was with the wind at our back. This time, we knew we had to just grind it out. And with young people we had to make sure that we were talking about what mattered. We were organizing. We were using all of the digital assets that we had. We had one of the greatest digital programs. These guys raised more money online than we did in 2008. They were mobilizing people in ways that no one thought we could in 2008. But that was the one segment demographic that we were the most worried about.

We knew from all of our analytics that we had strong support. The support was at the same level it was with African Americans and we felt very good about where the turnout was going to be there. It was going to take work but we knew we could get there. And I think we were aided, in some ways, in the primary by where the conversation went with Hispanic voters. We thought we could get some of the turnout numbers just based on how the demographics had changed at a pretty high level. But in terms of the percentage that we would get, I think we exceeded our own expectations in Colorado and Nevada and some other places. But youth was the most troublesome one early on.

DAN BALZ: I'll end with the last question that I asked Matt. That is, as you look back, what were the misconceptions or sort of strategic assumptions that you made at the time that turned out not to be the case, other than that you won?

JEREMY BIRD: It's always easier to have that conversation when you win. Personally, I think, and we had debate about this in the office, that we believed that the Republican primary would be over earlier than it was and that we would be facing a longer general election. It didn't really change so much about how we would prepare but we really did believe that it was going to be over sooner than it was, and I think that would have been a point for us.

DAN BALZ: What's the reason you made that assumption?

JEREMY BIRD: Just looking at who got in the race early on and how things were going, we just believed that the Romney camp would come out earlier. We had been in a tough primary too, and it just didn't feel like it would be that kind of length at the beginning. So that's one thing. Obviously, we knew that Mitt Romney was a good debater and the president hadn't debated in a long time, and so he did a lot of preparation. We were not necessarily ready for the outcome of the first debate and how that would change the electorate. But the thing that we did have is that we always believed it would be close. Some of the poll numbers that we would see in certain states would get people really excited—"Oh, look, we're up seven or so in Ohio." But it goes back to that underlying assumption we had that this was going to be a close race, that it was never going to be outside the margin, and that we were going to have to grind it out by running the best grassroots campaign that we could at the very local level by empowering people and really including them in the campaign. And, we knew we had to have multiple pathways to get to 270. We had to also have messages that really worked in some of those states. We had to push the auto message more in Ohio than we necessarily would in Florida.

DAN BALZ: One last one. Give us a sense, because I don't think we really have it, of the level of confidence of the president at the beginning of this campaign.

JEREMY BIRD: Messina and Axe can talk more about this tomorrow, because they know him better than I do and spent more time with him. But everybody that's been around him, many of you reporters certainly have, he's a pretty confident guy. He thought he could win this race from the beginning and he never wavered from that. And our analytics never wavered from that. We believed, even after the first debate, that we were still in a strong position because we fundamentally believed that what we were doing on the ground, with our paid media, with all the assets of the campaign, digitally, etcetera, that we were going to have an electorate that looked more like 2008 than 2010, and didn't look like 2004 either, just based on how the demographics had changed. So I think he started confident, and I think he was confident all the way through. I think he had a couple of moments that got him working a little harder.

DAN BALZ: October 3rd?

JEREMY BIRD: Yes.

RICK BERKE: Just a couple of things, Jeremy. One is, I want to get a sense for everyone of the president's engagement and how early that was. I know you said Axelrod and Messina saw him more but when was the first time you met in a meeting with the president where he talked about the reelection?

JEREMY BIRD: Honestly, that wasn't my role. My job was to be out in the battleground states. I learned this from Jon Carson, the field director in

2008. I don't think Jon Carson and the president ever saw each other in the 2008 campaign. And so it wasn't my job to be in any rooms with him. I was fortunate I did. So those guys will talk more about that. My job was to be in Ohio and Iowa and other places.

RICK BERKE: In your job, did you ever feel his hand directly in any way? Like, did anyone say Obama won't like that?

JEREMY BIRD: Sure, sure.

RICK BERKE: Give us an example.

JEREMY BIRD: Jim and Axe, and then when Plouffe was around, those guys were having meetings with him and relaying exactly where his head was, what he wanted to see, what we were showing him. So from the beginning, it wasn't like I was in the room with him, but those guys were in the room conveying what he wanted.

RICK BERKE: And, to give us a sense of his engagement and how sharp he was about this reelect, what are some of the things that were passed from him to you that you should be aware of?

JEREMY BIRD: So he came by the office, before the first debate but it was probably pretty close. Mitch Stewart[26] and I shared an office, had for four years, and I'm really glad that he stopped dipping. [*laughter*] So he came in our office and he was talking to both of us and it was very clear that he was engaged. We were talking numbers in Ohio. We were talking demographic numbers, we were talking polling numbers, we were talking how many offices, you know, what we were seeing from our voter contact. We were talking about the number of staff we have on the ground. It was very clear that he was engaged in what we were doing.

RICK BERKE: Obama was talking numbers.

JEREMY BIRD: Yes.

RICK BERKE: He knew all that off the top of his head? How early was that?

---

26. Mitch Stewart was the Obama campaign's battleground states director.

JEREMY BIRD: This was probably like September 2012, something like that. But he was engaged like that from the beginning. Obviously, he had a very big day job, and so he wasn't worried about how many offices I had open or staff I had in Ohio but, come September, he was very focused on battleground states. And when he went out, he became very close, I think, to a lot of our state directors. In 2008 the map was a little bit bigger. We were spending time in Montana and other places. He was in Ohio all the time. He was in Iowa all the time. And so he would talk to those guys or the ladies that ran our campaigns in these states, and he got to know them very well and knew what was happening in the states and would talk to them before his events in depth.

RICK BERKE: Let me also ask you, were the reelects of Bush and Clinton relevant to your campaign. Did you take away anything specifically from them?

JEREMY BIRD: Sure. And Messina is a better student of history than I am, but those guys read a lot of the books and studied a lot of what they did, particularly, you know, the best analogy was to look at what Bush did in 2004 and just learn from what he did and take what we could. I know they talked to folks that had been engaged in that but, more important-ly, read a lot about what had happened, looked at the maps, and looked at the analytics to try to learn from that. And then obviously we learned what we could from the Clinton folks and people that had been en-gaged in that. That was a very different election but there were still lessons to take from it.

RICK BERKE: My last question. That is, you said that you all thought Romney would be the nominee all along. Was there ever a fleeting moment in your head, Jeremy, where you thought for a second that one of the other candidates in this room just might win the nomination?

JEREMY BIRD: Personally?

RICK BERKE: Personally.

JEREMY BIRD: I think if Rick Santorum had built a grassroots campaign in some of these early states, and had the funding to do it, and things had gone a little bit different on election night in Iowa, where he won but it wasn't perceived that way, I think he potentially could have won, if he had built that grassroots campaign in some of those early states. I had worked in South Carolina in the 2008 primary, and I felt like that was going to be a very, very difficult state for the Romney folks. If somebody could come out early, get a win in Iowa, do well in New Hampshire, they could go down and win South Carolina and then put him in a really tough spot.

RICK BERKE: Was that the Jeremy theory or were other people thinking that?

JEREMY BIRD: That was my theory.

RICK BERKE: Well that counts for a lot. Thank you.

DAN BALZ: We'll hear the other theories tomorrow. Jeremy, thank you very much. [*applause*] We have come to the end. Thank you all. This is the appetizer for tomorrow's entrée. We'll find out how all the plans went awry, most of them. Thanks to all the campaigns.

2

THE REPUBLICAN PRIMARIES

TREY GRAYSON: This morning we are going to kick it off with a discussion on the Republican primaries. I want to introduce our two moderators this morning. They don't really need much of an introduction, but Jonathan Martin is a senior political reporter for *POLITICO* and Jan Crawford is a political correspondent and chief legal correspondent for *CBS News*. We are excited to have both of them here. Take it away, Jan and Jonathan.

JAN CRAWFORD: We only have a very short time to cover a lot of ground, and so to get the conversation started, Jonathan and I thought we are going to actually toss it out to you because you were there, from the beginning, formulating the strategies, seeing what your opponents were doing. So we are just going to say the first question and the floor is yours. What would you guys ask one of the other?

JONATHAN MARTIN: What are the questions that have been on your mind ever since the primaries, if you were curious about one of your opponents and their strategy? Please dive in.

••• THE EXTENDED REPUBLICAN PRIMARY •••

JAN CRAWFORD: Come on, Keith. All right, well, let's talk about perhaps the structure, the process of the campaign. There's a million kinds of general questions we'd like to ask all of you guys and then, of course, we have specific questions for each campaign. One of the things that we were obviously tossing around is the change in the rules to extend this campaign and the impact that proportional voting had.[1] Did that draw this campaign out longer? Was it ultimately to the nominee's detriment in the general? Or did that, as it was intended, allow for other candidates to come forward? Matt?

MATT RHOADES: Thanks, Jan. Obviously the process this time, and this is why when we were doing our early planning on the Romney campaign, we never expected to win this early, just because of the proportional allocation of the delegates. Early on, when the RNC was figuring out the rules, back in 2010, we knew that we didn't want an extended calendar. We wouldn't publicly say that though. But, behind the scenes, some of our supporters were focused on trying to keep the calendar a little less expansive. And so we knew, going into this, it wasn't going to be easy. Primaries aren't easy, first off.

JONATHAN MARTIN: Who was doing that?

MATT RHOADES: That would be individuals such as Ron Kaufman, who works at the RNC, who were focused on that. But, obviously when the rules changed, publicly we came out and said, "We're for it because those are the rules and you can't be against the rules." And, at the end of the day, we knew we had to be patient throughout the process and there would be people that rose up to the top, and we would have to just stick to our strategy in the primary. But, at the end of the day, we had to spend $87 million and we came out in April against an incumbent candidate that just had so much money. Maybe if it wasn't an incumbent president we were going against, it would have been great for everybody. I know a lot of people thought that the Obama-Hillary Clinton campaign made President Obama stronger, and there were certainly parts of the primary that made Governor Romney a better candidate. But, at the end of the day, when we've spent $87 million, and these are $2,500 checks that we can't collect until after the convention, it was a disadvantage.

JAN CRAWFORD: So do you think the bottom line would be that change ultimately hurt the nominee?

MATT RHOADES: Yes.

---

1.   In the 2012 cycle, new Republican rules required states that held nominating contests before April to award delegates proportionally.

JONATHAN MARTIN: Looking forward with the group here, should the parties stick with the system as is, the proportional vote, or should the parties revert to the winner-take-all style system for 2016? What do folks think? Who will dive in here? Dave Carney, I see you stepping up to the mic.

DAVE CARNEY: Well I'm not stepping, but rolling, sort of rambling. When you have an infrastructure and the depth of support of a front-runner, Governor Romney, you have some ability to affect the rules but generally candidates who get in the race in the normal cycle aren't running for the second time. The ability to impact the rules are minimal because, particularly if you try to affect the rules and lose, it can hurt your image and your respect amongst the party's activists and things like that. Do you care about primary voters? If you care about primary voters, then proportional is the way to go because if 40 percent voted for somebody and 30 voted for somebody else, those 30 percent should be represented at the convention.

JONATHAN MARTIN: So you think stick with it then?

DAVE CARNEY: No, no. I'm saying if you care what the primary voters have to say, then proportional is a fair way to do it. But, if you care about, let's get this thing and get this thing cooked so we go try to fight at the general election, then you want winner-take-all. And if you want the basic establishment, the guys with the money, the guys who have people like you fawning over them every day, you want to get this over with. In a year, everyone is going to know who the conventional wisdom says is going to be our nominee in '16 and that is going to help drive that candidate pretty far. But primary voters, and our party, is very small "d" democratic; they, I don't think, would stand for the ability to go back to the kingmaker, what they perceive as the insiders, telling them who is going to win.

JONATHAN MARTIN: It's here to stay though?

DAVE CARNEY: Yes.

JOHN BRABENDER: But I would say it worked, to some degree. I mean, and I'll represent Rick Santorum, he spent, between him and his super PAC, let's say $27 million and went pretty darn far because of the way the system was set up. I'm guessing probably the nominee spent with his campaign and super PAC in the $120 to $130 million range, yet we were able to have a continuous primary and not wrap this thing up after three states, which I think, for the party, was a positive thing. I would even argue that the prolonged debates were a positive thing and probably one of the reasons Mitt Romney won the first debate against the president. What I do think is a problem is when there's inconsistency. Florida, being a winner-take-all state, all of a sudden, in the middle of nowhere, changes strategies dramatically. Texas having to go to the end of the line because of changes down there changed the system dramatically. So I think it needs to be more balanced and more consistent, but I would argue that, to many degrees, the system worked.

••• THE DEBATES •••

JONATHAN MARTIN: Can we do a show of hands on this question? Were there too many debates? Yes, too many debates.

JAN CRAWFORD: Wait, did Vince raise his hand? Did you raise your hand?

JONATHAN MARTIN: We'll start with the Bachmann campaign, go.

Jonathan Martin and Jan Crawford listen to the managers give their view on whether there were too many debates.

BRETT O'DONNELL: I don't think there were too many debates. I mean the timing might have been bad on some of them, but certainly the debates had a huge impact both on the primary and the general election this time.

JONATHAN MARTIN: Now, full disclosure, Brett, you're a debate guy.

BRETT O'DONNELL: Well I understand that, but I think the airwaves were so crowded this time that voters really used the debates to make a lot of decisions about candidates, and that was seen in how the results bore out. I mean Gingrich's campaign came back twice on the back of debates, our campaign was put on the map because of two debates, and Florida and South Carolina swung because of debates. So I think debates mattered; they gave the public a chance to see the candidates outside of a paid media campaign, which I thought was pretty important.

JONATHAN MARTIN: Vince?

VINCE HALEY: Well no. We like debates, and in the course of the year different things happen in the public, whether it's the super committee, and voters want to know how the various candidates are going to speak about issues facing the country, whether it's a high price of gasoline in the spring, what are the candidates going to say? How are they going to illustrate leadership? And you mentioned a lot of television ad money is at times distortive of records. Well those can be clarified in debates and it's a very authentic reality, seeing the debates, as opposed to thirty-second attack ads.

JONATHAN MARTIN: So what's the downside of the debates? Ana Navarro is moving to the mic back there.

ANA NAVARRO: Maybe if our guy had been better at debates, we would like them better. [*laughter*] But since he wasn't, I actually thought we did have too many debates, and I also thought it hurt with the general.

JONATHAN MARTIN: What's the downside?

ANA NAVARRO: The downside was that they were trying to out right-wing each other and then we never came back to the middle in the general. The downside was that we had a terrible discussion that haunted Governor Romney all along about immigration that happened during the debates. So there were issues that came up during the debates, debate after debate, that I think just made it more difficult during the general.

LINDA HANSEN: We feel that the debates were very profitable. Obviously the first debate especially helped Mr. Cain get on the map, shall we say.

JAN CRAWFORD: Right. Of course, if you guys remember in that first debate on May 5th the focus group said that Herman Cain won.

LINDA HANSEN: Herman Cain won hands down. Not only that. We didn't have a lot of money, which was no secret, so the debates really helped to get our message out, but, in a sense as well, I was just talking with someone from Minnesota who said, other than the debates, they would have never really seen the candidates at all. They said especially like Governor Romney. They said other than the debates, they really never even had much contact. So I feel that the debates and extra debates are very, very helpful for citizens all across the country.

JONATHAN MARTIN: Well, Matt and Stuart, did the debates push your candidate too far to the right? Do you think it hurt you guys in the general?

STUART STEVENS: No, I don't think that's the problem. I think with these debates the cycle began with the best of intentions and spun sort of out of control. The biggest problem, from my perspective—and a lot of times when we do talk here, we'll be expressing our own opinions, there was not a unified opinion about things inside the Romney campaign but a difference of opinions on things—is that having the news organizations sponsor these began to give it a commercial quality that, at a certain point, became almost degrading to the candidates. They should have been more serious. There's something odd about this process.

JAN CRAWFORD: Can I interrupt? When you say degrading to the candidates, is there any moment or two, I mean right now, that jumps out at you as examples?

STUART STEVENS: Well I think the way that the candidates were being introduced, it was sort of more of an "American Idol" kind of model rather than a serious presidential debate, versus the way that they are done in the Commission of Presidential Debates where they are more serious. And there's also something very odd about the branding of these debates by large, multinational corporations, like the CNN debate, or the Fox debate or the NBC debate. I think in an ideal world you would have debates put on and news organizations would cover them, in the same way we do the rest of the campaign. We don't have a CBS-sponsored news conference or a CBS-sponsored rally, and, in the future, ideally you would have some mechanism to control this.

JONATHAN MARTIN: But, Stuart, just, if I could, to the first issue you gave, that you didn't think the debates hurt your candidate in terms of how he ran in the general. The word *self-deportation*[2] came out of your candidate's mouth at the debate in Tampa. If it wasn't for that debate, I don't think Governor Romney ever says that phrase. That wasn't helpful for the candidate in the fall, was it?

MATT RHOADES: Listen, I think he was expressing an opinion and it wasn't that damaging to him in the fall though.

JAN CRAWFORD: Going to Ana's point, the debates, because, again, you do have the media asking these questions and people are looking for interesting exchanges, did it sort of push Romney to the right?

MATT RHOADES: Listen, I don't have a problem with that. I think when you run for president, you should expect to get asked tough questions and you should expect to be placed in a lot of situations where you have to answer tough questions, and be that in an op-ed interview or wherever, there's no gotcha quality or ambush quality to the debate. Everybody knows what they are doing, they are up there.

JONATHAN MARTIN: But he wouldn't have used that phrase in a stump speech. He probably wouldn't have used that phrase in a print interview.

MATT RHOADES: Well I wouldn't make that assumption at all. He said what he wanted to say, but there's no pressure on that stage to outflank one another on the right when you are trying to get the Republican nomination. Listen, I think if you go back, one of the advantages that Governor Romney had in this process in general, and in these debates, was having gone through these debates before. And one of the things that we talked about was that debates are never about the room and you

---

2.   During a January 2012 Republican primary debate in Tampa, Florida, Romney, when asked how he would address illegal immigration, said, "The answer is self-deportation, which is people decide they can do better by going home because they can't find work here because they don't have legal documentation to allow them to work here. We're not going to round them up."

are going to get booed. And that was very true at the Tea Party debate, I think, in Orlando, which is a very raucous event, and we were laughing about it before, that this was going to be like rock'em sock'em, and they are going to boo everybody, and it happened. It was fine, it just happens.

JOHN BRABENDER: But that wasn't the structural problem with the debates. The structural problem was, particularly when there were ten candidates, or whatever it was, it was always Governor Romney versus whoever was the next-highest in the polling data. And what they would always say to us on the calls before time is we want equal time for every candidate. Great. The candidates, in many cases, who didn't have big budgets, that's how they get to be known. But, let's take when Governor Perry was up: the first question would go to Governor Romney or Governor Perry about the other candidate, and then they would do a rebuttal about the other candidate, and then they would be asked the same question about their candidate. And we would be halfway into the debate and half the participants didn't even have a question, and so the debates took on this air of who could knock off whatever candidate, other than Romney, was coming up and could we always make this somewhat of a referendum on Romney being the frontrunner.

STUART STEVENS: Well we would have rather them ask you the questions. That's why I think they need to be more serious.

JONATHAN MARTIN: Phil Musser with the Pawlenty Campaign, you guys had a memorable debate moment—

PHIL MUSSER: That's one way to put it. [*laughter*]

JONATHAN MARTIN: —that a lot of people think ultimately hurt the campaign.

JAN CRAWFORD: Do you think that it did?

PHIL MUSSER: Sure.

JAN CRAWFORD: Was that a defining moment for the campaign and for the candidate?

PHIL MUSSER: Yes. Obamacare wasn't forgotten. Look, it was a moment, and I don't think you blame the medium or the context of the moment. It was clearly, for our campaign, a key event that shaped the contour of our race from that point forward, but I wanted to turn your question a little bit forward looking because you asked about 2016, and here's what I think is going to happen because some of the viewpoints in this room are being reflected. I think that you are going to find, at the very beginning of this process, there was a good-faith effort to actually contain and limit the number of debates and a lot of people in this room sat around the table and said, "Is this a good idea or a bad idea?" The problem was we all had different interests, right? John Brabender and the Cain people and the Pawlenty people, to some different degrees, at the beginning of this race were looking at the right role for the party in the debates. The chief rub is, why are we outsourcing control of the debates to liberal news media organizations? Why are we not, to Stuart's point, putting some kind of framework around this that's got common sense and giving it to people that, frankly, are going to allow us to drive our message, as opposed to kind of play to the narrative of the scripts that the major news organizations write? So I think that process will be revisited formally in the next year and it's something that you should look for because I think there were probably too many of these things.

JAN CRAWFORD: Is that something the RNC would do? How would it happen?

PHIL MUSSER: Therein lies the rub because the structure of the national party committee versus the Tea Party Movement versus the interests and needs of the candidates are all very different, but I just think it's something that is clearly going to be rethought about again and discussed with more seriousness.

STUART STEVENS: It was very, very difficult trying to deal with organizations on the debates because, ultimately, the only power you have is that you won't show up.

JAN CRAWFORD: But is that much of a power?

STUART STEVENS: No, that's not much of a power. It's like okay, don't show up.

JAN CRAWFORD: Then that could be held against you, presumably?

STUART STEVENS: Exactly, which means we really don't have any power, which means you end up showing up, which means you lose control, and so you end up doing twenty debates.

JAN CRAWFORD: Let me go to Keith because when we were talking earlier about the differences in time in the questions that people got, I know that there was some frustration on the Bachmann campaign about some of the time.

KEITH NAHIGIAN: The first thing, and I'll get to the second, I would be overcautious on rechanging the system, whether it's the primary system or the debate system, based on an incumbent president election the next time there's an open cycle. I think it's a different landscape of having both parties looking for a nominee and vetting that nominee, so I would caution against overswinging a little bit in trying to make the system work for this campaign for the next cycle on certain aspects.

••• THE IOWA STRAW POLL •••

JAN CRAWFORD: Well, but on that point, some of the things that people are talking about now that would change four years from now, of course, would be the straw poll. Obviously that was something that was pretty successful for you, Keith, not so for you Phil. What are your thoughts on the straw poll?

KEITH NAHIGIAN: Well we debated it. We gave her the opportunity to get out of it, and she thought she needed to do it.

JONATHAN MARTIN: Why?

KEITH NAHIGIAN: I think the narrative of being her home state, the proximity to Minnesota. She is a very frugal person and did not want to spend money on stuff that didn't make any sense, and that was a pretty big hurdle.

JAN CRAWFORD: And you say the straw poll makes no sense? Is that what you are saying?

KEITH NAHIGIAN: Well it's a fundraiser. It's not a real thing. You are drawing from a circle of just a couple of hundred miles really. You may have people traveling longer distances in Iowa, but it's really a central Iowa caucus and not necessarily a statewide caucus. I would also just mention one thing. One of the biggest impacts we found on this campaign was the movement of the Florida primary.[3] Here we are, we built ourselves to get out of Iowa, have a prolonged New Hampshire experience and a South Carolina period, because there was a period in between, and then they moved Florida, and remember, it was like October or something like that. That happened very late. When you look back at that, and then everything else got compressed up, and we really didn't know when some of these caucuses and dates were going to occur. We locked in the debates and then you had other commitments that you had. We had a book tour and some other things. The debates way on the West Coast, travel days and a couple of holidays in there, it made it very difficult to then play in three states and it really compressed it. Even in my years of being in New Hampshire primaries and South Carolina primaries, I don't think those states got to have their fair share of their unique issues.

JAN CRAWFORD: Before you go onto that, let's stay on the straw poll though.

PHIL MUSSER: I hope that one of the legacies of the 2012 campaign is, talk to your presidential candidates; don't chase the shiny object in the straw poll. It's a circus, it's not a caucus. It's a joke. We made a fundamental, strategic miscalculation about the level of investment that we chose to deploy there, in part necessitated by the need to gain traction and momentum and try and secure financial support. But, ultimately, the straw poll, I think, has run its course, in terms of the contest for Iowa, in that it's unrepresentative of the broader contours of the caucus-going electorate that turns out, and, interestingly, it's really more of a celebrity contest. I've worked for Keith Nahigian in 1996. He's probably the best organizer I've ever met in Republican politics, and the fact that Michele Bachmann got in the race in May and managed to win the straw poll in August is amazing because it's not something you are just going to wake up and think about doing. It takes a lot of planning and time.

••• PAWLENTY'S PRIMARY STRATEGY •••

JONATHAN MARTIN: But it wasn't just the straw poll, Phil. Why did Governor Pawlenty feel the need to engage Congresswoman Bachmann that summer? Take us back to last summer, before the straw poll, why

---

3. In September 2011 Florida moved its primary up to January 31, 2012.

did he engage or why did he go negative on Bachmann? What did he see in the polling that said to do that?

PHIL MUSSER: Well we weren't polling at that particular time, in terms of any really specific depth, but it was clear that Michele was galvanizing the Tea Party support. We felt the need to kind of amplify the facts about her record and her background with respect to her service in the Congress. And, ultimately, I'm not sure but you can debate the merits of whether or not that was helpful to the broader cause of the race. I'm not necessarily sure it was impactful or helpful for us in the short-term, as it relates to the straw poll because, ultimately, that was a celebrity contest that I think was driven by a small faction of highly motivated, ideologically driven voters.

JAN CRAWFORD: When you saw the race unfold with candidates becoming the next alternative to Romney, was it just a mistake for Pawlenty to have gotten out so soon, or did he have no choice?

PHIL MUSSER: Well I think if you ask the governor, he would say this, which is we put together, I thought, a very good early plan. We were well positioned out of the gate. We put some big ideas on the table. We had a shot, and we missed our shot. The miscalculation was, I think we would all agree, that probably, from a strategic perspective, betting big in the Iowa straw poll, especially in the context of Governor Perry's entrance, which was imminent at that point in time, and Michele Bachmann's rise, we probably should have put a repause and a rethink on the whole thing. But, sure, had we kind of, I think, looked at the situation under a slightly less, lower level of post–New Hampshire debate duress and with the financial realities of the campaign crashing, the decision would have been to obviously stay because the lesson was pretty clear. If you hung around, you had your shot in the sun, and if Tim had had his shot in the sun, I think we felt that, to the discussion last night, if we were the alternative to Romney at the end that boasts on résumé, bio and background, we were going to be in a favorable position to compete.

JAN CRAWFORD: So was it a strategic decision to try to knock out the other alternatives to Romney and then that just failed? Were you trying to be the alternative to Romney early on, instead of the last man standing strategy?

PHIL MUSSER: Well we had put a lot of diligent work into building networks in the early two states that we thought, with application of visibility and resources, could grow to scale, and so we built a campaign that I think was more sophisticated and more developed than a lot of the other campaigns. And our goal was to essentially use the June month to start to raise the bar for ourselves so that we could build. You've got to remember Chris Christie was lingering around, and all these other candidates were and weren't running. Haley Barbour was in, Mike Pence was in and not in. What it did is it locked up a lot of the donor class, and so what we were trying to do was to unlock the donor class in June, do that on the springboard of a good debate in late June, and then use that to get momentum into Iowa.

••• GINGRICH'S PRIMARY STRATEGY •••

JONATHAN MARTIN: Okay, Rob Johnson and Dave Carney, you guys are here for the Governor Perry campaign but you worked for Newt before that. Yeah, nice and awkward. We heard so much from Newt about the consultant-driven campaign that he was forced to run in the early part of his bid. What exactly did he mean by that, from your perspective, and what did you guys want him to do that he pushed back on?

ROB JOHNSON: Well first of all, we couldn't force Newt to do anything so if it was consulting, it was Newt-driven.

JONATHAN MARTIN: Even back then it was Newt-driven?

ROB JOHNSON: Absolutely, and I think we were very honest when we departed that there was just a fundamental, to use his words, frankly [*laughter*], difference of opinion on how to run a campaign.

JONATHAN MARTIN: What did he want to do?

ROB JOHNSON: I wasn't a consultant, by the way. He was talking about Dave. I was the campaign manager, he was the consultant. [*laughter*] But we felt like he needed to go to the states and talk to the people and do it more than a day at a time.

JONATHAN MARTIN: What did he want to do?

ROB JOHNSON: He wanted to go to the states and talk to the people but a day at a time. He wanted to do television. He wanted to wait for the debates, and it turns out that was probably a pretty good strategy.

JONATHAN MARTIN: How much of that was driven by Callista, his wife?

ROB JOHNSON: The schedule?

JONATHAN MARTIN: Yeah.

ROB JOHNSON: They were a team, and so I think a lot was driven by the team. [*laughter*]

••• PERRY'S ENTRANCE INTO THE RACE •••

JONATHAN MARTIN: So when you guys left the Newt campaign—let that settle in for a minute—what did you know about Governor Perry's intentions?

ROB JOHNSON: I knew what he had said publicly.

JONATHAN MARTIN: That was it?

ROB JOHNSON: That was it. I knew what he had said publicly and, frankly, I didn't, at that point, believe it because I had had so many private conversations with him beforehand.

JONATHAN MARTIN: What did he say in those conversations?

ROB JOHNSON: I'm not running. I'm not going to do it.

JONATHAN MARTIN: Dave?

DAVE CARNEY: No, I mean for years he privately and publicly said he had no interest; he didn't want to do it. He thought he could have a bigger role impacting sort of the Federalist movement, the Tenth Amendment movement, from outside Washington, and that was a very radical departure from everything he had said. Everything we had done over the years to try to help lead that sort of states' rights/Federalist movement was designed to do that and not designed to be a candidate for president. Clearly, had he given any sort of indication, inkling, well, let's think about it or let's not rule it out or let's wait and see, anything like that, I think there are hundreds of things that we could have done differently that would get him better prepared to run. When you have never talked to legislators and county chairmen and political activists in the early states, when you are doing that days before getting in the race, and raising money and getting up to speed on issues, clearly that's not ideal.

JAN CRAWFORD: So did he have a grasp of how difficult it would be getting in so late? And when did it kind of dawn on him that playing catch-up was going to be that hard?

ROB JOHNSON: Before we answer that, I know Matt and Stuart read the book but, if he were going to run for president, we would have never written that book.[4] I mean it's what he believed, but he would have written that book later.

DAVE CARNEY: I just want to finish up on the Newt thing. First of all, he is a brilliant guy, and he has millions of ideas, and he's looking for help, he's not looking for correction. But I think, fundamentally, it comes down to finances. He did not have the resources. He did not have the financial infrastructure to support him and paying a bunch of consultants hanging around to design and implement a campaign that he was not going to have the resources to execute. Basically, originally we were going to do both. We were going to have a really aggressive, multi-million-dollar field operation and we were going to do all of this new engagement in social media and have basically a cutting edge, sort of third way to run a campaign.

JONATHAN MARTIN: Let's stick with Perry for a second. The straw poll was August 13th. That's also the same day that Governor Perry gets in the race. When though did Governor Perry actually decide to run? He announced on August 13th, but when did he decide, this is a go, I'm going to run? What day?

DAVE CARNEY: The actual final decision, where there was sort of no going back, was like August 6th or 7th.

JONATHAN MARTIN: It was that close to the actual announcement?

ROB JOHNSON: It was right after we had a big event in Houston.

JONATHAN MARTIN: The prayer rally at the Astrodome, right?

---

4. In his 2010 book *Fed Up!*, Perry called Social Security a "Ponzi scheme."

ROB JOHNSON: Over 30,000 people showed up, and it was pretty close to right after that.

JAN CRAWFORD: What did it? What did it? You say he changed his mind. What was it that said, "Look, I've got to do this"?

DAVE CARNEY: Honestly, I don't know. I know that he was getting great encouragement to run from folks privately and publicly, both in Texas and outside of Texas. I think the reason there was 1,700 candidates in the race over the course of the campaign was there was always a feeling there was something missing in the Romney candidacy. And whether it was policy ideas or whether it was passion and enthusiasm, whether it was debate, I don't know what it is, but there was just something there and I think he felt that. I think he has, on paper, an excellent record to be able to communicate when the country is really off track and losing jobs, and we had a pretty good jobs message. I don't think it was a single thing. I don't believe he woke up on August 6th and said, "Okay, let's go." I mean it was a very short but thoughtful process to get there.

ROB JOHNSON: And we always knew we could raise a lot of money out of Texas, but I think something else that was encouraging—I guess encouraging is the right word—in the latter part of July, we reached out to a national network led by Peter Terpeluk,[5] God bless his soul, and we would invite ten people and a hundred people would show up in Austin, Texas, and we were doing this three times a week. So we were seeing three hundred national fundraisers, bundlers, a week and, at the time, only one in five of the McCain elite donor bundlers were engaged in the race. So four out of five weren't. And they were showing up in Austin, Texas, to meet Rick Perry, and it was very encouraging.

JONATHAN MARTIN: Matt Rhoades, how did the entry of Governor Perry into the campaign change your strategy?

MATT RHOADES: First off, up to the point of Governor Perry getting in the race, the candidate in the race that we were most concerned about was Governor Pawlenty because, to the point that Phil Musser has made, with their strategy of, if Governor Pawlenty was able to get through the travails of the Iowa straw poll and was to be able to go on and win the Iowa Caucus, he was one of those candidates that could pull off, with his retail politic way, both Iowa and New Hampshire.

---

5. Peter Terpeluk Jr. was a powerhouse fundraiser for the Republican Party who served as U.S. ambassador to Luxembourg from 2002 to 2005 and as finance chairman of the Republican National Committee in 2009 and 2010. He died in October 2011.

JONATHAN MARTIN: Right.

MATT RHOADES: And if we had lost Iowa and New Hampshire to Governor Pawlenty, things would have been pretty bleak for our campaign. When Governor Perry got in the race, certainly we had a lot of respect for his record when it came to jobs and the economy because the way people were talking at that time, you would think every job in America that was created was actually created in Texas. [*laughter*] And up to that point we had put an onus or an emphasis, excuse me, on running a campaign focused on jobs and the economy. And so we knew that this was going to be an obstacle to us moving forward and that's why, very quickly, during the course of Governor Perry's entrance into the race, Governor Pawlenty had left, and we made it a point to contrast on Governor Perry's record, and it included the initial debates and the interactions on those stages. And obviously Rob made a point about "Fed Up!," and I give credit to Stuart Stevens as the individual on the strategy behind it. With Stuart's guidance, we decided to put an emphasis on Governor Perry's position on Social Security and not go after jobs and the economy.

JONATHAN MARTIN: Did your polling show that that was Perry's biggest vulnerability?

STUART STEVENS: I don't think we ever really polled it.

JONATHAN MARTIN: Okay. Matt, you actually said something very interesting. You said before Governor Perry got in, you got most concerned about Governor Pawlenty. What I'm curious about, of the candidates who didn't run, and there were a lot of candidates who didn't run this cycle, which of those candidates were you guys most concerned about? Was it Chris Christie? Was it Jeb Bush? Sarah Palin? Who was it?

MATT RHOADES: To win your party's nomination, you have to run your campaign, and it goes to the point again that Phil made. We made a decision. We weren't going to chase shiny objects, we weren't going to do straw polls. We had done straw polls the last time. Obviously the debates are important in the Republican primary process but one of the reasons why twenty-plus debates is a bit too much is because it takes away your ability to run your campaign.

JONATHAN MARTIN: Who were you most concerned about who didn't run?

MATT RHOADES: We had respect for a lot of people whose names were floated, but if you're not in the race, you're not in the race.

JAN CRAWFORD: Let me go back to Governor Perry. Obviously, the narrative coming out of his withdrawal was that the debates did him in, the three agencies.[6] What happened? What happened with that campaign? Why, after jumping in and skyrocketing to the top, becoming the candidate that the Romney guys were most concerned about, then it just all fell apart. Why? Was it the debates? That he got in too late? That it was never viable? The money? I mean, what was it?

DAVE CARNEY: Well I could talk to my therapist. [*laughter*] I still haven't got the right answer but it's one of two things. I mean, we made a lot of mistakes.

JAN CRAWFORD: Like what?

DAVE CARNEY: Just small mistakes, but the big tactical or strategic mistake is we should have, if he was going to do this, started it years ago. As governor of Texas, the session of the legislature meets 140 days every two years. He has a lot of time on his hands. He could have been doing lots of things, going to help other people around the country, going to meet people, become very helpful in Ohio and Iowa and New Hampshire and South Carolina, some of these important states, and meet donors and things like that. So we didn't have that luxury of time. And two is we should have waited. I mean we should have waited actually longer to get in when we decided okay, let's take a look at it and was it a possibility. Rob taught me these three questions that we tried to answer and put a framework and plan together. It was based on that we needed to get in because Romney started locking people up more than he had, which was he had a lot of people locked up already, and I'm not sure of the fundraising but I think we had an unlimited ability to raise money, that was never a problem, it was a matter of how to collect it.

Our problem was the political side, the political support, and Governor Romney's team was excellent and had a long head start and was locking people up. A lot of people were waiting to see if he was getting in the race and we were concerned. We should have waited. We should have waited until November, maybe, or maybe the middle of October because of the Florida move-up and having the declaration by

---

6. In a November 2011 CNBC Republican primary debate, Perry tried to name the three federal agencies he would like to eliminate if he is elected president, but he only remembered two—the Commerce and Education Departments.

the secretary of state to be on the ballot. It would have given us more time to be prepared, more time to do some of the groundwork that's necessary, get better prepared on the issues and things.

JAN CRAWFORD: You wouldn't have had the September debates.

DAVE CARNEY: Right. I mean, listen, this is the craziest thing about debates.

JONATHAN MARTIN: First of all, they were panels, they weren't debates.

DAVE CARNEY: Whatever. Yeah, exactly. This is, like, crazy. The president of the United States never debates. It's a skill that is unrequired, unnecessary. [laughter] He's not the prime minister, he doesn't stand there and take questions for a half-hour. Nobody ever questions the president in public. You do not argue on the red phone. I mean this is crazy. [laughter]

Number two, the RNC has never, ever enforced anything. I mean the idea that the RNC, like they did last time in Minnesota, fixed this problem, that's crazy. It's the establishment candidate who is not going to want to do debates, the frontrunner, and everybody who has no money wants to get on national cable TV for twelve minutes because it's their shot and it's free. And the idea that you go from California to Florida to California with a holiday in between, in ten days, that's illuminating? Whatever happened to the town meeting? Matt is a hundred percent right: candidates have got to run their own campaigns.

JONATHAN MARTIN: But the Roemer folks, the debates were your guys only shot.

DAVE CARNEY: What kind of crazy idea is that? [laughter]

JONATHAN MARTIN: Carlos, tell him.

CARLOS SIERRA: We hated the debates. We really hated the debates. I think we do need some debate reform. I think Stuart made a great point that it's basically corporate sponsored. It's very undemocratic.

JONATHAN MARTIN: You guys were pining to get into these debates, now you are knocking them?

CARLOS SIERRA: Everyone had their time to shine, and it was because of the debates. Michele Bachmann shined. Perry shined.

ROB JOHNSON: We shined before the debates. [*laughter*]

CARLOS SIERRA: Exactly. Like I said last night, part of our strategy was the debates and, unfortunately, we never got in. I know Gary Johnson[7] never got in. We do need debate reform though. It's sad there were two governors who were not allowed in.

LINDA HANSEN: One of the things that I think we need to remember about the debates is who we're ultimately trying to serve, and that would be the citizens of the country. That would be the voters who are looking for information, many of whom never get to live in Iowa and see the candidates every breakfast, lunch, and dinner. Who do we serve? And, as journalists, what is your job? Your job is to give factual information to the citizens of this country. And so we need to remember what's the purpose of the debates, and there's positives and negatives about how many, where they were, all that. And Stuart brought up a really good point about who is in charge of the questioning.

••• A ROMNEY-PAUL ALLIANCE? •••

JONATHAN MARTIN: Okay. Trygve Olson, you were sitting next to Matt Rhoades, which is fitting to a lot of folks in this room because there was much chatter about the Romney-Ron Paul alliance. What was the nature of the contact between the Paul campaign and the Romney campaign? Were you talking?

TRYGVE OLSON: I'm going to use my own debate strategy and I'm going to answer the question I want to talk about, rather than talking about what you asked. [*laughter*] This is a typical media attack.

JONATHAN MARTIN: The Newt Gingrich strategy.

TRYGVE OLSON: I think the thing with the debates, there was some effort, and it started with the conversation between Jesse Benton and Ginsberg[8] based off of 2008 to try to get all the campaigns together to talk about the debates. The problem with the number of debates is you can't really get at it because everybody has their own interests, so what

---

7.   Gary Johnson, the former governor of New Mexico, was the Libertarian Party nominee for president in 2012.
8.   Jesse Benton was Ron Paul's political director, and Ben Ginsberg was the Romney campaign's national counsel.

ended up happening is we're not going over ninety minutes, we don't want to have a green room that's six thousand miles away so Stuart and I have to ride around in a golf cart with a guy who gets lost because he doesn't know where he's going on the University of Tampa campus. And if you want to know why Stuart and I are on the same golf cart, it's because it only reinforces the notion we have an alliance from people like you. [*laughter*]

But the important thing, one of the things that I think is missing from this conversation that matters and the debates reinforces is, I don't know how to refer to it any differently, there's kind of the seventh-grade girls, and I don't mean any disrespect to seventh-grade girls, component to this in that all the candidates are spending so much time with debates and like, Bob likes Joe and Joe doesn't like Frank and whatever. And so, like last time, Huckabee and McCain—there's been a lot reported about this—really didn't want Romney to get the nomination, and so they ganged up. This time, there was a tendency for candidates, as somebody would rise, everybody would gang up on him.

The question I would like to ask to Carney, the one thing that I couldn't understand with you guys is when you guys did roll in, you had seven state troopers. Simi Valley was the first appearance with everybody else and all the rest of the campaigns were sitting around, well, here comes Rick Perry: He's riding high in the polls. He's got seven state troopers with him. He's got this entourage. Who does he think he is, the prime minister of Britain? Let's all get him. And so, I don't know if there's a way around it, but I always wondered if the optics of your rolling into this dynamic of people who had been traveling entered into the equation because I do think it mattered. It certainly mattered in my guy going after you on Hillary Care.

JAN CRAWFORD: So did you put your own X on your back? That's the point, right?

TRYGVE OLSON: Yeah.

JAN CRAWFORD: Did you paint the X on his back?

DAVE CARNEY: It goes to, I guess, the success of the Texas Rangers to think that there were only seven there. Believe me, there was a lot more than seven. [*laughter*] It's just a fact of life that there's a tremendous effort in dealing with an incumbent, and security issues to balance, the same with the president. It's a constant fight between the protectee's people and the protectors, and it's just sort of life. In hindsight, would we have preferred not to have gotten in the race and had things gone so well, and things happen and the poll numbers, and temporarily looking really great? No, I wouldn't trade that. I would rather have a longer ramp-up time, but once you get in, you want that. We were not structurally sufficient to support that sort of meteoritic rise, and we became a target, just like most everybody else for their fifteen days in the sunshine were a target. We just didn't have the infrastructure in place to support that, that the candidates need in order to be supported. But security is always an issue. It's a high-profile job; there's a lot of people. It's difficult, and it's a constant battle. They would prefer to have machine guns actually out, not hidden, and many of them never leave the confines of a bulletproof, bombproof tunnel underneath the Capitol.

JONATHAN MARTIN: Stuart, you want to go there?

STUART STEVENS: I just think it's really important to note that having run for president before, which is a great advantage for Governor Romney, I think it would be a great mistake to think that the candidates who were in this race that ended up not getting the nomination or maybe didn't have such a good debate here or there are not candidates who could be president and who would not do a lot better next time they run. There is nothing like running for president of the United States, and having run before is a great experience. I think there were a bunch of tremendously talented candidates that would do really well. And I think it's a real mistake to say, "Okay, we had this number or that number, well, that means that that person is not up to that level of playing the game." Watch these candidates. I think a lot of them will come back and do really well.

JAN CRAWFORD: Let me go back to the point that Jonathan was making about Dr. Paul in the debates. They were a major part of this primary for different reasons for different candidates. There would always be this effort by the alternatives to attack Romney. But, Dr. Paul really didn't do that in those debates, and it looked like there clearly was some kind of bond or alliance that he had struck with Romney. Why was that?

TRYGVE OLSON: Matt, do you want to tell me what I should say?

MATT RHOADES: No.

TRYGVE OLSON: There's been a lot made of the idea that we didn't attack, that we didn't draw a contrast with Mitt Romney in the way that we drew a contrast with other candidates, whether it was in the debates or through our paid media. The reality is we had lots of pieces of mail that drew contrast. The Romney folks liked to remind us about the day Mitt Romney announced we raised $1.7 million off of that with a pretty scathing Mitt Romney as the establishment piece, but, strategically, we were never in a place where we were competing with Mitt Romney for essentially establishment votes, and so I think that matters. I think the other thing that matters is, on a personal level, and Stuart alluded to this, it matters to have done it before for a lot of reasons, but one of the things that mattered in that relationship is, and this has been documented a lot, Ann Romney and Carol Paul became friends. Ron Paul considers Mitt Romney somebody that's a friend. They had shared a journey that had gone on for four years and, to some degree, they're at a similar station in life; they have five kids. So there were issues, certainly on foreign policy, where he disagreed with Governor Romney, but, strategically, it was more important to draw a contrast with Rick Perry when he got in the race because he was taking votes, Tea Party–type voters, from us in Iowa.

JONATHAN MARTIN: I want to ask a question.

MATT RHOADES: Jonathan, can I just add one thing?

JONATHAN MARTIN: Please.

MATT RHOADES: One of the lessons learned in running, like Stuart said, you learn so much from running before, and one of the things in the 2008 campaign, we, many of us, were full of Bush/Cheney staffers, and we divvied up amongst various campaigns, and we just weren't very respectful of each other. We'd run into each other at debates, and it was just like a level of immaturity, über-competition. That was a mistake that I learned personally, running in 2008, and I think in politics it's so important, and this goes to the personal relationship between Governor Romney and Dr. Paul, to show a little respect for each other. They debated each other, I think, thirty-four times over two campaigns.

••• THE HUNTSMAN-ROMNEY RELATIONSHIP •••

JONATHAN MARTIN: Well, speaking of relationships, Matt, you and Matt David, I know, are long friends, but your candidates didn't seem terribly fond of one another. Matt David, can you talk about Governor Huntsman's relationship with Governor Romney and sort of his view of Governor Romney?

Trygve Olson listens as Matt Rhoades talks about the relationship between Mitt Romney and Ron Paul.

MATT DAVID: Well first, on the debate topic, Stuart is absolutely right that it's really the circus nature of these, the "American Idol," thirty seconds to explain your position on immigration, raise your hand, the ten-to-one question. That's what really kind of killed us. I think for the outside public watching those debates, it kind of framed the entire party in a negative light. And then Carney is right too though that if you are an underdog in the race, and you don't have money, you need to earn media opportunities.

JAN CRAWFORD: Can I stop you there though? I just want to make sure. You said the debates. I mean you're talking more broadly, but you believe that those debates actually harmed the party itself?

MATT DAVID: Absolutely. I remember we did a debate, and I talked to a friend that was outside of politics the next day, and he was like, were you at that crazy Fox debate? I was like, well it was actually CNN but, yes, I was there. That tells me a lot. So, yeah, I think it did hurt the party.

JAN CRAWFORD: Why? Because the candidates looked less presidential? Does everyone agree with this?

MATT DAVID: It's like Stuart said. When we walk on stage and it's like it's a cross between "American Idol" and a football game, being announced onto the field.

JONATHAN MARTIN: All right, Matt, talk about your boss's relationship with Governor Romney because it's one of the most fascinating dynamics of this race.

MATT DAVID: Did you like that dodge?

JONATHAN MARTIN: Answer the question.

MATT DAVID: I think the media wanted there to be a competition for a variety of reasons.

JONATHAN MARTIN: Oh, come on. Governor Huntsman didn't do anything for Romney after the primary ended. He barely endorsed him.

MATT DAVID: They told us to be candid about it.

JONATHAN MARTIN: What's the back story on that relationship?

MATT DAVID: Here's what I believe on this. You had the Olympics story that everyone wrote about, that Huntsman wanted it and then Romney came in. I talked to Huntsman at length about this, and he honestly felt that that whole story was overblown. It was really a process issue, it wasn't a personality conflict. But, here's what I believe. I think they are both very successful, very driven, very competitive people. So I think if you are in a situation where you are running for president of the United States, you want to win it. And they do have some family connections, a lot of friends, they are both Mormons, so I think that increases the level of competition.

JONATHAN MARTIN: What was the nature of the preparations that you guys put in place while Governor Huntsman was in China, as the U.S. ambassador, to get the campaign ready? How much did you guys do and what did you do?

MATT DAVID: We laid out what we thought our path was going to be. We started doing opposition research on the candidates.

JONATHAN MARTIN: This is you, John Weaver, who else?

MATT DAVID: And Tim Miller.

JONATHAN MARTIN: Did Governor Huntsman ask you to do this? Were you guys doing it without his knowledge?

MATT DAVID: At one point, I had ruled out doing 2012.

JONATHAN MARTIN: But you were assuming the ambassador for China wanted to have all this stuff laid out for him.

MATT DAVID: Yeah.

JONATHAN MARTIN: And not talking to him about it?

MATT DAVID: Yeah. The first meeting was a little awkward. [*laughter*] I'm like, "Here's your plan to run for president, literally."

JONATHAN MARTIN: And what did he say?

MATT DAVID: He said, "We'll look at it," and then we immediately started briefing him on the issues. Where are you at on this? How do you feel about your cap-and-trade position going to be an issue for you? How would you answer that now? And you could just tell like his wheels had been spinning on this.

JONATHAN MARTIN: That was late April of 2011. It was the weekend of the correspondents' dinner.

MATT DAVID: It was the early morning after the correspondents' dinner, right.

JONATHAN MARTIN: Did he, at that point, tell you he was in the race, that he was going to run in the race?

MATT DAVID: I could tell by that conversation that he was going to go.

JONATHAN MARTIN: And that was your first meeting?

MATT DAVID: Yeah, but he said he wanted to spend a couple of weeks talking to his family. We were going to test the waters going to New Hampshire and South Carolina.

PHIL MUSSER: Can I just say one thing on the inside game?

JONATHAN MARTIN: Please.

PHIL MUSSER: Irrespective of the personal relationships between the principals that ran for president in this campaign, one thing you've got to give Matt and the Romney campaign enormous credit for, and other people in this room as well, is they did a remarkable job at the inside relationship game. So Matt and other members of the Romney team were in constant contact with the other people who were leading the other enterprises. And they did so in a way that, as the campaign progressed and people got out of the race, it softened the willingness for others to get behind the campaign. And it's really, really a testimonial to Matt's leadership, in particular, but it's something that I think was totally missing in 2008 and that he did a terrific job of because I know that all of us in this room talked to some degree. He led this effort, and it made a big difference for his candidate as the primary progressed.

••• THE ATTACKS ON GINGRICH •••

JAN CRAWFORD: I want to follow up on something Matt was saying, talking about respect. There's one campaign in this room who may feel they didn't get a lot of respect, and that's the Gingrich campaign on some of the ads that you guys ran. So I'm going to ask you this, Vince: Do you think, in addition to the negative ads that you were faced with in Iowa and Florida that the party leaders also were trying to tip the scales for Romney?

VINCE HALEY: Well it certainly felt that way at times. Rush Limbaugh gave an interview to Greta at the end of December last year where he talked about his belief, because Greta asked him about all this ganging up on Gingrich, and he responded that he thought that there was an inside-the-beltway establishment that was wired in and had a heart for Romney. Now, whether that was true or not, at times it felt that way. As I said last night, we were trying to run a positive campaign. Newt always believed that the voting public was sick of negative campaigns. That was a lesson from 1994 when they did the Contract with America, and it was not going to just be an attack on Bill Clinton in the '94 bi-election, it was going to be offering a positive program. And, in a similar way, he wanted to offer a positive program. Dave mentioned the financial limitations of the campaign, which made it very difficult to respond to negative attacks when they came. Gingrich, I think, was very successful in his approach, not just in the debates. He did very well in the debates, but in several public gatherings in Iowa, in key moments in October and November, he wowed the audiences. So he was winning in many ways, lots of support on the ground, not just in debates. But, we were not prepared to deal with the onslaught of ads against us in Iowa.

JAN CRAWFORD: So did you feel like, after South Carolina, you may have had Romney on the ropes but you just didn't have the money?

VINCE HALEY: Well Newt has often talked about how you can have waves and, take South Carolina, we had two debates that week before the vote. I forget exactly what the polling was that week. I don't know how close it was. But, the first debate took place, and I think Newt had two standing ovations, had enormous momentum. And then, of course, the second debate, if you all remember, there was this question that John King led off the debate with about *ABC News*'s interview with Newt's ex-wife.[9] And Newt gave an answer, and the place erupted in a standing ovation. And I turned to somebody on our team, and I said, "Newt either won the primary right then and there or lost it."

JONATHAN MARTIN: Did he tell you guys before that debate that he was going to give that answer if the question came up?

VINCE HALEY: No, not me.

JONATHAN MARTIN: You didn't know?

VINCE HALEY: No. So if the figures are correct, there was a 30 percent bump up in turnout in South Carolina. It shattered the record from 2000. So there was very positive momentum. Then you go to Florida, which has eight media markets. If there was a place to stop him, it had to be Florida, and they committed resources to do it.

---

9. In a January 2012 CNN Republican primary debate, Gingrich earned a standing ovation from a South Carolina crowd when he angrily rebuked moderator John King for opening the debate with a question about allegations by his ex-wife Marianne that he'd asked her for an "open marriage."

JAN CRAWFORD: Was that your firewall? Florida? I mean, were you guys the only one that had the money?

STUART STEVENS: Had we lost Florida, I wouldn't have said it was a firewall. [*laughter*] And, to go to Vince's point, I do remember the polling from that debate, and I don't remember it precisely, but I think it was a double-digit shift toward Newt after that first debate, ten to fifteen points. And if you go back and look at the second debate, the governor did not attack Newt because it was not a moment where Newt was attacking him. It was just one of these things that happened that Newt, to his credit, seized the moment. He's very good at that, and there wasn't anything he could do, just kind of get out of the way. We always felt very comfortable about winning Florida, but we also felt that after we won New Hampshire, we could lose states and just stay in and we would win. We might lose some, win some, maybe this thing would go to June, but we planned to stay to June. We went to the convention, we stayed at the convention. We were going to do what it took to win time-wise, and we couldn't control that calendar. We were very steady and calm about it.

JAN CRAWFORD: How alarmed were you after South Carolina?

STUART STEVENS: Not at all, to be honest.

JAN CRAWFORD: I mean, your polls had you up though. You must have been surprised.

STUART STEVENS: Listen, in politics things happen, and Newt had great moments. The governor grew his vote from four years earlier. He came in third. We didn't see anything happening that was damaging to the candidacy. He didn't lose because he had stumbled. He didn't lose because he had been attacked. His negatives didn't skyrocket. Newt had a good week. I mean, give him credit.

VINCE HALEY: And in Florida, Governor Romney had two great debates, and, at a practical level, Rhoades led an operation which I think was very aggressive on the early vote in Florida. We were not as organized in that way to get the early vote, and I think they were running ads well earlier than even the South Carolina debate, so they had quite an advantage on us. But you did have to spend a lot of money on ads in Florida, nevertheless.

MATT RHOADES: Let me just echo first what Stuart said. We had to stay calm during South Carolina, but I can tell you fifteen minutes into the first debate in South Carolina, that was the last moment I thought about South Carolina the rest of the campaign. I simply just shifted focus to Florida.

JAN CRAWFORD: Really? You knew that?

MATT RHOADES: You knew. It was a great moment for the Speaker.

JONATHAN MARTIN: This is the Myrtle Beach debate on Fox?

MATT RHOADES: That very first debate in South Carolina.

JONATHAN MARTIN: Right.

MATT RHOADES: Within fifteen minutes of the first debate, I shifted my focus on Florida. And that's when we went and doubled down on our efforts in Florida. I forget the specific amounts of money that we spent, but traditionally you do a thousand-point TV buy. And for the Florida primary, we upped that to at least 1,500, maybe more. I don't remember the exact numbers.

JONATHAN MARTIN: Going to those debates in Florida where obviously Governor Romney had two strong performances, what was your guys' advice to Governor Romney in terms of engaging Newt?

JAN CRAWFORD: Also, we have Brett here too who worked on those debates.

JONATHAN MARTIN: Yeah.

BRETT O'DONNELL: I'll defer to my friends across the table.

MATT RHOADES: Well obviously we knew the debates were going to be very important coming back from the two great performances the Speaker had in South Carolina. And, each debate is an event in and of itself, and you shift your strategy and focus in each one of those. You usually go into each debate, at least in the primaries it's a little less complicated, with probably three goals. And certainly, our goal going into the Florida debates was to do contrast with the Speaker. I don't know if you want to add anything, Stuart, you were a big part of that.

STUART STEVENS: Before each of these debates, we went through this process of what are our goals for this debate? And how do we accomplish those goals? And we tried to accomplish those goals in the debates. It was clear that the major competitor that emerged was the Speaker, so we needed to engage the Speaker. There's a rule of thumb, and Brett could speak to this better than I, but a large percentage of the time the most aggressive person in a debate, when people are engaging, will win that debate. And we had pretty clear-cut, simple goals. We needed to engage and win.

••• PERRY'S BACK PROBLEMS •••

JONATHAN MARTIN: I want to ask Dave Carney something before we forget this, and that is the question of Governor Perry's health. To what degree did his back problems impact his debate performance?[10]

DAVE CARNEY: I think it had a big impact.

JONATHAN MARTIN: How so? Because of pain?

DAVE CARNEY: Well originally what the doctors and the patient thought, in terms of recovery time, it was supposed to be a very short period before he could get back to his regular routine. The whole campaign was built upon a very aggressive, arduous schedule of travel in order to make up for lost time, and the situation during the summer and early fall, or in the fall, was never completely right. It was supposed to be two weeks or something like that, and it was four months, and it was still a problem. It's just a fact; it's not an excuse. I think we passed tort reform in Texas, so we can't actually sue the doctors for what they told him. If my doctor tells me I need to lose a few pounds, I may not exactly listen to what he had to say. I listen to what I think I want to hear, so it could have been the patient [*laughter*] wanting to think it was two weeks, and everything will be fine. But this little procedure was minor in everybody's minds, in the governor's mind, in the office, our minds. It was not a big deal in the slightest. It was an in-and-out operation.

JAN CRAWFORD: But do you think it had an effect on his debates?

DAVE CARNEY: Yes.

---

10. Governor Perry underwent surgery that involved a spinal fusion and a nerve decompression on July 1, 2012, to correct a recurring back ailment.

JAN CRAWFORD: Was he on medication? Was it just the standing? Having to stand and he was in pain?

DAVE CARNEY: Yeah, it was the standing, and it was the inability to get a decent night's sleep. You know, when you travel it was grueling on his body, so just more difficult to study, more difficult to get comfortable. And, again, this is our specific problem because we had no time. So we would go to a debate site to do something, and we wanted to meet with fifty people, have different meetings and try to reach out, to introduce Perry to different types of people that we would have spent the last five years doing. And you can't do that when you're in pain. It's a negative meeting, so you don't want to have it. You end up really hurting yourself because the debate prep takes so much time. It was definitely a factor, not an excuse. We made many other mistakes, but it was a problem.

••• BACHMANN AS THE WOMAN CANDIDATE •••

JAN CRAWFORD: There was another health issue that was raised on the campaign trail, and that involved Michele Bachmann. Keith, do you think that had an impact on her campaigning or at least on the public's perception and the media's perception of her as the candidate?

KEITH NAHIGIAN: It was incredible how much coverage it got. I mean with a person who has headaches it went to the question of commander-in-chief, the button, the phone, that kind of thing, and I think it's a higher standard for a woman running for office, especially in a state like Iowa.

JAN CRAWFORD: What do you mean a higher standard? You mean women have to be healthier?

KEITH NAHIGIAN: Yeah. Women don't get out of Iowa. Mrs. Clinton didn't get out of Iowa.

JONATHAN MARTIN: So why did you campaign there in the first place?

KEITH NAHIGIAN: Well it was a decision we collectively had to make. But if you look at the number of statewide elected officials, there's no women in the state senate, there's no congressional members that are women. You just saw a woman First Lady get beat in Iowa. It's a different place, and I think the impact of that on a state like Iowa was a little bit more.

JAN CRAWFORD: You mean that the migraines had resonated with voters more?

KEITH NAHIGIAN: Yeah. I think it was a bigger issue, and, remember, it was an issue for like two weeks. It was kind of amazing. I mean, I was on the John McCain campaign in 2000, and we had to open up our medical records of John McCain and the post-POW camp kind of thing, and that was kind of interesting. But here we were. We were running against a guy with stage-four cancer, and they didn't ask him a question about his health at all. It was overblown, considerably, and I was with her every day on the entire campaign. I never saw her have any issues at all.

JAN CRAWFORD: Never?

KEITH NAHIGIAN: No.

BRETT O'DONNELL: We literally had reporters jumping into us to ask questions about the migraine headache thing. It was absurd, and we also saw this in other ways. We saw stories about her nails and about the dresses she wore, and nobody ever wrote about Mitt Romney's tie.

JONATHAN MARTIN: They do it all the time. That's not true.

BRETT O'DONNELL: There were way more stories about what dress she wore or what colors she wore or why it was a bad color or her hair. I mean, I think there were a lot of stories that were gender specific.

JONATHAN MARTIN: All right.

BRETT O'DONNELL: I thought that the coverage was way over the top, and the migraine headaches opened the door to that.

LINDA HANSEN: You brought up Mr. Cain's cancer, and I think one of the reasons maybe that wasn't a huge issue was because he was open about that from the very, very beginning. He spoke very, very openly about it. So in defense of the media in that regard, he was very open about it. The point still remains that there is a double standard. They don't talk about, oh my gosh, how much did Mitt Romney pay for his shoes? They talk about different things about women, and why is that?

We have kind of a joke on our campaigns with our team. It's like, if I would say something intelligent, they would look at me, and I would say there's not just air between these ears. And it's a joke. But every woman knows exactly what I'm talking about, and I think every man might because there is this mild double standard. We say there's no glass ceiling, but there is, in a way, because we focus on things that are inconsequential when it comes to women candidates. And I think that we could learn from what you brought up.

KEITH NAHIGIAN: It kind of rolled into our *Newsweek* cover.[11] I remember that. We sat down with a photographer who said, "My job is to come and take a bad picture of you." There was the first conversation he had with her where he said, "My editors don't want me to take a good picture of you," and we were about to cut the whole thing off. Like I said, I've done seven of these, working with males, females, working with Governor Whitman in New Jersey, and it's a different game. I remember when Governor Whitman had an ovarian cyst when she was the governor and the *New York Times* had a picture this big of her anatomy of what was going to happen. And then, six months later, Guiliani had prostate cancer and the press said, "Let's give him his privacy." It's just a world of difference, and I think that particular issue lingered much longer than it actually was. They were looking for a story that didn't exist, and they almost couldn't take the answer no throughout.

••• CAIN'S PROBLEMS—AND EXIT FROM THE RACE •••

JAN CRAWFORD: Let me shift gears here just a little bit because when we are thinking about how the race progressed and the next candidates who would come up, it almost felt like at times you guys were just playing Whack-a-Mole. Like there would be someone who would come up, and you would knock them down. And then someone else would come up, and then Mr. Cain obviously had his moment. When were you two aware of the allegations of sexual harassment?[12] Did you know

---

11. On August 7, 2011, *Newsweek* ran an unflattering picture of Bachmann on its cover, with the headline "The Queen of Rage."

12. In the 1990s, when Herman Cain was president and CEO of the National Restaurant Association, two female employees complained to colleagues and senior association officials about inappropriate behavior by Cain and the sexual harassment allegations led to settlements with the two employees—one for approximately $45,000 and another in the mid-$30,000s. Cain said he was falsely accused and that a thorough investigation found the claims had no basis.

about those when he declared his candidacy? Were you aware right before they were alleged? When did you find out about that?

MARK BLOCK: Well we didn't have an opposition research department. Just like when you sit down with a candidate, you ask him what's going to come up. We were very aware of the National Restaurant Association.

JAN CRAWFORD: So when he got in the race, you knew about what had happened at the association?

MARK BLOCK: Yes. We knew about it, and there was nothing there. One of the things that I would say that we did wrong is not respond forcefully sooner to the National Restaurant Association allegations because we knew there was nothing there. He made the decision, I'm not going to chase something that I know there's no substance to, all right? It spun out of control, and, if I had to do it all over again, on Halloween day we would have came out with the news conference and tried to put it to bed.

LINDA HANSEN: The other thing that I've said often that I think we could have done a better job of in that regard is actually preparing his family for the rigors. They were great. They were a hundred percent supportive. Mrs. Cain is a hundred percent supportive. She was with him all the way through, every bit, but when the media came on their family so much, it took a physical toll. And that's when Mr. Cain decided he needed to think because the physical toll it was beginning to take on his family, not only his wife but many people know he had his fourth grandchild born January 1st, so his daughter-in-law was in the late trimester of pregnancy. So he's looking at that in terms of my first job as a leader is to be leader of this family, take care of my family.

JONATHAN MARTIN: Why didn't Mrs. Cain campaign more for Mr. Cain, both before the story but also in the aftermath of that, when she could have been a pretty powerful character witness?

LINDA HANSEN: She was great, a hundred percent supportive.

MARK BLOCK: Mrs. Cain was the deciding factor when he decided to run for president, a hundred and ten percent supportive. And she did campaign with him, but not as rigorously as other candidates. Mr. Cain will tell you it was for two reasons. She wasn't running for president, he was, and he didn't want to put her under the media buzz saw that he knew he was walking into. And, quite frankly, I think it has been written that she has a little challenge in traveling because of her health, and he didn't want to put her through the rigors of that.

LINDA HANSEN: I think she felt a little bit like Laura Bush did when George Bush proposed to her and she said, "Well I'll be happy to marry you, as long as I never have to give a speech." But Mrs. Cain was someone who is very classy. She's very articulate. She's very opinionated. She would have risen quite well into the role of not only the nominee's wife, but she would have been a great First Lady.

MARK BLOCK: You know, Jonathan, if you remember the Greta interview with Mrs. Cain, she made the decision to do that.

JONATHAN MARTIN: Mrs. Cain did?

MARK BLOCK: Mrs. Cain did. They didn't ask us. She didn't ask him. She said, "I want to do this." It came from Mrs. Cain.

JAN CRAWFORD: Well you're asking why she didn't campaign for her husband. Why, when he got out of the race, didn't Mr. Cain campaign for Governor Romney?

MARK BLOCK: Excuse me? Why didn't he? He did. Wait a minute, time out.

JAN CRAWFORD: Did you see him as someone who could have been a powerful surrogate? Could you have used him more?

MARK BLOCK: He was.

MATT RHOADES: He did. He did a ton of college stuff for us. He came by the headquarters. He did campaign for us.

JONATHAN MARTIN: Well he didn't appear on national TV for you guys as a surrogate in the fall campaign. Right?

LINDA HANSEN: Mark, feel free to jump in here, but one of the things about Herman Cain is that he was really trying to make sure the message got out afterwards, apart from a label. So you go in with a label, an "R", whether it be Romney or Republican, a lot of the times you can't reach some of the very people you need to have come over to your side of the ticket. So he was not this absolute, card-carrying surrogate, but in terms of promoting the issues, promoting the ideas and policies that would really help this country, he was out there every day.

••• SANTORUM'S RISE •••

JONATHAN MARTIN: I want to get John Brabender in the conversation with Senator Santorum. John, one of the things I know folks in this room were fascinated by for a long time was this dynamic of having both Santorum and Gingrich in the race, dividing the conservative vote while running against Governor Romney. Can you talk to us about the nature of the conversations that your boss, Senator Santorum, had with Newt during that period of time, because they were talking, I believe, on the phone and occasionally at debates? What were they talking about? Was it ever considered that one would drop out and carry the banner? Can you just sort of tell us about that?

JOHN BRABENDER: Well most of those conversations were staff to staff. Rick and Newt did talk a couple of times, but I remember Santorum telling me that Newt gave him some historical reference to the 1920s type of thing of how it was going to play out again. And I think Rick reminded me it was a senator that had won that year, but, anyhow, when we got to what I would say was the final stage of the campaign, we felt there were three things for us still to do to get to the delegate count to win, that had to happen. Number one was, first, to win Pennsylvania. Number two was Texas, which was having at least some discussions to going potentially to winner-take-all because they were so late in the process. And, number three, we had to get Gingrich out. And it wasn't where we were competitive with Gingrich but in many cases it was where he was getting now four percent of the vote but it was killing us.

JONATHAN MARTIN: Was there a discussion to get him out of the race, and, if so, what did you say?

JOHN BRABENDER: There were clear discussions between our staff and their staff. I got the sense that their staff felt it would be in the best interest if Newt Gingrich would step aside and there would be some unifying nature. I believe it was very close to that happening.

JONATHAN MARTIN: When? Do you recall?

JOHN BRABENDER: Early April. I remember receiving a call saying that Newt personally had decided he did not want to do that.

JONATHAN MARTIN: Who was the call from? Do you recall?

JOHN BRABENDER: I know, but I'm not going to share that.

JONATHAN MARTIN: Yeah, yeah. And if that had happened, do you think your candidate would have gotten the nomination?

JOHN BRABENDER: Well I think it would have helped. I mean, I think that if you look in retrospect, people forget how close maybe Rick did come to getting the nomination.

JONATHAN MARTIN: Yeah.

JOHN BRABENDER: I really believe, first of all, it hurt a tremendous deal not winning Iowa on Iowa night. We did not get the type of luxuries that you would have, being on the cover of *Time* and *Newsweek*, those type of things, the money that comes with it. But I really believe if we would have won Michigan, which was relatively close, that we would have won Ohio the next week and we would have been the nominee, quite frankly.

JONATHAN MARTIN: Vince, how close was Newt to getting out of the race during this time and what compelled him to stay in?

VINCE HALEY: Well I think there was discussion of that. In terms of what compelled him to stay in, I think part of the polling showed that the Gingrich vote was not necessarily all going to go to Santorum. There was going to be a split—some going to Santorum, some to Romney. And I think he also felt that, and this is speculation on my part, that it would be seen more as sort of an alliance against Romney that I don't think he felt comfortable with. And he held out hope for doing well in Delaware and possibly a Reagan-style comeback in North Carolina, but that was a long range hope and it was slight and tenuous, but those are some of the reasons.

JAN CRAWFORD: After Florida, he kind of backed off his pledge to remain positive and really sharpened his attacks on Romney. Does he have any regret about that? Does he think that may have ultimately hurt Romney in the general and ultimately paved the way for the president, or was that something that may have helped Romney in sharpening his responses?

VINCE HALEY: One of the things that, in hindsight, we would have done much better, hopefully, would have been a much stronger surrogate operation because it's always better when others can deliver messages, as opposed to from him. Or, you deliver those messages through paid media television ads. So, absent those resources, Newt used the term one time that if he's a running back or full back coming through the line and no one is blocking the nose guard, then he's going to run over the nose guard. So it became up to him to be the one to call out some of the inaccuracies in the ads that were opposing him. Running for president is a very personal thing. Newt has been a national figure for thirty years. He's been a builder of the Republican Party, a builder of the Conservative movement, so one cannot simply take some of those ads and just sort of wash it away and say, "Oh, it's all part of a big political game, and it's all ironic and amusing."

JAN CRAWFORD: So he took it quite personally?

VINCE HALEY: Well, I mean, from my vantage point you can't but help take it personally, to some degree. And I think that the challenge will always be, how do you take negative attack ads and either match them to some degree on television, or find a way either to transcend it because you have such an overwhelmingly positive vision of the future that those ads then sort of lose their potency or do it in a sort of a charismatic way by tossing it aside. We didn't find that right way to do that. And so it's a very human thing and maybe he could have done it in a better way, but there you are.

JAN CRAWFORD: Keith?

KEITH NAHIGIAN: If one of the goals of this forum is to kind of look back at the process, I do think one thing that didn't match up with this open percentage delegates, as you would go through and it was going to prolong the whole thing was—and it didn't really get written about in depth—the burden of ballot access. Getting on the ballot in these states was dramatic and certainly Romney had a huge advantage. He had money, he had started early. But, these states have figured out that it's a shakedown now. It's unbelievable. They just make up a price. You want to be on the ballot in the District of Columbia? I don't know, let's make it a hundred grand. It's an unbelievable burden for the natural growing of a campaign if you have to build it to go until June and you are starting in the beginning and you have to suddenly take a million dollars to get on these couple of ballots. It's going to really be a hurdle. We always say the RNC can't reform anything but it may be something they need to address so there is some kind of a consistency, at least in the first, maybe a couple of them. We experienced Virginia. You had to make a decision. Are we going to be able to be on Virginia's ballot? If we would have been the alternative to Romney, we wouldn't have been on the ballot in a lot of these states. And I think some of the other campaigns weren't on the ballot.

JONATHAN MARTIN: There was something of a divide in this primary between what I would call the sort of ragtag colonial army versus the sort of well-polished lobsterbacks from Great Britain. The lobsterbacks won in this case but, let me ask John Brabender, Santorum only had three chances—Michigan, Ohio, and Wisconsin—as I recall, to knock off Governor Romney. How much would a more professionalized, well-financed campaign have helped that cause? The Romney campaign in Michigan I know banked a lot of early votes going into primary day. You guys did that robo-call to try and get some Democrats out at the end because you just needed to move some votes, find some votes. Looking back at those three states especially, what was the advantage that Romney had, in terms of his organization versus you guys?

JOHN BRABENDER: Well actually I would argue it wasn't the organization as much as it was their super PAC because the way the dynamics changed, we could fight a battle in one state at a time with the Romney people and do it quite efficiently, we found. The problem is while we're fighting in Michigan, the super PAC is hitting us with ads in Ohio and Illinois. That was the big problem that we were running into—we could not control the message further down the road like they could.

JONATHAN MARTIN: I stand corrected, Michigan, Ohio, Illinois was the order.

JOHN BRABENDER: Right.

••• ROMNEY'S PRIMARY STRATEGY •••

JAN CRAWFORD: Looking at your primary strategy, you talked last night, Matt, about how you ran this kind of lean, disciplined campaign, but we come to the convention and Romney has been campaigning for 18 months this time around and we're talking about how that was the chance to introduce Romney to the American people. Were there missed opportunities in the primaries where you could have done that better? I mean, say, Michigan? These were states that you were going to be contesting in the general election.

STUART STEVENS: We were going back and reviewing what ads we had run for this thing, because we forget. The spot that we were in by a large percentage, more than any other spot in the primary, was a spot that we call Mass Record, which we ran because it worked, which was about the Governor's record in Massachusetts. If we had it here, you would say, "Oh yeah, that one." And I think though that what you were able to do in each of these states on the media was completely dwarfed by the conversation that was being held, and that conversation became a loud argument between candidates, and that dwarfed anything that each of the candidates was able to do. So when we came out of these states and finally secured the nomination and started testing, we found a remarkable number of people thought that Governor Romney was Catholic and was against contraception. It's because he had been in these debates and it's sort of like, you're in a restaurant and you're not really paying attention but you hear this argument at this table over here and you get bits and pieces of it. You don't really know what they are saying. That's how most of the public looks at the primary.

JONATHAN MARTIN: Stuart, you said earlier that the debates didn't hurt the candidate in terms of pushing him to the right, but now you are saying that he was seen, because of those debates, as being against contraception. That sounds to me like it hurt pretty badly.

STUART STEVENS: It's not just the debates because after Arizona, there weren't anymore debates. It's what you are seeing on the evening news. It's just how it's being covered.

JONATHAN MARTIN: You bring up a topic I'm really fascinated by and that is, to what degree was your primary strategy geared around general election viability? How much did being strong against Obama inform your primary strategy? I mean certainly not wanting to retreat on health care was part of that because you didn't want to apologize for creating this health care law here in Massachusetts. But, what issues especially were you guys very, very driven by in terms of not wanting to hurt yourself too much for the general?

MATT RHOADES: Well obviously we put a premium on just talking about jobs and the economy and the president's record and that's what we tried to make the primary campaign about. Obviously that's forward looking into the general. But when you are running for the nomination, you've got to win the nomination. And if you are looking beyond securing that nomination too much, you are jeopardizing your chances of winning that nomination.

JONATHAN MARTIN: Could you have run without trying to outflank Perry on the right on immigration in the primary, Matt?

MATT RHOADES: I regret that. I truly believe that people were shocked that we were going after Governor Perry in a Republican primary on Social Security. They were critical of us at the time, saying we were hitting them from the left. And if you look through the unwinding of the Perry campaign, a lot of people put a focus on that one infamous debate moment, but it was the very early debates, the first and second debates.

JONATHAN MARTIN: The heartless. [13]

MATT RHOADES: By the third debate, and this is well before the other moment, I think Governor Perry was badly hurt and I, in retrospect, believe that we could have probably just beaten Governor Perry with the Social Security hit.

JONATHAN MARTIN: Interesting. Dave, do you want to comment?

DAVE CARNEY: Yeah. I think it was the third debate that was sort of killer. I wish we had forgotten that one. The first debate actually worked out pretty well when Williams asked about the death penalty. [14] That helped us. In the second debate, it was going to be a disaster, the whole idea of, you think this is going to be $5,000? Well how much would you, okay, what is it, $10,000, $50,000, $100,000? [15] And the back and forth with Congresswoman Bachmann. I mean, four times he goes, I want to respond to that. Why are we responding to that? And if she had not said right after that, "Gardasil makes people crazy," or whatever, that sort of

---

13. In a September debate in Orlando, Perry said his opponents who opposed Texas's in-state tuition plan for some illegal immigrants had no "heart."

14. In a September 2011 Republican primary debate at the Reagan Library in California, comoderator Brian Williams asked Perry whether he has "struggled to sleep at night" with the idea that any one of the inmates executed in Texas might have been innocent. Perry responded no.

15. In a September 2011 Republican primary debate, when Bachmann suggested Perry pushed for the HPV vaccine at the bidding of Pharma giant Merck, he responded, "If you're saying that I can be bought for $5,000, I'm offended."

saved us. We couldn't get anybody to do that for us in the third debate and that whole thing in Orlando, things just, you know, filtered out of control. There's things we could have done systematically and structurally to come back but, at that point, you're right, Matt.

JONATHAN MARTIN: Stuart, did you not know that you guys were always going to play in Iowa or were you genuinely uncertain about what your chances were going to be in the caucuses?

STUART STEVENS: We were completely uncertain about what we were doing in Iowa.

JONATHAN MARTIN: For how long?

STUART STEVENS: Until we were certain. I don't know. [*laughter*]

JONATHAN MARTIN: But what was the moment that you guys decided to engage there?

STUART STEVENS: We didn't go on television. It's one of the interesting subjects through this whole campaign that plays into the debate, that we didn't go on television until after Thanksgiving, and we went on very modestly then. So we ran basically a month of television in Iowa and spent eight days on the ground in Iowa. I would say definitely a post-Thanksgiving decision.

JAN CRAWFORD: When was the moment inside the campaign when you realized Romney was the nominee?

STUART STEVENS: When Senator Santorum withdrew from Pennsylvania.

JONATHAN MARTIN: It was not before that?

STUART STEVENS: No.

JAN CRAWFORD: So it was an open question throughout?

STUART STEVENS: You can't be in a fight and not be in the fight.

••• HUNTSMAN'S EXIT FROM THE RACE •••

JONATHAN MARTIN: Yeah. Let me ask Matt David and Ana about something that I think fascinates all of us in this room, and that is when the candidates decided to drop out. You guys came in third place in New Hampshire. It wasn't a close third but you still went to South Carolina. Yet, after a few days in South Carolina, you decided to drop out. What changed in those days between staying in after New Hampshire and then ultimately dropping out?

MATT DAVID: His conversations with his family. He made the decision after New Hampshire.

JONATHAN MARTIN: Was it a financial issue?

MATT DAVID: No. When we had the conversation, you could literally see it on his face. I remember it vividly. I mean he was done. And, at that point, we thought, internally, that Romney was going to win but we felt we could stay in, peel off some more delegates and then our endorsement could mean more in the end. But, when your candidate is done, he's done.

Matt David and Ana Navarro discuss Jon Huntsman's decision to quit the race.

ANA NAVARRO: He also understood that his role in South Carolina would be the spoiler role and that was something he wasn't willing to play. I do think the finances had something to do with it. I mean Jon Huntsman is one of the most frugal billionaires you've ever met. [*laughter*]

JONATHAN MARTIN: Right.

MATT DAVID: The only thing I would say is finances were an issue the entire campaign, so it wasn't the decisive one.

ANA NAVARRO: They had an unlimited ability to raise money. We had an unlimited inability to raise money.

••• PERRY'S EXIT FROM THE RACE •••

JONATHAN MARTIN: And, Rob and Dave, it was widely expected that your candidate, Governor Perry, was going to drop out after Iowa. Yet he then went for a jog and took out his BlackBerry or his iPhone and tweeted he was staying in. Did that catch you guys by surprise when he did that?

ROB JOHNSON: Yes. [*laughter*]

JONATHAN MARTIN: Why did he decide to stay in? What did he say?

DAVE CARNEY: The same reason he got in the race to begin with. He talked about his family and the people. He just thought it was the same call to serve the country and to basically try to rectify and move forward. I mean, he is a very confident guy, and he just knew there were a lot of things he could do better.

JONATHAN MARTIN: But before South Carolina was over, he also pulled out of the race, so what informed that decision?

DAVE CARNEY: I only talked with him once during that day that he got out and, basically, you know, he was clearly not going anywhere. And the infrastructure was just not there to continue. My advice to him was not to basically embarrass yourself by losing South Carolina, which we should have won. Three months later, we should have won South Carolina.

JONATHAN MARTIN: Well did he know that he would both, (a) drop out and (b) endorse Newt? Or did you guys discuss that and sort of hash that out a little bit?

ROB JOHNSON: No. That was his decision.

JONATHAN MARTIN: To both?

ROB JOHNSON: To both. To Dave's point, the governor just realized there was no clear pathway to winning the nomination, and he felt, at that moment in time, he had an ability to influence the South Carolina primary by endorsing Newt, the Speaker. I would argue that Newt probably would have lost by ten points if we hadn't have done that. [*laughter*]

STUART STEVENS: I think there's something that's difficult to realize unless you've been through this and seen how hard this is for candidates and their families and how much candidates and their families are real people and how much that affects the flow of campaigns. No one runs for president at this level who is not a tremendously accomplished, talented person, and a very driven person. And each of these decisions become very difficult, but it's very, very tough on families, very tough. And it's a very difficult thing to report on because you're going to get close to the family usually, but, for a campaign and these people, it is a driving force that is at the center of so much.

JAN CRAWFORD: You could see the emotion on Ms. Romney's face on election night. You could just tell she had been crying. How have they since processed that? The governor is meeting today with the president. Has it been harder for her to accept? How would you characterize their reactions to the loss now?

STUART STEVENS: Let me just say I thought on election night she handled it very well.

JAN CRAWFORD: Oh, no, I'm not saying that she didn't.

STUART STEVENS: I was actually struck by how—I don't know exactly what the right word is—steady she was. I think that there was a realization that, had Governor Romney been president, it would have been difficult for the family. I think that they understood that on a personal level, but it's very difficult to speak to what someone else is thinking.

JONATHAN MARTIN: We talked a lot about tactics. I want to talk about message for a minute because in the aftermath of the campaign this month there's been a wide range of discussion among Republicans as to how to take back the White House in 2016. We've heard talk about being more moderate. We've heard talk about being more populist. I want to go to Matt David, Phil Musser, John Brabender certainly—Santorum, Pawlenty, Huntsman—because all of you guys at some point or another were trying to figure out more of a populist campaign, more of a moderate campaign, and it seems like this is an important conversation going forward for 2016.

••• ROMNEY DEFINING ROMNEY •••

JAN CRAWFORD: Before we move forward to that, I have one more strategy question. We are supposed to be going through the conventions on our panel, and one thing I would like to ask the Romney campaign is, what was the strategy in the summer when you were allowing the president to define Romney so that you came to the convention having to introduce your candidate to the American people when he had been the target of attack ads for months?

MATT RHOADES: Let me start it off by saying we made the decision going into the general that the thing the voters needed to learn first and foremost about Governor Romney is what he would do as president. And so that's why we went with "day one, job one," and that was the focus of our paid advertising over the summer. To the first question, we had in the very beginning, unfortunately, gone through a long primary process that we call the long slog, and we had spent $87 million to secure the nomination, become the presumptive nominee. And, we were not going to take matching funds so that we could be more competitive down the stretch. So that meant that we were being outspent over the summer, and we always understood that that was going to be one of the bigger challenges that we had, even to the point where we did take out a loan at the end of the primary process, going into the convention, so we could stay up on TV for a longer period of time. So that was our initial thoughts. Stuart, I don't know if you have anything to add.

STUART STEVENS: I want to make three points on this because I think it's really often misunderstood here. First, the day that Mitt Romney announced in June, he had, what, 25 percent of the electorate in the Republican primary. President Obama had close to the amount of votes that he got on Election Day. So when you think about that, that means, what was Governor Romney's task? He had to win the primary against a bunch of formidable opponents, and I think these opponents have been underestimated by the press, frankly, and then present himself to the public and garner a majority of the electorate nationally. That's a tough process. What did the president have to do? The president had to hold onto the votes that he had, and that is a very different process. If you actually looked at it, the president's campaign probably lost votes over that year, but they thought it was enough votes to win. You come out of a primary, you are forced to look at the situation of what do you need to do when you have to triage this. And every day in that campaign, in those situations, it's "Sophie's Choice." And when people say, "You should be doing this. You should be doing that," my answer is "You're right." It's like scheduling. They say, "You should be in Richmond, and you should be in Des Moines." You're right, but you can only be in one. And we tested this extensively and what voters—and this makes sense when you think about it—wanted to know most is what Mitt Romney would do as president. They desired more information about Mitt Romney. But what they really wanted to know was what would this guy do as president. That was the essential element that we had to fill with voters to get them. I would just say that the premise of the Obama campaign was to define Mitt Romney such that by the debates—we heard this spin over and over again—that there would not be enough persuadable voters, etcetera. That didn't happen. It didn't. In all the national polls, his favorability was the same or was higher than Barack Obama.

JAN CRAWFORD: So you don't believe that the attack ads that they ran in the key toss-up states, which people in other states didn't get, created a level of resistance that was just impossible for you to overcome?

STUART STEVENS: No, no. I don't believe that, no. The other thing is just the amount of money they had to spend that we didn't have to spend.

••• THE ROLE OF SUPER PACs •••

JONATHAN MARTIN: We talked a lot about the debates, and for good reason, but we haven't talked about one of the other major factors in this primary—super PACs—that much. Matt and Stuart, I think Carl Forti and Charlie Spears were here. You guys couldn't coordinate during the campaign, but now those restraints are gone, the truth can be told. What did you guys expect the super PAC that supported you to be doing during the campaign? What were you hoping for? What was the discussion in the campaign?

STUART STEVENS: We didn't talk about it. There was never a discussion about this massive entity outside that was blasting Newt. Jonathan, you don't have time to sit around and talk about what other people are doing. You are so busy worrying about what you are doing.

JONATHAN MARTIN: So there was never a discussion about what Carl and those guys were doing?

STUART STEVENS: No.

JONATHAN MARTIN: What you hoped they would do in Iowa? Anything like that?

MATT RHOADES: There were parts during the course of the campaign where super PACs were helpful to Governor Romney's campaign, no doubt about it. And I think the most obvious example is the baggage ad[16] that Restore Our Future did in Iowa. Stuart and I were just reflecting, and we should have looked this up, I'm not sure if our campaign actually did a negative Newt Gingrich ad in December leading up to Iowa. I think we were positive, so certainly that was helpful for the Romney campaign. Then again, of course, you live by the sword, you die by the sword. Super PACs were not helpful to Governor Romney in South Carolina, for example.

JONATHAN MARTIN: I wanted to ask you about that because the Newt super PAC went after you guys pretty fiercely, thanks to the man in Las Vegas,[17] on the issue of Bain Capital. Did that guy, did those attacks on Bain prepare you guys at all for the general election or, if not, why weren't you guys more prepared in the general for the Bain attacks?

MATT RHOADES: Obviously we knew Bain would come up during the course of the campaign, and it had certainly come up during Governor Romney's Senate campaign in 1994. It came up in his gubernatorial campaign in 2002. It even came up a little bit in the primary in 2008,

---

16. Restore Our Future, a super PAC supporting Mitt Romney, ran a TV ad assailing Newt Gingrich and his political baggage.
17. Las Vegas casino magnate Sheldon Adelson funded a Gingrich-affiliated super PAC, spending $16.5 million to help Gingrich's presidential campaign.

with some of Governor Huckabee's supporters. So during the course of the primary season, the chairman of our campaign, Bob White, who is one of the founders of Bain, set up a task force, which included staffers on the campaign. It included former Bain employees. They just started war gaming this all out in the fall, literally up on the white board, what the attacks were going to be.

JONATHAN MARTIN: In the fall of '11?

MATT RHOADES: Yeah, in the fall of 2011.

JONATHAN MARTIN: How much did the Newt and Perry Bain attacks hurt you guys, do you think, in the primary?

MATT RHOADES: In the primary what happened was there was a super PAC ad that was called "King of Bain" or the film.[18] And within twenty-four to forty-eight hours, our Bain team was able to go through the film and the ads and find out that it was related to a company that was sold after Bain had actually owned it, so it was viewed as inaccurate. So what we were able to do was fact check that and really make a push and an argument in a primary that this was an attack on capitalism. I think that we were successful because we had organizations, news entities, like the *Wall Street Journal* editorial board, conservative newspapers like the *Washington Examiner,* who called out Speaker Gingrich and the super PACs that were perpetuating these attacks on capitalism. We even did an ad when we had all those ads going up in Florida that defended Governor Romney's record at Bain and pointed towards these attacks on capitalism. So in the primary, I think we were successful in responding to that. Certainly, like I said, we set this group up in the fall of 2011. We thought that these attacks could occur in the primary. We were a little bit surprised at the intensity in a Republican primary on them but we dealt with them.

JAN CRAWFORD: Well they came out pretty early on in New Hampshire, right?

MATT RHOADES: South Carolina.

VINCE HALEY: Well if I could just answer, I would say one thing is to change these rules so the money can flow to the campaign. The reform

---

18.   In January 2012 supporters of Newt Gingrich bought the rights to a short movie made by former Romney supporters, called "King of Bain, When Mitt Romney Came to Town," that was very critical of Mitt Romney's tenure as head of Bain Capital.

should be that you should have unlimited money but with twenty-four-hour reporting and full disclosure. Our campaign wouldn't have wanted the Bain attack. We would have wanted more attacks on the Massachusetts record.

JONATHAN MARTIN: You guys didn't want the Bain attack?

VINCE HALEY: No, it came completely out of the blue. It came up for the first time in one of the debates. Gingrich was not talking about "The King of Bain." He was talking about Mitt, the Massachusetts moderate. He was talking about his record. This was completely off the topic that we wanted to talk about and the media became consumed by it. Now, maybe there was an incidental benefit in that Santorum was completely washed out of the conversation for a couple of days in New Hampshire because of all this attack on capitalism but, as Matt said, it was very effectively rebutted by Gingrich being seen as attacking capitalism. And we had many supporters who were quite displeased by what was happening. And there were times in South Carolina when the question could have been, do we continue on that vein, "The King of Bain"? We didn't. We focused on other things.

JONATHAN MARTIN: Was there longer term damage do you think, just from the branding of vulture capitalism? And, did that sort of stink start to really surround Governor Romney at that point?

STUART STEVENS: I don't think there's a binary answer to that. There's not a "yes" or a "no" answer to that. Look, you run for president, people are going to attack you. They are going to attack you for something. If it's not this, it's going to be something else.

DAVE CARNEY: Stuart is right. These aren't secrets. The White House letter from Huntsman to Obama[19] wasn't put out by anybody sitting at this table. These people are very good at what they do on the other side and they knew about Bain. They didn't need Rick Perry to come up with a clever phrase or the ads that the Speaker did. They were going to do that anyway.

JONATHAN MARTIN: If you guys could run through the super PAC, what would have been the one thing you could have gotten your super PAC to have done for you? Either Newt or Romney?

---

19. In April 2011 the *Daily Caller* released a handwritten letter from two years earlier from Huntsman to President Obama calling Obama a "remarkable leader."

JOHN BRABENDER: I would argue Rick Santorum ultimately was the biggest beneficiary of it, and ironically he was the only one, I think, that actually defended the governor on the whole issue.

TRYGVE OLSON: The one thing that I would point out is we ran a lot of ads attacking other candidates, but we didn't have a super PAC to do that for us. Ron Paul had more small-dollar donors than anybody, which is something that, theoretically, we would like to encourage in the process. When we put up ads hitting Newt Gingrich or Al Gore's Texas cheerleader or hypocrisy, or whatever, Ron Paul had put his own name on it, whereas when Restore Our Future was hitting Newt in Iowa, they could do it under somebody else's name. I think, really, when you look at 2016, the first thing that everybody is going to run and do is, you are going to want to run and get a super PAC to do your dirty work for you so that you don't have to do that. You are going to try and get Jon Downs[20] or your meanest ad guy, in terms of talent, going to the super PAC, rather than internally, but then it's outside the control of the candidate, which is unfortunate.

••• LESSONS LEARNED •••

JAN CRAWFORD: Last question, and I guess we are going to have to do some kind of closing thoughts, so let me try to segue this. When we think about some of the lessons learned or what the big truths were going forward, I just want to pick up on what you were saying. Did you not have the money to aggressively defend yourselves against the president's attempts to define you over the summer? Was that why you didn't? You said you spent $87 million during the primary.

STUART STEVENS: Look, we spent all the money we had. It's not complicated. We had a primary that cost us, I don't know, $137 million or something. The president didn't have a primary. He had four years to build a war chest. We didn't. We had to go out and raise a lot of money in that summer. We spent all the money that we had. We had to choose what we were doing. And in states like Ohio, we were being outspent three and four to one. We watched this very carefully and did what we felt and what our testing showed us was the most effective responses, given the limited options that we had. They had more bullets in their gun, and it's not an unusual circumstance.

---

20. Jon Downs created ads for Ron Paul's 2012 presidential campaign.

The Bachmann and Perry teams listen to the Romney camp's view of the long primary.

MATT RHOADES: I think there also was, over the course of the summer obviously, pro-Romney super PACs and there also was the RNC's independent expenditure, which we didn't coordinate with but certainly the money that we raised over the summer funded. And that's where Trygve's friend Jon Downs was and others, and they were out there doing contrast ads against the president. So there were Romney contrast ads going on.

JAN CRAWFORD: If we're looking forward thinking, was that a direct result of the elongated primary process and the proportional allocation that you guys then were in a situation where you couldn't run as effectively? Was that a direct impact of the change in the rules?

STUART STEVENS: It's hard to say because the Democratic primary went on until June four years earlier, which wasn't a result of the RNC rules. So primaries end when they end, and they end for different reasons. I think everyone would say that it's your advantage to end a primary sooner—and for twenty or thirty years people have said this—and be able to focus on the general election faster.

JONATHAN MARTIN: Matt David, one of the bets that Jon Huntsman seemed to make after the '08 election was that the defeat of John McCain was going to usher in a period where the Republicans would embrace something close to a DLC-style moderation. There was an opening for somebody in the party on the environment, perhaps on gay rights, to sort of move a bit to the middle. That calculation was probably mistaken, in hindsight, but can you just talk to me about your candidate and the sort of broader themes that he struggled with of one day trying to be the conservative, but also trying to be more of a moderating force? And do you think the next time around we are going to see more candidates in the GOP primary take a Huntsman-like course, in terms of trying to move more to the middle, to a more pragmatic approach?

MATT DAVID: Well yeah. This was actually reflected in the super PAC conversation too because we waited forever for the super PAC to come in and then when they did, they came in in New Hampshire with an ad talking about how conservative we were, which is not really our message in New Hampshire. [*laughter*] So it was very unhelpful. We struggled with, as I laid out last night, we thought our initial path was to the left of Romney but what we had going for us, at the end of the day, was he actually had a very conservative governing record in Utah when you looked at it. We hoped at the end of the day the conservatives would come back and give us a look. It just never happened.

JONATHAN MARTIN: Going forward though, in terms of a moderate force in the Republican Party, are we going to see even more candidates that take the approach that at times your candidate took of trying to say, "Look, we're not going to win a general election by shouting at each other and trying to appeal to just our narrow base?" Are more candidates going to be emboldened in '16 to take that approach, do you think?

MATT DAVID: I think we're going to have to moderate on some issues— immigration, gay marriage—but I think Stuart wrote about this the other day in his column, it's very difficult to beat an incumbent president, very, very difficult. So while we've got to make some changes, I don't think it's a freak-out moment for us. I think actually one area, and we were talking about this last night, where we do have to catch up and we should freak out a little bit is on the technology front. I mean listening to Jeremy talk last night about their analytics and their data and the technology, that's somewhere we need to step up.

JONATHAN MARTIN: In terms of a populist approach, we've read so much about Tim Pawlenty and Sam's Club for so long, and it seemed like the most promising message for your candidate was to be the populist running against the rich son of a governor and a CEO. And here's the son himself, St. Paul, but he never fully embraced the Sam's Club message and ran against Wall Street and ran that real populist campaign. Is that an opening, do you think, in the party going forward? More of a populist approach that Pawlenty talked about but never fully embraced?

PHIL MUSSER: Yeah, possibly. Just to build on Matt's point, beating incumbents is very, very challenging, and as you look at the potential field in 2016, I'm not sure that the Obama coalition that turned out in '08 and '12 can be reconstituted again by a nominee Cuomo or a nominee Clinton against a nominee Rubio or nominee Santorum, or nominee whoever may well run. And credit to the Obama campaign for churning out that coalition. I agree on the technology front. I think there's obviously lessons to be learned there, and I suspect that the party will, in due diligence, focus on that. And, frankly, having no designated leader will lead to a period of somewhat organized chaos where a lot of this will get kicked around. That's probably a healthy process, if an unruly one. And then, finally, I think the demographic challenge, most explicitly illustrated with the Latino community, is one that has instructive lessons. We probably didn't spend enough money communicating there early enough. If you want to understand functionally where El Salvadorans, Nicaraguans, Mexicans, and Cubans get their information, it's overwhelmingly from basically two places on television, which are Univision and Telemundo.

I would hope our party would look at developing a growth-oriented prosperity agenda aimed at showing working class Latinos how the conservatives' principles can be good for them, and I would encourage our party to take the last $100 million that went out the door at the very end of the campaign and look at starting to communicate that at the beginning of the cycle.

JONATHAN MARTIN: Well we're going to wrap up here but we want to close by going around the table. The big take-away from this campaign and the biggest surprise to you of this campaign, or you can answer the two questions with one answer.

CARLOS SIERRA: I also want to comment really fast on that, and it will include that. I think if Bachmann, Cain, or Santorum would have gotten the nomination, it would have been more of an ass-kicking. I think our party does need to moderate. I think minority outreach is huge. Our party is dead unless there's a shake-up.

JONATHAN MARTIN: So you are saying if you guys had nominated a conservative, like Bachmann or Santorum—

CARLOS SIERRA: It would have been more of an ass-kicking.

JONATHAN MARTIN: Vince?

VINCE HALEY: Obviously, money matters, message matters. I don't know if I have a particular grand insight other than we have to grow the party and we can offer conservative governing solutions to the country and attract a big majority. I don't think it's this idea of whether we're a conservative, populist or a moderate, or what have you. I think we're talking about, how do we make people's lives better through a set of policies? And the definition of what that is can come later but conservative governing solutions will be the way of the future.

DAVE CARNEY: I would say the biggest takeaway for me of the whole election cycle is that people have this misconception that there's a party where people sit around and make decisions. Voters make the decisions. Jeff Larson[21] and Ben Key[22] don't sit there and say "Okay, we're going to be moderate here." That's crap. Candidates are good. They have a good message. They are going to win. Candidates are bad. They have a bad message. They are going to lose. And the media and the elite want things nice and tidy and clean and not messy, which is what everybody here but Romney became, and they don't like that. They're like, "Let's get this thing over in January so we have a whole year to beat up on the president." People think that the headquarters of the RNC does something other than be a legal entity to raise money and do technical things.

ROB JOHNSON: I agree with everything he said. I think another interesting point, or thing that I learned, was how important *Fox News* was in the Republican primary. You could sit in Washington, D.C., and talk to 70 percent of Iowans or 60 percent of people from South Carolina. And I think that Newt was on to something with that point. And I agree with Matt completely: we've got to catch up on technology.

---

21.   Jeff Larson was chief of staff at the Republican National Committee.
22.   Ben Key was executive director of the Platform Committee of the Republican National Convention.

JONATHAN MARTIN: Well will that impact, do you think, future campaigns in terms of going to Iowa and New Hampshire? Will the candidates do less of it because they can go to Fox and be on TV nationally?

ROB JOHNSON: No. The candidates without money will do it. The candidates with money will go press the flesh and get on Fox from Des Moines.

JONATHAN MARTIN: Keith and Brett?

BRETT O'DONNELL: I think my takeaway is for the future and that is I think our party has to get back to real conservatism, being able to show demonstrable differences in how we are going to govern, the philosophy of government, smaller government, and on the fiscal side as well. I think that's the big thing to attract a wider audience.

KEITH NAHIGIAN: I think people who do a presidential campaign sometimes overreact and think that they are in the most unique year of all times. Firing a sitting president is one of the hardest things you can possibly do. In 1996, you were talking about this huge dynamic in the summer, wow, these new super PACs. In 1996, Bob Dole lost the race between June and August with Clinton ads up in the targeted states, so I think maybe overanalyzing is perhaps not the right thing to necessarily do. I think every time you lose a race, you refocus your messages, and you move forward. I think Matt and his team did an unbelievable job of trying to unseat a very popular president who had unbelievable skills, and it wasn't going to be easy. And, they had to do it in a very short period of time. I think they did a great job of keeping us collected, as kind of the dean of the candidates, and moving this forward.

JONATHAN MARTIN: Matt?

MATT DAVID: I would say keeping perspective is so difficult—and, Jonathan, you have written about this—when you're in this vacuum and trying to feed the beast that is Twitter and Facebook. So keeping perspective about what you are seeing as a campaign, versus what voters are seeing, those are two different things.

JONATHAN MARTIN: Matt, yes or no, will there be a Republican in '16 in the primary who is for gay marriage?

MATT DAVID: Yes.

JONATHAN MARTIN: John Brabender?

JOHN BRABENDER: The lessons I think we learned, at least as a campaign, is: One, winning a Saturday primary means nothing. Number two is we are getting into dangerous ground I think, as Republicans, saying, oh, let's start acting more like Democrats. I think the biggest lesson we learned in the primary is that there are a lot of blue collar people who feel we no longer represent or understand their lives, and I think that was also reflected in the general election.

MARK BLOCK: December 5th, when Mr. Cain withdrew from the race, was extremely painful for all of us. I could share hundreds of stories, but the one that resonates and always will in my life is when Linda and I had breakfast with Henry Kissinger and Mr. Cain. As we were walking out, Mr. Kissinger said, "All the other candidates came here to ask me what I should say on the Sunday shows, you asked me what you should do as president."

LINDA HANSEN: That was very telling and it's kind of like what I said before, what is our purpose? Our purpose is really to serve the citizens of this country. Our motive from the very beginning was to promote those common sense solutions. I think Mr. Cain resonated because I often said he said what a lot of people were saying in their living rooms as they were throwing their Nerf footballs at their TVs. We learned that it was the people who really were speaking in a new way this election and it was chilling at times.

JONATHAN MARTIN: Trygve?

TRYGVE OLSON: I'll be fast. Biggest surprise, how the media and the pundits were overbuying into the notion that Obama's coalition is a democratic demographic coalition.

JONATHAN MARTIN: This is the primary discussion that we're talking about now.

TRYGVE OLSON: Oh, well, I think that's true in the primary too. [*laughter*] The second one is I think the Republican Party needs to do better among younger voters, and there are real lessons in Ron Paul's message to attract younger voters.

JONATHAN MARTIN: National security? Should the party be less hawkish, do you think?

TRYGVE OLSON: I think you can have a discussion about national security that may not be where Ron Paul is but may be someplace not where John Bolton is.

JAN CRAWFORD: But what is Ron Paul's message, do you think, to attract younger voters?

TRYGVE OLSON: Economic empowerment is a huge one. An emphasis on the fact that if you are thirty years old, you were in college when 9/11 happened. You've seen friends go to Iraq, Afghanistan, come back as different people, you've had two recessions, and Ron Paul is speaking to them about the fact that government is not necessarily the answer to their problems and that they shouldn't sit around saying we need to rely on government. Jeremy yesterday said that the demographic group that Obama was worried about was younger voters. There's a huge opportunity there. Ron Paul, 13,000 people at the University of California-Los Angeles Campus, 6,000 at the University of Wisconsin-Madison.

JONATHAN MARTIN: All right, the same with Matt, yes or no, will there be a candidate in the '16 Primary, Trygve, that is for marijuana legalization?

TRYGVE OLSON: What candidate are you thinking about, Jonathan? [*laughter*]

JONATHAN MARTIN: Yes or no?

TRGVE OLSON: I have no idea. I don't predict the future.

JONATHAN MARTIN: Is Ron going to run in '16?

TRYGVE OLSON: I would be arrogant to try and make an announcement for Ron Paul, but I'm sure you'll be the first one to know if he does.

JONATHAN MARTIN: Matt?

MATT RHOADES: Take-away? One of the luxuries of working for Governor Romney is no matter how hard you were working, he was working harder. And if you want to win your party's nomination, you have to go out and take it. One of the big reasons why, at the end of the day, in April, Senator Santorum was going head to head with Governor Romney is the guy worked tirelessly. He sat out there in Iowa when no one was paying attention to him and that matters, and I think sometimes people forget how much that is a factor in who becomes the nominee. Surprise? The debates. The debates were important in 2008, but in the 2012 primary it was just shocking how they shook up the race week after week and how many people were watching these things.

STUART STEVENS: I think my biggest surprise was the degree to which Governor Romney was considered a frontrunner, even though he never led in the polls. It was sort of odd. And a take-away is that we seem to be at a moment now that is very narrative driven. If we go back and look at the November/December 2004 moment, it was filled with why there was a Republican lock on the electoral college, why it was unlikely for a Democrat to be elected president in the near future. I think it's a similar moment here. And I think that the primary process, in four years, is likely to serve us very well and to produce a nominee that is likely to win the presidency and we should remember that.

PHIL MUSSER: I agree with both of those. I'm going to go on debates as well because the ability to reveal singular authentic moments was shape shifting. In tandem with that, the rise of social media, specifically, Twitter, in terms of setting the narrative both during and postdebate. And the implication of essentially a Twitter narrative on your ability to raise funds, frame the outcome, fundamentally reshaped, I think, both the debate process and has implications for the future as we go forward to 2016. I think it will probably provide a whole new medium in which debates are discussed.

JONATHAN MARTIN: Thank you all so much. Appreciate it very much. [*applause*]

TREY GRAYSON: Just for a point of reference, there was a Gary Johnson representative who was going to be here but canceled at the last minute.

3

THE DEMOCRATIC STRATEGY THROUGH THE CONVENTION

TREY GRAYSON: Let's get this session started. Obviously there are fewer participants this time and we're going to talk about why we have fewer participants. This panel is going to be moderated by Lois Romano, a former IOP Fellow and senior reporter for *POLITICO*, and Jonathan Karl, the chief political correspondent for *ABC News*. This conversation is going to be about the Democratic primary time period leading up through the convention. Lois and John, take it away.

••• LAYING THE GROUNDWORK •••

JONATHAN KARL: All right, excellent. Thank you. Well it's great to be here and great to have the full force of the Obama campaign across from us, so thank you very much. Because you guys look so happy, can I rewind a little bit and go back to November of 2010. Obviously, there was that election, which I'm sure you guys recall, but you guys were just getting ready to start the reelect. Unemployment was at 9.8 percent. The president's approval rating at 39 percent, right track/wrong track, way under water. If this reelection you were preparing to do was going to be a referendum on the president, he was going to lose. So how soon and what were the first steps you did to make sure that this was going to be a choice election? That you were going to make the Republican alternative—who looked, even at that point, like it was quite likely going to be Mitt Romney—unacceptable?

**Jonathan Karl and Lois Romano lead a discussion on the Obama campaign's strate-
gy during the Republican primary season.**

DAVID AXELROD: Well, first of all, I remember saying to the president
the day after the election that I thought the seeds for reelection had
been planted in that midterm election. And I told this to a group last
night, and it reminded me of the Winston Churchill story about when
he lost the prime ministership and someone said it was a blessing in
disguise, and he said, "Well it's rather well disguised." [*laughter*] But
the fact is that we lost the midterm elections because of the difference
between the turnout, and so one thing we obviously had to work on was
turnout. The bigger thing was, we knew that the electorate in the general election in 2012 would look much different than it did in 2010. But
you are talking about 2010, right?

JONATHAN KARL: Yes.

DAVID AXELROD: The other thing is that it was clear that the gravitational
pull in the Republican Party was very much to the right and that any
candidate who ran for president on the Republican side was going to
have to pass through that toll booth in order to be nominated. What you
saw after that, sequentially, were a number of sort of center-right Republicans dropping out of the race or opting out of the race, I think, in

part, because they knew they would have to go through that process. Governor Romney was willing to make those Faustian bargains, and they turned out to be quite costly. So we've seen this before. We saw it with the Gingrich Congress in '94. It set us up to, I think, seize the middle and you can see in our election that we did win moderates by more than a few points.

JONATHAN KARL: But, going back to that point and a few months forward. You went to Chicago in, what was it, January of—

DAVID AXELROD: 2011.

JONATHAN KARL: '11, yeah. When did it become clear to you that it was likely to be Mitt Romney, and what were your first steps to say, "Okay, here's how we are going to begin to make the case against him," because it was early?

DAVID AXELROD: Well, first of all, my working assumption from the time we won the election in 2008 was that Romney was the likely nominee, just because I believe in the opposites theory of presidential politics. People never look for the replica of what they have. They look for the remedy. And so, in contrast to Obama, the sort of businessman, and we knew the economy was going to be the issue because we were headed into this huge recession, so it seemed like he would be the likely guy. I want to disabuse you of one notion. We weren't sitting around in November of 2010 saying, "How can we take Mitt Romney down?" That's not what we were thinking about. We were thinking more in macro terms about the positioning of the Republican Party.

••• DEFINING THE OPPONENT: MITT ROMNEY •••

LOIS ROMANO: You used that period though. You had a great time element on your side and you did use that period to start to define Romney, correct?

DAVID AXELROD: Not that period. I think the definition of Romney came much later.

LOIS ROMANO: Okay well, let's just talk about whenever it was. Somewhere in there you made a decision to define him as a right-winger, an extremist, and then the subtext was that he was just a rich, out-of-touch corporate businessman.

DAVID AXELROD: Okay that does it. [*laughter*]

LOIS ROMANO: Well you know. But, as some of us wrote about at the time, you did not go heavy on the whole flip-flopper thing, and my question is, Stephanie, you had a lot of that information obviously from Kennedy, McCain put out memos on it, why did you not take up the flip-flopper mantle initially?

STEPHANIE CUTTER: So 2011, Axe just walked us through thinking about the impact of the 2010 midterms. We watched what was happening in the Republican primary through 2011. We also were deeply enmeshed in some of our own battles—budget, debt limits—but we were watching the Republican Party. And over the course of the summer and into the fall, we watched how Mitt Romney was increasingly taking some of those conservative positions that he was being forced to because of the nature of his party, the outcome of the 2010 elections, what he needed to do, presumably, to get the nomination, and they were piling up. We also looked at how voters were receiving that information and, while the argument that Romney had no core was a powerful argument, to build the foundation to get there, you really had to paint him as having positions that were not in the mainstream, whether it was on corporations are people too,[1] or all the immigration positions through the debates. We were watching that very closely, and it started to pile up on him.

DAVID AXELROD: Let me just say we viewed this in two phases. We introduced it, and I talked about it. We had a press call on it. David Plouffe went on television and made the core argument. And we did that as an argument to foment discussion within the Republican primaries. We were surprised, frankly, that none of the Republican candidates had challenged Romney early on on these shifts in position, and we thought that by introducing the issue of the alacrity with which he switched positions, we could lengthen the Republican primary process because core Republicans would be doubtful of his commitment. I think you are right in that, in the long run, flip-flopper was not a very good argument for us in a general election context because we didn't want to give people an out to say, "Well yeah. His ideas seem kind of nutty but he doesn't really mean them." I had someone say, who was

---

1.   In August 2011 at the Iowa State Fair when a protester shouted, "Corporations!," to urge Romney to raise taxes on corporations that have benefited from loopholes in the tax code, Romney said, "Corporations are people, my friend."

close to him but not involved in the campaign, I said, "Well how are you going to segue back to the center after taking all these positions?" And the guy said, "Well, you know Mitt is full of whatever, and everybody knows that. So people will just say, 'That's Mitt,' but they know he doesn't really believe that stuff." And that became hard for him to do when the time came because he never did solidify the base, and one of the reasons he didn't solidify the base is because we introduced this notion of the flip-flopping into the primary process.

JONATHAN KARL: How did you do that?

STEPHANIE CUTTER: Well we did a little bit of it hands on, but the media had a lot to do with this too because there was already a narrative of Mitt Romney, similar to what David was just saying about people who were close to Romney, that he has been a flip-flopper. That was covered a little bit in 2008. It certainly was covered in his campaigns here in Massachusetts, so it wasn't hard to convince anybody of that, but it was necessary to make sure that that was part of the conversation through the Republican primary. The first time he was actually challenged publicly about being a flip-flopper was on *Fox News*, and obviously we don't impact *Fox News*.

That really set the stage, and that was around the time where there was a press call and Plouffe went out and said that he had no core. That was a good "poking the bear" moment for us, and then it kind of took off. At the same time, and I'm a little bit repeating what Axe was saying, because he was being challenged as a flip-flopper, he had to move further to the right to convince people, you know, I'm a severe conservative, I'm an ideal Tea Party candidate. Those were things that he had to do to convince people that he would be okay; he would carry their party line and their agenda. So it was a two-part strategy.

JIM MARGOLIS: That was the point that I was going to make and we did put a little bit behind it. We did video that was moved out to everyone. We did an ad that sort of pushed people to the Mitt v. Mitt, but it was all in the context of what would be a primary conversation for him, not something that we were looking at as a long-term strategy for the general election.

JONATHAN KARL: You guys were playing in the Republican primary?

JIM MARGOLIS: Well.

STEPHANIE CUTTER: Well.

JONATHAN KARL: That's what you were describing. He was running an ad against Romney.

JIM MARGOLIS: It was an online message to everyone.

JIM MESSINA: None of us had an idea, at that time, how right he was going to go in the primary. When we were building this thing in March and April of '11, we couldn't have assumed he went so far to the right on immigration. To Stephanie's point, he got kind of forced into it. He did the personhood thing on the Huckabee show.[2] He did some things that would later damage him greatly in the general election. So we never thought that the no core argument was a general election argument, but it certainly caused the primary to go longer and did him some damage. But, at the time, we couldn't have seen how far he was going to move to the right.

••• ANYONE BUT ROMNEY? •••

JONATHAN KARL: Was there ever a moment you thought one of the other guys could win?

JIM MESSINA: No.

JONATHAN KARL: We had a nodding from Stephanie. [*laughter*]

LOIS ROMANO: Okay we're going to have to poll here.

JIM MESSINA: Every Friday we rated them in order for our weekly memos, and Romney was number one every single week, never went to number two, and so we always assumed he was going to be the nominee. Yeah people moved up and down. Perry moved up the list pretty high at the end. Santorum was on the list. But Romney never went to number two.

DAVID AXELROD: My supposition was, and I think many of you shared it, that in theory, Perry was a potential threat to Romney for all the reasons that we've discussed. If there was an authentic conservative who was

---

2. In November 2011 TV show host and former Arkansas Governor Huckabee asked Romney, "Would you have supported the constitutional amendment that would have established the definition of life at conception?" Romney replied, "Absolutely."

well funded and plausible, that was the greatest threat to Romney in the primary process and, on paper, that was Governor Perry, I guess until he spoke. [*laughter*]

LOIS ROMANO: To what extent did Huntsman play into your heads early on as a potential problem during the general?

JONATHAN KARL: Was he ever number two on your list?

DAVID AXELROD: Not after November of 2010.

JEREMY BIRD: Getting to what you just talked about, there's no way, coming out of that, that he was going to win the Republican primary.

DAVID AXELROD: His candidacy was hard to understand in the context of Republicans and the Republican Party. Maybe you have some of his folks here, but the theory, I think, was that he was what they needed to win a general election. But you had to get from here to there, and there was no way. And, frankly, we didn't appoint Huntsman ambassador to China with a notion of disqualifying him in 2012. No we really didn't. But his association with us was probably not a net plus for the primary. [*laughter*] He was the perfect man to be ambassador to China, but it didn't hurt to put a potential challenger in Beijing. At no time did we have a meeting in the White House saying, let's find something for Huntsman to do so he won't run for president. He really was well qualified for that job. Look I was there; I heard him introduce the president in Mandarin.

JONATHAN KARL: He spoke Chinese in one of the debates too.

DAVID AXELROD: That probably didn't help him either. [*laughter*]

••• **THE BAIN ATTACKS** •••

LOIS ROMANO: We just heard Matt Rhoades talk about how he was surprised at the intensity of the Bain attacks during the primaries. Did you guys have a little bit of a hand in that?

DAVID AXELROD: I mean—[*laughter*] we raised the issue. We were surprised, frankly, at some of the intensity of the attacks. Ironically it was Sheldon Adelson who funded some of the most intense attacks on him

Stephanie Cutter listens to David Axelrod talk about the Bain attacks on Romney.

on Bain. We were surprised at the vehemence with which they went after him and, frankly, also just slightly concerned that, by potentially going overboard, that would spoil the issue moving forward.

LOIS ROMANO: Well it didn't, right?

STEPHANIE CUTTER: But it took them a while to get there. That was January, right?

DAVID AXELROD: Yeah, it was the South Carolina primary, January.

STEPHANIE CUTTER: We thought it would happen much earlier on the Republican side and were a little surprised that it took that long. We didn't think it would happen with the veracity that it did, and we were worried that maybe there was a little bit of overshooting the runway on it, and it would take the issue off the table for the general election. We had obviously nothing to do with what Republicans did on the issue, but we did start to introduce the subject through the Republican primaries, having some of those now infamous Bain guys travel around—Randy

Johnson[3] and others—into the primary states and, through the DNC, do some press events just to remind people that the issue was there. But then a few of his primary opponents picked it up and ran with it much further than we thought.

DAVID AXELROD: I think it underscored some of the difficulties within the Republican base because you had a divided party and you had the sort of corporate Republicans, and then you had these more populist Republicans. For the corporate Republicans it was unthinkable that raising the mistreatment of workers, outsourcing, and so on would be an issue in the Republican primaries. For the more populist Republicans, they had a receptive audience. So the reason we were surprised was because there was this tug and pull within the party and these guys played a heavy card there.

JONATHAN KARL: You also had the tug and pull when we moved forward, after he clinched the nomination, and obviously that was Cory Booker and others who were critical of the way you guys used Bain. Jim, how much were you hearing on that? I mean, were you getting supporters of the president in the business world saying, come on, lay off this?

JIM MESSINA: Yeah. I think it was an ongoing conversation for a short amount of time. But, to Stephanie's point, once the Republicans finally went after it and did it on their own, it sort of was easy for me to say to some folks on our side that this is fair game and everyone is doing it. And here's the truth: it was a very small amount of people. The majority of our supporters understood exactly what this was about and what we were doing. It's a presidential campaign. Everyone is going to have an opinion.

DAVID AXELROD: Before you go forward, I know there's a fascination with tactics, but tactics really don't mean anything unless they are informed by a strategy. And, Simas, you ought to talk a little bit about the context of this. Our whole campaign was predicated on an argument and that argument was that we needed to build an economy that worked for the middle class and that the middle class had been pummeled over a long period of time. And within the context of that, the Bain argument was really quite relevant and important. It wasn't just a tactic. It was a reflection of an attitude. David, why don't you talk a little bit about the research?

---

3. Randy Johnson was a former factory worker whose company folded under Bain's watch.

LOIS ROMANO: Also in talking about it, take the next step, and tell us how well it worked for you. You did the research and then, we understand, it worked well in certain states. Go ahead.

DAVID SIMAS: In early 2011 it was very important for us, knowing that the economy was going to be the fundamental issue, to understand the president's strengths and weaknesses relative towards it and the same thing with Governor Romney. Here is the tone and tenor of what we heard in a lot of the focus groups. I like the president, and these are undecided, independent voters, for the most part. I think he's trying really hard, I think that he shares my values, but I'm concerned that things either haven't turned around fast enough or they haven't turned around. When they would talk about Governor Romney, they would talk about his technical expertise. Here's a guy that seems to me that he's been successful at different things that he's done. And, to David's point about the strength of Romney in this environment, that technical knowledge that he had about the economy was very, very important. The importance of Bain was to basically give him the technical expertise but essentially say, "Just because he's been successful doesn't mean that you, middle-class family, are going to benefit from that."

And so that was the important thing on a very meta, meta level is essentially, look, the guy has been successful at everything he's ever done, but when he wins, it doesn't necessarily mean that you are going to. One additional point that I think is important, that our quantitative, especially Joel Benenson's[4] work, did on this. There's a fascinating question we began running in 2011 that talked about, what's the best way to grow the economy: a strong and vibrant private sector or a strong middle class? And, frankly, I was surprised that by a margin of about 55 to 38–39, across the board, there's this idea that a vibrant and strong middle class was really the key. And in the focus groups—group after group after group after group—we would hear these undecided, independent voters saying things like, "Look, I need a guy, a president who, from the beginning to the end, his entire focus is going to be on things that grow the middle class because that's the way you grow the economy."

JONATHAN KARL: I know it wasn't your ad but the Priorities USA cancer ad,[5] what kind of an impact did that have?

---

4.   Joel Benenson was the Obama campaign's lead pollster.
5.   In August 2012 Priorities USA, a super PAC supporting President Obama, ran an ad that tied Romney to a family's loss of health insurance and a woman's subsequent death from cancer. The ad focused on a former worker at a company closed by Bain.

DAVID SIMAS: We didn't look at a specific ad.

JONATHAN KARL: But that dominated the story for several days.

DAVID SIMAS: Let's just put this in context though because you're talking about an ad that ran twice. This was an obsession with you guys, but for the average voter this just wasn't really on the radar screen. I mean there wasn't this recoil from something they had never seen. It wasn't a discussion in the focus groups. This is one of those places where there are two universes: there's the universe in which we all live, and then there's the real world.

JONATHAN KARL: Jim, could you ever see yourself making an ad like that?

JIM MARGOLIS: I don't think that would have been the tone and tenor of where we would have gone and I just want to underscore what David is saying. We were having a hard enough time when we were putting 2,000 points behind a spot, let alone when it gets played two or three times. Among voters this was not something that penetrated.

JONATHAN KARL: What was the reaction in Chicago? I mean, when you first saw that ad? I know what you told us at the time, you kind of deflected it, but now it's all over, what were you thinking when you saw that? Were you like, "Oh my God, what are they doing now?" or "Brilliant!"?

DAVID AXELROD: No, no, no. We felt that the ad went farther than it needed to go. I mean the fact is that the indictment was not an unfair indictment. I think the implication was less clear than you guys did, short of implying that there was a direct link between Romney's decisions and this woman's death—

JONATHAN KARL: Do you think that's an okay argument, that there was a direct link?

DAVID AXELORD: No I said it isn't a direct argument.

JONATHAN KARL: Oh okay.

DAVID AXELROD: And we said at the time that it wasn't, and we could not communicate with the Priorities people. I presume that the things we said had something to do with their decision not to run the ad anywhere. And really more than anything, it is a little parable about how coverage of modern politics is done today because the ad dominated coverage, but it didn't dominate the race. Now I will say there are other ads that Priorities did during the course of the campaign, including the coffin ad[6]—that was very, very effective—and most of their ads were very, I think, down Main Street on this issue of middle class viability and Romney's practices and business and what that might say about his philosophy. So I'm not here to condemn all the work that they did. On that particular ad, we thought that it went too far, and we said it went too far.

••• THE VEEP SELECTION •••

LOIS ROMANO: I'm going to jump around a little bit because we want to get a lot in here. Paul Ryan, tell us a little bit of your reaction when he was picked. I know some of you did not expect it, and you thought it was going to be maybe Pawlenty. At what point did you realize it was going to be him? What was your reaction? And since it was two weeks before the convention, how did that impact your strategies?

STEPHANIE CUTTER: Well we had the same strategy no matter who it was really because if you looked at each one of the potential VP picks, it fit right into the story line that it was doubling down on the policies of the past that crashed the economy in the first place and punished the middle class. Each one of them had a record that supported that in a pretty big way. Now Ryan was incredibly well known amongst everybody in this room but also in the progressive base for what he stood for, so that made our job a little bit easier. But in a larger sense it really just was a doubling down of everything that Mitt Romney had stood for on the economy and on the wrong side of the middle class. So I think that we all thought that it could have been Pawlenty. It could have been Ryan or Portman. Those were probably the top three, and we were ready for either one of them. We were a little surprised that Romney had called Ryan "the intellectual leader of the Republican Party," and that it seemed as though they weren't ready to answer questions about whether Romney supported Ryan's agenda because Ryan was so well known for that agenda, and they didn't have clean answers on whether he

---

6.   In June 2012 Priorities USA, the super PAC supporting President Obama, released a new ad against Mitt Romney in which a worker says he built his own "coffin" after Romney's private equity firm bought his paper plant. Former Marion, Indiana, paper plant worker Mike Earnest said he and other employees of the American Pad and Paper plant were asked to build a stage from which company officials told them the news that their plant was being closed.

supported the Ryan budget. I just remember a lot of back and forth about, "Well, you know, I'm the candidate, he's the vice. I'm at the top of the ticket. It's my agenda now." But we had Romney on record for so long embracing the Ryan budget.

DAVID AXELROD: Yes, he wanted the benefit of appointing the idea man without embracing his ideas, but that was impossible. It was impossible to make that separation in picking Ryan. Teddy, you ought to speak in a second here to the impact on our own base and on social media when Ryan was chosen, but we did expect a Portman or Pawlenty.

JONATHAN KARL: Was Rubio ever anywhere on your list?

DAVID AXELROD: Not in our thinking.

LOIS ROMANO: Would one of them have done better, in your view, against you guys?

DAVID AXELROD: That remains to be seen. You can make the argument we won Ohio. Now I think it's widened out to three points, but perhaps he would have made a difference there. But they did this sort of rapid fire, and I know this is this afternoon's topic, repositioning over the course of six weeks. Here's my observation of the Romney campaign. It seems to me that they always were doing what they needed to to get through the next thing on the theory that just being on the ballot against Barack Obama, as vulnerable as he was, was enough. And so if you had to run to the right of Perry on immigration, you run to the right of Perry on immigration. If you have to run to the right of Santorum on social issues, you run to the right of Santorum. And now they're approaching a convention that was largely a hostile convention for him. He still hadn't won over the hearts and minds of the Republican base, and so Ryan was a popular choice with that base. It bought him more enthusiasm among the base and in that convention. But what it also did was make Medicare a front-and-center issue in a way that didn't end up to their benefit, so we were debating Medicare instead of the economy. It tied him to the Republican Congress when Congress was polling at, what, 10 or 12 percent, and they were in danger of falling within the margin of error so that nobody in America might like Congress. And he's the idea man behind this. I think one of the best lines in the campaign was former Congressman Tom Perriello who said, "Only Mitt Romney could point to this Republican Congress and say I want the brains behind that operation." [*laughter*] But I think it had a galvanizing effect on our own base, and, Teddy, why don't you talk about what happened around that time in social media?

TEDDY GOFF: I do think it had a galvanizing effect to be sure. I mean we came out of the gate that morning when he made that pick with a website and a video and all that stuff. He was the kind of person that was really well suited to be discussed and obsessed over on social media. When you think about the moments that really broke through, I think about his convention speech, and I know we don't want to move that far forward, but the Janesville argument[7] that he made was one of these things. The social media world lives in a bubble, the same way Axe was talking about the Washington press. The voter doesn't necessarily hear this stuff that is trending on Twitter, for the most part. The Janesville thing, they did. And there were a couple of other examples of that. Even sort of atmospheric stuff about him, like those photos that were taken for *Time*,[8] I mean he was just sort of a perfect, I think, kind of object for this election and for the kind of impact the social media had on this election. He was very galvanizing for us, and he, frankly, raised us a lot of money and recruited a lot of volunteers for us and all that stuff.

DAVID AXELROD: Wasn't that night one of the five biggest fundraising nights we got online? The night they picked Ryan?

TEDDY GOFF: The night they picked Ryan was up there, and then certainly the night that he gave his convention speech was one of the biggest. In terms of money that was probably fourth or fifth, something like that.

LOIS ROMANO: Wow.

JEREMY BIRD: One of the things that it did that's very counterintuitive at the state level is that Paul Ryan helped us in Wisconsin. Here's why. Our folks in Wisconsin were totally demoralized. They had just gone through all these recall elections and we had lost, and it was the hardest state for me, as a field director, to mobilize our volunteers.

JONATHAN KARL: One more fight.

---

7. In his speech at the Republican National Convention, Congressman Ryan blamed Obama for the shuttering of an auto plant in his hometown of Janesville, Wisconsin, that closed while President George W. Bush was in office.

8. In October 2012, as part of an issue featuring a profile of Ryan, *Time* magazine did a photo shoot of his workout.

JEREMY BIRD: We put everything into it, and we had lost. And Paul Ryan regalvanized all of our troops in Wisconsin in a way that no other pick would have. And so I think you saw in some of the polling numbers that Wisconsin was getting a little closer, but, for us, it was actually a boost. That pick got our folks really excited across the board, but it really, really helped us in Wisconsin in a way that we didn't see coming, I don't think.

JONATHAN KARL: I want to get to the convention, but I have a very quick last question on Ryan. You guys still lost amongst seniors in the key states. Ryan may not have helped Romney, but he didn't hurt them for the reason many of you and us thought he would.

DAVID SIMAS: Well, first of all, the Democratic Party, since I think 1972, has not had a very successful record winning the senior vote. The more important piece around Ryan and Medicare is what we were hearing from voters, these undecided, independent voters. When they heard Medicare cuts, they put it right into that middle class security bucket, regardless of age, so these aren't sixty-five-plus voters, although there were many of those, but look, if you are over fifty-five, you don't have to worry about it. I love the guy in a focus group in Des Moines, who is fifty-three, who turned to the guy and said, "Well I guess they are coming for me." And so it helped with the overall middle-class security message, which was key to what we were doing.

••• THE CONVENTIONS •••

JONATHAN KARL: I want to move quickly onto the convention. It's got to be an advantage to go second, right? I mean you get a chance to watch their convention, to see what they did, and I'm just wondering, Jim—because you were obviously busy in Charlotte getting ready—how closely were you watching what was going on in Tampa and what moves did you make based on what was happening up there to adjust what you were doing down in Charlotte?

JIM MARGOLIS: Look, we were pretty clear about what we wanted to do in the convention for some time, and there was a series of objectives that we had that were spelled out—unfortunately spelled out in *POLITICO* and some other places because the memo was leaked—but that was pretty consistent with what we tried to have happen. And that was prior to the Republican Convention. Now, as we were watching the convention, clearly there were moments that sort of jumped out at you.

LOIS ROMANO: Such as?

JIM MARGOLIS: Well look, that provided a lot of fodder within the speeches that people would get up and communicate to millions of people back home. That was something that was obviously an indelible moment, but from an overall perspective of what is it that we were trying to achieve, those objectives really didn't change.

LOIS ROMANO: Did you tweak anything? I mean, for example, you came out pretty quickly about Romney not thanking the troops. And I'm sure you had something in your convention, but did you beef that up a little bit, for example?

JIM MARGOLIS: Yeah, those were the nuances. We had speechwriters who were refining speeches and so on, but the basic contours of the convention were ones that we had settled on long before the convention: the importance of this fundamental middle class message, the importance of a Bill Clinton who is going to be able to deliver what he delivered that night to America. That was obviously incredibly important to us. Those kinds of things were really locked down and didn't change.

DAVID AXELROD: There was an architecture to the convention as we planned it and the first day was going to be very much the personal connection between the president and the middle class and what motivated him around these issues. The second day was going to be largely dominated by Clinton taking apart the Republican economic argument, and the third day was going to be Biden testifying to the character of the president's leadership and then the president's speech itself. And of course our keynote on the first night was important to us: Mayor Castro of San Antonio.

JONATHAN KARL: Who broke the news to Biden that Clinton was going to have his slot?

DAVID AXELROD: It turned out to be a pretty good deal because he got better numbers actually where he was. Yeah, yeah, so everybody was happy.

JONATHAN KARL: Well who broke the news? [*laughter*]

LOIS ROMANO: Were you all surprised by the Republican Convention, that it didn't hang together?

DAVID AXELROD: They had the unlucky circumstance of the weather. And I think Rush said we were to blame, but I don't think we were. But yeah, I mean partly because it was compressed, but it was a lack of coherency. But the bigger thing was that rather than pivoting toward a general election audience, this was really a rally of a base, and they further estranged themselves from key constituencies that were going to be important in the general election instead of using it as an opportunity to improve their relations or their outreach to those constituencies. So like I said, I think it was a base-oriented convention. What was odd about it was that Romney was sort of an apparition in many ways there and it seemed like there was more enthusiasm in the room for Ryan than there was for Romney.

JIM MARGOLIS: I just wanted to comment, there was also either some bad luck or maybe somebody made a misjudgment, but, for example, I thought the video that they did for Governor Romney that ran in New Orleans, when I looked at it, I was just kind of, "Goddamn, I hope this thing ends before ten o'clock because it was terrific." I don't know whether Stuart produced that or who did it, but it really was the kind of thing that I think could have had a lot of impact. But it hit before primetime.

LOIS ROMANO: Just one more question, then we'll move on from the convention. Did anyone think that Clint Eastwood might play well after watching it?

JONATHAN KARL: What was the reaction when you were watching it?

LOIS ROMANO: What was the reaction? How did you think it was going to come down the next day, given that he is beloved?

JIM MESSINA: Well I remember Teddy running into my office saying this thing was exploding online, and you could see immediately what a disaster it was for him—both with our people, the swing voters, our daily analysis of social trends. No one thought it was a good moment.

JONATHAN KARL: So you ran in while he was still up there?

TEDDY GOFF: While or maybe slightly after. That was the night that we did, and maybe some of you guys remember, that tweet that said "this seat's taken," and it was a photo of the back of the president's head. That was, at the time, the second-most retweeted thing we ever did, ever, since the Barack Obama account was created in 2007 or maybe 2008—second only to the same-sex marriage announcement. So I mean it was really something that stood out, and it had a similar kind of resonance on Facebook. And then the next week we get to Charlotte, and people were selling T-shirts with that photo saying, "seat's taken." So I mean that was obviously something that our people found offensive, in a really visceral way. Hearing Romney attack the economy or whatever doesn't do it but such a personal sort of show of disrespect for the president was very helpful to us.

DAVID AXELROD: Good fundraising. It was a huge fundraising opportunity for us at their convention. I think there was energy in the field after their convention.

TEDDY GOFF: Certainly on the fundraising side, that day, the following day, it helped. I hope the Republicans always time their convention to be the day before an FEC deadline because the combination of the Romney speech and, to whatever extent, the Clint Eastwood thing motivated our people even more.

LOIS ROMANO: You had one of your biggest fundraising days?

TEDDY GOFF: Yeah our second, if I remember correctly.

••• A DATA-DRIVEN CAMPAIGN •••

LOIS ROMANO: Let's stick with you, Teddy, for a second. We've been learning more and more about your very sophisticated and much-heralded digital operation, so I have a multipart question. Are the POLITICOs and pundits overrating the part that it played in this campaign?

TEDDY GOFF: Yes.

LOIS ROMANO: Okay, but wait. Have you really revolutionized the way campaigns will now tackle an electorate? I mean, are voters now really turning into just stats?

JONATHAN KARL: Logarithms.

LOIS ROMANO: Logarithms, yeah.

TEDDY GOFF: We didn't talk much about logarithms. [*laughter*] I think a couple of things: First of all, I think it's important to keep in mind that the fundamental goals of the campaign haven't changed in four years and in forty years. We were trying to do a very limited number of things. We were trying to recruit volunteers, register voters, raise money, persuade people, and turn them out, and that was it. And so I think technology and social media can help you do that a little faster and a little more efficiently.

LOIS ROMANO: Tell us how it changed from 2008 in your answer too.

TEDDY GOFF: Sure. Well with regard to that question specifically, the 2008 campaign was obviously very celebrated for its effectiveness in the use of digital media, and I worked on that. Almost all of us did. It was really groundbreaking and really a marvel. The fact is that Facebook was about a tenth of the size it is now. Twitter was nowhere. I mean, we never talked about it once. Even the smart phone—now it's sort of hard to imagine or remember a time when you weren't checking your phone every five minutes—but the iPhone had been invented during that campaign, in the summer of 2007, and so these things really came a long way. And I think there are a lot of things that we did for the first time in this cycle that people sort of wrongly attribute to earlier campaigns and think that we did them then too. We honestly didn't.

JONATHAN KARL: Like what?

TEDDY GOFF: All those things. Facebook and Twitter were effectively new to us this cycle, and so that changes your mindset, certainly, from my perspective and from my team's perspective.

LOIS ROMANO: How you used Facebook? Is that what you are saying?

TEDDY GOFF: I mean even thinking about it, even it being a significant part of the strategy. In 2008 Dan Wagner[9] did an analysis after the election and concluded that 99 percent of all our e-mail lists voted. And so we entered into this election with an understanding that anybody we

---

9. Dan Wagner was the chief analytics officer for Obama 2012.

were talking to directly, the vast preponderance of those people were going to vote for us. And so the question was not, "How can we serve them with content that's going to really make them turn out and vote?" The question was, "How can we serve them with content and experience, and all that, and tools and resources and information that's going to make them go out and get their friends?" Because while 99 percent of our people, at least on e-mail and Facebook and Twitter—presumably a lower share but still a very high share—are going to vote for us, Barack Obama's now thirty-three million Facebook fans in the United States or Facebook fans globally, they are friends with about 98 percent of the U.S.-based Facebook population. That's more than the number of people who vote. So we knew all along that if we were treating our people with an experience and with content and, again, with information and resources and tools—not that would get them excited but that would keep them engaged and go out and get their friends excited—we knew that we could reach literally almost everyone in the United States. That was a totally new dynamic that didn't exist in 2008.

JEREMY BIRD: I just want to add there the difference between '08 and 2012 in the digital world is that Teddy's team got very close to erasing the barrier between the organizer in Des Moines and Chicago, in terms of what we were doing. In 2008 there was an online program, and then there were the field offices and what I was doing in Ohio and what people were doing in states. In 2012 the digital tools that we had and the analytics that everybody has hyped up was about serving that organizer and that volunteer in order to do the things that Teddy talked about, whether it was registering the voter in that area because that's what we needed to do to win, whether it was persuading folks, or whether it was turning them out or raising money or building the organization to do all those things. And that integration took a lot of time to figure out, but it allowed us to basically run ward races or run neighborhood races, run local races, where all the tools that we were creating, from Dashboard to the follow-up e-mails that we would do, were about mobilizing people to go do one of those things on the ground. And then to also do that knowing that not everybody we were going to reach had a phone number or an address or some other way for us to get them. We were reaching a lot of people through their social networks on the ground and online. The merger of those two things was the biggest difference, in my mind, between 2008 and 2012.

TEDDY GOFF: And, very quickly, that last thing about people we couldn't reach via phone is incredibly important. Of our GOTV targets, eighteen to twenty-nine years old, 50 percent of them we couldn't reach by phone. So they either don't have a land line, or we didn't have their cell number, or whatever it was. Of that group, 85 percent of them we could reach via a friend of Barack Obama on Facebook. If Jeremy is running the biggest and the best volunteer operation in history, it could have been twice its size. We still couldn't reach these people because we didn't have their phone numbers.

LOIS ROMANO: Are you talking about targeted sharing?

TEDDY GOFF: I am, but even just Facebook generally. We had an ability to reach these people who just simply couldn't otherwise be reached.

JONATHAN KARL: So is the robo-call dead? Were you doing much of it?

DAVID SIMAS: I'll let Jim speak to that, but the robo-call and what we were seeing—how we were seeing people react to thirty-second spots— in some ways goes to what Teddy and Jeremy just mentioned. We would hear people go, "Romney says A. Obama says B. I don't know what to believe because I go to this site, and it verifies that. I go to another site, and it verifies something else. Well what do you believe? What's the basis of trust?" Someone on Facebook that I know. A volunteer that comes to the door and engages in a conversation over and over and over again. So the fact that we had people at the door in districts, what Jeremy said, is spot on. We ran ward races throughout the country based upon trust, and that is much more powerful than a robo-call or anything else that you can do. And for me, besides the fact that candidates matter more than anything else, the organization underneath allowed us to run thousands of ward races throughout the country.

••• THE GROUND GAME •••

JONATHAN KARL: So Jeremy, bring me into that ground game. Republicans talk about the ground game being just so important here. I was watching a lot of counties on election night but especially just kind of blown away by Hamilton County and Hillsborough County.[10] What was going on there? These were two counties that Republicans just have to win. I mean they had their convention in Hillsborough County, and you guys won. It was one of the few counties they actually ran more ads in than you guys ran, and you guys won in Hamilton County, in a Republican county. You guys went in there.

---

10.   Hamilton County is in Ohio and Hillsborough County is in Florida.

JEREMY BIRD: So I could talk about this for a long time. I'll try to be as brief as possible. Maybe I'll start with your robo-call question. So you guys did a lot of calls in the room here, clearly, and you would release the results and would have a debate about a lot of things. But one of the things that Republicans started talking about towards the end, and other folks would talk about this, is when you did a poll of how many percent of the voters you were talking to had been contacted by a campaign. In some places, it would look about equal. And, in fact, in a couple of states they might have been a little bit ahead, but you never asked the second question, how? You never asked the second question, and no poll did. How were they contacted? We looked at this every day when we would look at our analytics. We would say, "Were you contacted by us? Were you contacted by the Romney campaign?" And then we would ask how, and we would get beat by robo-calls. We would get beat by mail. We would never get beat in any state by door-to door, face-to-face, or personal phone calls from a volunteer. The robo-call is a tactic, and it can work to turn out people for an event or do some other things. But that alone is nothing. It had to be part of a bigger strategy. And I talked about this a little bit last night, our strategy was that we believed that people on the ground building real relationships in their neighborhoods and talking to people outside of the traditional campaign tactics, as well as the campaign tactics, these people, our volunteer neighborhood team leaders, owned the campaign. At the bottom of their e-mail they would say, you know, "David Simas, neighborhood team leader, Hillsborough County." They knew their goals. They had eight or ten precincts that they owned as a neighborhood team leader. They knew how many people they needed to register. They knew how many people they needed to persuade. They knew where the polling locations were because their kids went to school there, because they went to church there. They knew where the barber shops and beauty salons were in the African American community. They knew where the grocery stores and the small businesses were in the Latino community. They knew their community at Ohio State University because they were students there. They weren't paid staffers. Our staffers were there to support those people that lived in those neighborhoods and they worked those lists. And it was hard, but what we did in 2011 was we got the 20 percent of people that were going to be the leadership, the foundation that we were going to build on, so that when people started paying more attention in 2012, we could build on that.

LOIS ROMANO: And how did you get them?

JEREMY BIRD: It was a combination, all the different ways. We'd call people. We'd e-mail people. We knew who had given money. Jim talks about this all the time: too often we treat donors and volunteers as separate universes. These are people that care about the president. They are supporters. And a lot of people became volunteers because they first gave five dollars. And a lot of people gave five dollars when Teddy asked because they had been volunteers and they owned the campaign and they wanted to do more.

JIM MESSINA: An important point here is Obama. This organization re-flected him and people were that loyal and spent all this time because he stood for things they cared about, because he involved them, be-cause we ran a campaign—he ran a campaign—about big issues that they cared about. I remember about two months before the election I went to Columbus, Ohio. Jeremy had me do a neighborhood team leader convention, and this woman said the single smartest thing. And at that moment I thought, "Okay, we are doing this campaign right," when she said, "Jim, I've been a neighborhood team leader for Barack Obama in Columbus, Ohio, for five years. I know every single person in my neighborhood. I know the Democrats who might not vote. I know the Independents who are going to make up their mind the final days of this campaign. I know the Republicans who we could never get." She's like, "The Romney person who got here a month ago was from out of state. Who do you think is going to do better the last week of this campaign?" And it was true. We knew exactly who we had to go get, and that, in part, is why we got the turnout numbers that mattered. But you built an organization around the president, and people were motivated by him. That's why so many people basically became full-time volun-teers. We had over 30,000 neighborhood team leaders who did almost nothing but volunteer for us full time.

••• THE AD WARS •••

JONATHAN KARL: I want to ask about the air war component of this because something that just fascinates me—

JIM MARGOLIS: You mean advertising matters there?

JONATHAN KARL: Yes. Well it's a good question: how much does it mat-ter? But, before you answer that, I looked at the numbers. The Wesley-an Media Project goes through and crunches how many ads ran, how

Jim Margolis and Teddy Goff discuss the Obama campaign's advertising strategy.

much money was spent. The numbers blow me away because you guys ran, according to them, 503,000 ads, thirty-second spots. Mitt Romney ran 190,000. You guys ran more ads even on your side than they ran including the super PACs. They spent more money; you guys ran more ads. What were you doing? I mean I've heard stories of you guys going in and being able to buy cable at better rates because you bought national cable when the local cable stations were jacking up rates in the key states. How did you guys work this?

JIM MARGOLIS: Let me do this pretty briefly because probably a lot of people aren't going to be that interested in it. There's a couple of things that are the forces here at work. First, you sort of have to look at this as Obama and allies and Romney and allies, and when you do that, I think it comes out to about $550 million that was spent by Obama and allies and about $685 million for Romney and allies.

JONATHAN KARL: But you guys ran a lot more ads. How? I mean, he's the business guy.

JIM MARGOLIS: Of the money that was spent, we spent $450 million of the $550 million total out of Obama for America. Out of that $685 million, it was about $225 million that was spent by Romney—$225 to $450. So we spent about twice as much out of OFA as the Romney people did out of the Romney for President campaign. And the difference there then is we're getting the lowest unit rate time. That's one of the big factors. In other words, every federal candidate is allowed to purchase time at the lowest unit rate of their best advertiser. And so we got a rate that was often, as you got into the end of the campaign, half—even sometimes a third—of what the super PACs were paying for that advertising. So there was a real difference there. Second, there were two other important parts of this. One of them is what we called "the optimizer," which was the analytics operation that was awesome through this campaign, where we were able to—and I really don't think you probably want to go through this whole thing now—use the analytics operation inside the OFA headquarters. And it was just unbelievable. Dan Wagner and his team—we should just be doing shout-outs all day long for Teddy and all the different people who were really looking at this stuff that allowed us to, in a much more targeted way, speak to the people we wanted to speak to, either in persuading them or being able to turn them out ultimately and go to the shows that the people that we were most interested in watch.

JONATHAN KARL: Give us an example.

JIM MARGOLIS: The example is, traditionally, you would go get ratings from Nielsen and traditional sources. If you have Direct TV, if you have satellite TV, if you have a set top box, we could look through an organization called Rent Track at the second-by-second changes that you were making on your television set: when you went onto an ad, when you went off, what show you were watching, when you changed. That information could then be combined with the voter file. We would make clear we weren't looking at individuals because this was done by a third party, so there's a wall. We don't know exactly what Lois Romano is watching. What we know is what demographically she is, whether that person is a persuadable voter. Done on the outside, put together with a voter file, following all the other information that you have, we can now take people like Lois and say, "Wow, here's where they are skewing, in terms of the programming that they are looking at." It optimizes the ability to go in and talk to people. So, for example, we were a little heavier on things like TV Land than we would have been previously. We probably got about 15 percent additional efficiency in what we were able to do.

JONATHAN KARL: And was Romney advertising at all on TV Land?

JIM MARGOLIS: I don't think he ever went to TV Land, but I mean that's just one example. So where were those women? Where were those key persuadable voters? And, again, it's the combination of traditional—it's the combination of when you bought. We bought much, much earlier. We bought so that we could get the programming that we want, and then we had this incredible tool from incredible people who were just doing an amazing job with data.

LOIS ROMANO: Did you, as you were studying all these models, figure out somewhere in there that not everybody was getting their information from TV?

JIM MARGOLIS: Well we know that it's changed.

LOIS ROMANO: Can you talk about that a little bit?

JIM MARGOLIS: Maybe we should do this in combination. Teddy should be part of this as well.

LOIS ROMANO: The whole online stuff, yeah.

JIM MARGOLIS: Because a lot of our younger voters are not tuning in. They are going to Hulu, or they are going to a million other places. Teddy, why don't you jump in?

TEDDY GOFF: Sure, and Simas and Jim should jump in as well. A lot of people aren't watching TV, and so we spent—I don't know what the ultimate percentage was—but probably 15 or 20 percent of our overall ad spending was online, just on persuasion stuff.

JIM MARGOLIS: What would that have been in 2008? Just in comparison?

TEDDY GOFF: I'm guessing it was probably more in the 5 to 6 percent, 7 percent, something like that, significantly more. But as Simas was saying, people really trust their friends, and they don't really trust political advertising for the most part.

JONATHAN KARL: Not even his?

TEDDY GOFF: They trust Jim's more than anybody else's. So that's why we put so much effort into making sure that all of our people were effective ambassadors for the campaign. And one of the things that was sort of consistently amusing to all of us, I think, is there was so much chatter about what a negative campaign this ostensibly was. The fact of the matter is if we posted something on Facebook, ten million people would see that—if it was an effective post. Ten million people in the United States. And for all of the sort of back and forth of press releases and that kind of thing, millions of people weren't experiencing that campaign. They were experiencing a whole different campaign that was largely positive, that was largely about what their friends were saying. The negative stuff really doesn't move as well as the positive stuff online. And so what they were experiencing was this uplifting stuff about supporting the middle class, about fighting for education, about fighting for that kind of thing, and it was a whole different campaign that millions of these people were experiencing, some from the paid side but also some from just sort of the natural mechanics of social media.

DAVID AXELROD: First of all, on Romney, one of the things we were aware of was that they were buying news adjacencies very, very heavily, which is sort of the traditional way to buy media on the theory that people who watch the news are likely to vote. Our strategy was, for our purposes, much more effective. But essentially your question is, did we spend $550 million or, in our case, $450 million on something that has no impact?

JONATHAN KARL: Yes.

DAVID AXELROD: Are you guys idiots? [*laughter*] And I think the truth of television in a presidential campaign is that it becomes less relevant the deeper you get into the race and probably because by the time you get to the postconvention period, coverage is so intense, and then debates take over, for better and worse. Debates take over coverage during the period in which those debates are going on. So for a full month debates were the center of the discussion, and it renders ads much less impactful. And so one of the key decisions that we made, and Jim was in the middle of this, was to frontload our spending on television from May through August on the theory that that's when it would have the greatest impact. I don't think there is, in the modern age, an example of a television ad after Labor Day that was decisive in a presidential race. When you think of all the ads that we typically think of as having been impactful, most of them, or virtually all of them that I can think of, ran before the convention. And so we gambled on frontloading, not knowing exactly whether we could fill in the gaps, and there was some concern at times as to whether we could fill in those gaps. We got a little bit of a break because there was a great reaction to our convention, we raised more money than we thought. September was better than we thought. But I would say one of the key decisions we made was to frontload our media.

DAVID SIMAS: Finally, to David's point about how effective that was from our perspective, while we did not see movement in the horse race, what we did see throughout the summer, were changes both in the qualitative and in the quantitative research. First in the quantitative, Governor Romney's unfavorables among voters in swing states were increasing, especially the very unfavorable, and that became very important later on when we were trying to determine how folks were going to break. That was the first thing. In the qualitative we were hearing voter after voter after voter basically echo back the messages that we were giving them, saying that Governor Romney didn't care about the middle class, that even though he may have been successful in business, that didn't mean that it was going to help me. So that frontloading helped to really set the stage in these voters' minds. And then when the 47 percent video came out later on, all of that work that had been done put that in the appropriate context for these undecided voters.

••• THE FUTURE OF POLLING •••

JONATHAN KARL: Jim, you said that polling is broken. I think that was the phrase you used. I'm wondering, I know how much different what the Romney team was seeing was than what we were seeing in the public polling but, for you guys, what was different? You were doing a lot of your own polling, a lot more sophisticated, frankly, than a lot of what the media polls were showing. How was it different from what we were seeing in our polls?

JIM MESSINA: Well I want Simas to join us for this, but we had three different looks at the electorate. Benenson was doing battleground state polls which were going to macro what we're all seeing in the battleground states.

JONATHAN KARL: Daily tracking?

JIM MESSINA: Not daily until the end, but weekly or every two weeks into the spring. And then we had state pollsters who were very experienced in their states. We had Diane Feldman and John Anzalone who had been in these states for a very long time. And then our analytics team

David Simas and Jeremy Bird listen on as Jim Messina explains the Obama campaign's elaborate polling operation.

was doing eight or nine thousand random samples every night in the battleground states, giving us a very deep look, and that's how we did some of the modeling that Margolis just talked about in the media stuff that we thought was very helpful. So we were getting three different looks at the electorate. And why I think David and I had so much confidence the last couple of weeks of the election was all three of them were saying the same thing. Wagner was seeing exactly what Joel was seeing, exactly what Anzalone was seeing in Florida, in a way that gave us real confidence—that, combined with the early vote numbers. Every morning at 8:55, Jeremy would walk in with the early vote numbers from the day before, and you could see our people voting and our sporadic people voting. You took those three polling devices we had, plus the early voting, and we thought we knew exactly where the electorate was.

DAVID AXELROD: This is really a fundamental question for you guys. There was a proliferation of public polls, and each of them was treated as equally accurate. There was an obsession with the Gallup polling. We now know the Gallup Poll was probably on the far end of wrong, and yet it would become sort of a motif of the coverage—why you're losing

Independents, the gender gap is gone. And I think David can speak to the fact that because we did have a lot of resources with which to do research, we researched this and tried to make some judgments as to why it was that these media polls were so off. And we found that as many as 20 percent of people who were actually going to vote were not making the media screen on unlikely voters. And so there are a lot of questions to be explored on how these polls are done and whether they should be accorded the kind of status they are accorded because what happens is then it just becomes a big horse-race story, and you guys don't even know where the horses really are.

DAVID SIMAS: At the beginning of the race, we brought people in basically to look at all three types of polling and basically deconstruct everything: do an analysis of what we were doing wrong, where we needed to bulk up. Look, we needed to do a certain percentage of cell phone calls because if we didn't do that, we weren't going to get African Americans; we weren't going to get young. We needed to make sure that the voter list that we were using was really rigorous and quality controlled and make sure that it was a good list to work from. There were all kinds of recommendations that went to all the pollsters. They adopted them. And throughout the campaign, Jim would call me in and he'd say, "Look, here's this public poll that says X, Y, and Z. That's completely different than anything of what we are seeing." What we would do with every single one, and we had a couple of people devoted to this, was take a look at the assumptions. Are they doing cell phones? Are they doing voter list calls? And deconstruct it so I could go back to him and say, "Here's why we believe this is wrong for the following reasons." But we questioned our assumptions from beginning to end. The good news for us is, with about a month out, we had our Benenson Poll at 50 to 46. We had our state aggregate pollsters where you take Feldman, Anzalone, Harstad, you roll them all up together, they were at 50–46. And you take the analytics nightly poll, think about this, 9,000 interviews per night.

JONATHAN KARL: Spread across the nine states? Eight states?

DAVID SIMAS: I think it was ten states. And their aggregate numbers were the same.

JONATHAN KARL: What was the tenth?

JEREMY BIRD: Are you counting North Carolina?

DAVID SIMAS: Yeah.

JONATHAN KARL: What's the tenth? Nevada?

JEREMY BIRD: Colorado, Iowa, Wisconsin.

JIM MESSINA: I want to reiterate something Axe said because it's a very important point. The ABC/*Washington Post* poll kept bouncing around. One week they had us down 15 with Independents.

JONATHAN KARL: The total, by the way, was dead accurate in its last day.

JIM MESSINA: Lots of polls were accurate the last day. So we took their screen, and 20 percent of people who had already voted would have been kicked out of their screen, 20 percent, especially young people. And so that's why, back to your original point, I do think public polling needs to be looked at very carefully about what their screens are, what their demographics are, how much cell phone usage there is, because you are just missing huge chunks of the electorate.

DAVID AXELROD: And I would tell you that from April—and probably earlier—through November, we were never, in our own polling, behind in the race, never. And the race trended almost consistently within a band, whether it was the larger survey or when we went skinny down to the battleground states, of 2 to 4 points, a lead of 2 to 4. Maybe we got down to 1 at one point. After our convention and the 47 percent debacle, we went to 6 or 7 percent but then, after the first debate, it came back to the 3 or 4. There was this illusion of volatility that was created by the public polls and perhaps by some artful spinning on the other side, but we knew the reality was that this race was fundamentally stable throughout. And so, again, we are talking about the two universes: the real world and the world in which all of us live.

••• LESSONS LEARNED •••

LOIS ROMANO: Just a final question because we are going to wrap it up here. In this period between the primaries and up through the convention, is there anything you would have done differently? Are there any miscalculations you made? It's hard to argue with success, I know, but in advising someone who comes behind you in 2016, what would you say?

JIM MESSINA: I think one mistake we made—I think we made it for the right reasons—but we waited too long to jump into the super PAC world. And when we did it, it looked like a complete flip-flop. It was hard. Priorities was out there a long time trying to raise money without us, and that was hard for them. And I think we underestimated how much the other side was going to raise. When we were building this thing in February and March of '11, I don't think we thought half-a-billion dollars of super PAC ads.

LOIS ROMANO: Anything else? All right, well thank you guys. [*applause*]

4

SUPER PACs

GWEN IFILL: Hi everybody. I'm Gwen Ifill with PBS, and along with Rick Berke with the *New York Times*, we're going to talk about money today. We will have kind of a freewheeling, wide-ranging discussion about the $6 billion campaign and why it happened, how it happened, how it came to be, and what effect it had. I want to start by relaying a conversation I had with a voter yesterday in Dallas, Texas, who raised his hand and said, "So after all this money was spent, can you tell me whether it made a difference in who won and who lost?" And I realized I honestly didn't have an answer, but that you guys might. So I want to start by going down the line and asking your thought about that. When you look at the numbers, when you look at the outcomes, and you look at the money that you raised and the records that you broke, what difference did it make? After all the worry about *Citizens United* and all the concerns about outside spending and individual spending, did it make a big difference? Nick Ryan, I'll start with you.

••• IMPACT OF THE HUNDREDS OF
MILLIONS OF DOLLARS SPENT •••

NICK RYAN: I think it had a big effect in the Republican primary. I think that if you look at the work that Restore Our Future did, they were incredibly effective at assisting Governor Romney get through the primary. And without the super PAC that I ran for Senator Santorum, I don't think he would have been able to have the success or the funds necessary to be competitive. As you went through the process and you headed into a general election against an incumbent president that's

Gwen Ifill and Rick Berke moderate a discussion on the role of super PACs in the 2012 presidential race.

well liked and well defined already, it's more challenging to be effective in that big of a race. The smaller the race is, you are able to affect the outcome much more.

GWEN IFILL: I should also add, as we go down the line here and as we continue this conversation, Rick or I are going to encourage you to have conversations with each other if you hear a description of events which you may disagree with or which you saw differently. Bill?

BILL BURTON: Why would you say that—

GWEN IFILL: I don't know why, I just came to you. [*laughter*]

BILL BURTON: I think Nick is right. In the primary the super PACs made a huge difference. I don't think that Mitt Romney would have been the nominee if it weren't for Restore Our Future. In the general election I feel like the work that we did defining Romney's business experience was something that stayed with voters all the way to Election Day, and some of the other projects we engaged in, like with Hispanic voters, I think they were able to help undercut what was already a growing problem for Mitt Romney. But if you look at the broad picture, at the hundreds and hundreds of millions of dollars, I understand that voter's confusion about whether or not it made a bit difference because here you look at the final outcome, and it's a 50-50 country basically. But that's like saying, "If you were in a war where two countries were firing missiles at each other, did the missiles make any difference?" And if one of those countries isn't firing missiles, you can see what that difference is a lot more than you can if both countries are firing the missiles. So I think that they do make a big difference, and I think that in 2016 you will see a proliferation of outside groups far beyond what you saw this time around.

STEVEN LAW: I find myself in the uncomfortable position of agreeing with everything that Bill Burton said. [*laughter*]

GWEN IFILL: Don't make that a habit.

STEVEN LAW: Right. I try not to. But—to maybe add a little more detail to the picture with respect to American Crossroads and Crossroads GPS—we looked at the election year, from our perspective, the critical time period was going to be the period between the end of the Republican primaries and the conventions, during which time we assumed what ended up happening, which was that the Obama campaign would frontload their spending, would try to make Mitt Romney an absolutely impossible alternative choice for voters, and would try to put it away as much as they possibly could before the conventions. And we ended up frontloading a lot of our spending as well during that particular time period, which we dubbed the interregnum, between April and August. In fact, we were not disappointed that Obama outspent Romney by about a hundred million dollars during that time period, and outside groups—between us, Restore Our Future, and Americans for Prosperity—ended up making up that deficit very significantly. As a result, two things happened from our perspective. One is that the ballot test from the end of the primaries up until close to the conventions was essentially frozen in place. But more significantly, from our purposes, when we looked at the election from the very beginning, our view was that the critical metric for us to drive was whether voters believed that President Obama's economic policies were helping the country, helping the economy or hurting. And we found, in all of our regression analyses, that if we pushed people into the box of saying that, on balance, his policies were hurting the economy, they could become a voter who would switch from having voted for Obama in 2008 to voting for Romney in '12. And during the course of that period, those numbers did in fact change from the plurality saying, he was making the economy better too, on the eve of the conventions, saying that Obama's policies made the economy worse. So from our perspective, at sort of critical points, outside spending both in the primary season and at other points had a material effect on the progress of the races.

RICK BERKE: A quick follow-up. When you say you agree with Bill Burton, do you agree that had it not been for Restore Our Future, Romney wouldn't be the nominee?

STEVEN LAW: Well I didn't pay as close attention to the primaries, that was the job of the person on my right, but it did seem to me that most of the impactful advertising, particularly advertising against potential competitors to Romney, was done by Restore Our Future.

RICK BERKE: So you would agree they led to Romney's getting the nomination?

STEVEN LAW: I think they were a critical factor, I don't know if they were the ultimate one.

RICK BERKE: And Carl or Charlie, would you say that's the case?

CARL FORTI: Absolutely. I mean, look, I think that super PACs impacted the debates both in the primary and in the general elections. When you look at the fact that between April 1st and Labor Day, Obama outspent Romney by over $100 million, we would not be talking about this race the way we are right now. It wouldn't have existed like it did in September and October if that was allowed to happen unchecked and so, from that standpoint, we did have an impact. Steven's point that in all of our polling and in all of our focus groups, we determined that we had to convince people, or bring them over, to make the decision that Obama's policies were hurting the country and, by the time we got to the convention, for the first time, a plurality in our polling thought that and that's where I think our impact was.

RICK BERKE: So were it not for your impact, who would be the nominee? Who would have been?

CARL FORTI: I don't know that we know.

RICK BERKE: Who do you think?

CARL FORTI: Well I mean Rick Santorum was the last man standing but had super PACs not been involved the whole way along, Rick might have won it out of the gate.

CHARLIE SPIES: I agree with basically everything that's been said. I think it was certainly a key factor in the primary. It's trite but obviously the candidate is the most important factor and a super PAC can't make up for deficiencies of a campaign, but I think we were a key ally in that effort. Two things. One is, when we started by talking about these massive amounts of money being spent, I think one thing we learned in this cycle is the timing of money is just as important as the amounts of money.

GWEN IFILL: Give us a specific example where the timing made a difference.

CHARLIE SPIES: I was at the Republican Governors Association meeting two weeks ago and one of the governors said to me, if your super PAC had just spent a few million over the summer doing voter registration and voter ID work, and not spent it at the end, in the closing week, on TV ads, you would have won my state. And I just sort of smiled and nodded. What are you going to say? But we didn't have the extra money over the summer. Money ended up getting backloaded and spent in the closing six weeks and in the closing month because that's when the money came in and that's when people were most enthused. You heard on the previous panel the Obama strategists talking about frontloading their spending. That's a luxury that an incumbent campaign has. It's not something that, at least as a super PAC that was candidate-specific, like Restore Our Future was, that we had the ability to do.

The other thing I hope we do talk about, I know we've got plenty of time, is that there's a lot of journalists here who wrote a lot of articles about how awful super PACs were going to be and how they were going to distort democracy and how this was going to lead to Watergate style corruption. I think one thing that's notable is, over the last couple of years, in my opinion, you really haven't seen—I mean the usual self-reform groups that make money off claiming there's problems put out press releases—scandals involving super PACs. If there were campaign finance scandals, that's probably maybe foreign money to the Obama campaign and that's the campaign itself, not the super PACs.

GWEN IFILL: We'll get back to this. [*laughter*] I promise you but, first, Brian?

BRIAN BAKER: Well I would agree with all the points made and I would say, for us, we were what I call a boutique super PAC in that we focused on issues and we were not only in the presidential race but also in senatorial races. I think in some of the primaries super PACs played a big role there. I think the other thing that's interesting about super PACs, to pick up where Charlie left off, in terms of the reporting, is a lot of folks focused on the negative but, in fact, at least on our side, our super PAC ran all positive advertising featuring people who voted for President Obama in 2008 who had decided they didn't like his performance in office and switched to support Governor Romney. And I think some of the more memorable ads from Restore Our Future were the positive ads, like the family of the young girl that Governor Romney helped save when he was at Bain Capital. So I feel like the media didn't focus enough on the fact that a lot of the super PACs were really actually bringing positive information flow about candidates out there and I think that's an important role for super PACs as well.

GWEN IFILL: But did it work? Back to the original question.

BRIAN BAKER: Certainly, if you judge it by whether or not it worked in terms of Governor Romney lost, so you could say no but, on the other hand, given all of the things that were said about him, in terms of him causing cancer and all these terrible things that Bill's super PAC was saying about the governor, I feel like the super PACs on our side did a good job of humanizing Governor Romney and really pointing out the positive aspects of his record. So it probably brought it more to parity and gave the campaign an opportunity to get their message out.

RICK BERKE: Now, you guys said that it was largely what you all did that helped deliver the nomination to Romney. Did he not hold up his end of the bargain in the general? I mean it's pretty well known that there was some distress among your ranks that some of his ad strategies were inefficient, focusing on things that were done in the '80s, like *Wheel of Fortune*, *Jeopardy*, instead of the better targeting? How much do you blame the ad people on the campaign and the strategists on the campaign for what happened in the end?

CHARLIE SPIES: I'll take a first crack at that, and I would not say at all that they didn't uphold their end of the bargain. I thought they ran a very good campaign, and it was a very, very close election. And maybe other people said what you are alluding to, but I certainly haven't said that. To the extent that there was a lot of discussion about, could there have been more positive framing of Governor Romney and more to define him, I don't know the answer. And I think the campaign has good answers for why more resources weren't more focused on that. But if experts were to conclude that there should have been more positive definition, I would say that it's very difficult to do from the outside.

RICK BERKE: Let me ask Carl and see, was there anything you would have done differently if you were the Romney campaign? How do you think they handled those closing months in their ad strategy, or do you think it was picture perfect?

CARL FORTI: I don't think we can possibly answer that question. I mean we were each making decisions in our own bubble, and they were doing what they thought was best.

RICK BERKE: But your frustration was no secret.

CARL FORTI: I don't think any of us expressed real frustration. The only thing that made it difficult for us to do our job was, as somebody pointed out on the Obama panel before, they placed back in July for the

Steven Law listens on as Carl Forti discusses Restore Our Future's decision-making processes.

whole fall and Romney was placing week to week. That's obviously their choice. There's nothing wrong with that, other than the fact that there were no signals there then for us, the super PACs, to know what was most important or where to go. We kind of had to make our own decisions.

STEVEN LAW: I think that it also just reflects a larger issue which became a strategic constraint on the campaign that had nothing to do with tactical decision making. They were at a significant financial disadvantage vis-a-vis the Obama campaign throughout, not only in the summer but through the fall. In the end, as it was said, that they were outspent by about $154 million on TV. That's $30 million in Ohio alone. That's the equivalent of six weeks of unanswered television, which, from our perspective, probably put constraints on their ability to do triage messaging. But, from our perspective, in some ways it made it very clear to us that our role was to continue to keep the pressure and the attention on Obama's policies and the impact of those policies as a means of at least keeping voters locked in place for as long as possible.

GWEN IFILL: Did you feel at any point that you were hamstrung by a campaign strategy that was not keeping what you saw as a useful political strategy?

STEVEN LAW: No. I mean we knew what we needed to do. In fact, it was interesting. I was listening to Matt Rhoades last night talk about the policy. It was sort of the way that they viewed the campaign, and it was the first time I've ever heard him articulate that because obviously we didn't talk during the campaign. But it was precisely the same frame of reference that we used. So from the vantage point of continuing to focus on the economy and jobs, it was entirely in keeping with the direction that we felt we needed to head.

••• THE CANCER AD •••

GWEN IFILL: The reason I asked you that question—I'm not picking on you—is because I'm coming back to Mr. Burton. David Axelrod said earlier today that he was not crazy about that "Mitt Romney gave my wife cancer" ad. That was your ad. Was that something where you were out of step with the campaign?

BILL BURTON: I think you could rightfully say that they wouldn't have run the ad that we put together, but I think there's a bunch of different pieces of this. First, I think you guys are being much kinder to the Romney campaign than maybe I would be if I were in your shoes because, given the fact that there was message confusion, no clear direction from Boston, I think for reporters, for voters, for anybody, on where they were taking the message of the campaign, it must have been really difficult for you guys to figure out where exactly to go. And I think Crossroads and Restore focused a lot on jobs and debt, but if you look at what AFP was doing with Solyndra[1] and all these other attacks, and you've got the Romney campaign doing welfare reform and the war on religion. At any given moment, if you're a voter, you probably don't have a very clear sense. So if you are a super PAC supporting the campaign, you probably also don't have a very clear sense of what can be most helpful. Your point on the spending is a much bigger deficit than I think people might initially realize. To not know where the campaign thinks are the most important targets makes it impossible for a super PAC to target your own funds. And you had so much money but, not knowing exactly where the campaign was going to put it, puts you at an even bigger disadvantage as a super PAC because you are spending so much more money, especially as you get closer to the election. Not being able to plan that out in advance is very difficult. The last thing that I would say on this is that I don't think enough attention has been given to the fact that Mitt Romney—who is a spectacularly wealthy man—at a point where he was being attacked relentlessly, didn't put any of his own money into the campaign. I don't know at what point he decided that he wasn't going to spend a dime to help his own effort, no matter how bad things got, particularly in May and June when we were doing the Bain attacks and the campaign was doing their series of attacks. The fact that nobody was out there responding to that—and they could have—is probably a mistake that led to the loss.

GWEN IFILL: I don't want to get away from the cancer ad. Do you regret doing that?

BILL BURTON: No, I don't. Because if you look at what happened with that spot, for starters, we didn't say that Mitt Romney caused someone to get cancer, and I think you have to presuppose that voters are idiots to think that they would take that from that ad. I don't think anybody

---

1. In January 2012 Americans for Prosperity began running ads criticizing President Obama's handling of Solyndra, the solar-energy firm that went bankrupt after receiving grants from the government. The ads criticized Obama for supporting the company and pointed out that the company's major investors were campaign supporters of Mr. Obama.

who watched it thought that. I think that what people saw was that there were real-life consequences to what happens when somebody comes to town, shuts down a factory, and people lose their jobs and promised health care benefits. And in Joe Soptic's case, and I talked to him about this, he doesn't blame Mitt Romney for his wife getting cancer. What he blamed him for was the fact that, at a point of terror in any person's life, when a family member gets diagnosed with a terminal illness, he didn't have health insurance that was promised to him. And regardless of any other facts that came out, that was true. If you look at what happened politically during that entire period, there was probably a week where we were just getting pounded by a lot of the folks in this room, by folks all over Washington. But the ultimate result of that was we spent a week talking about Mitt Romney's business experience, after which there's probably not a lot of people who walked away from it thinking, "Oh, that was a positive thing, that Mitt Romney had that business experience." And two, none of that accrued to the president. Even though the campaign had to answer questions about it, and the president at one point answered a question about it, it wasn't like voters thought, "Oh, the president is getting too nasty and negative here." It was a message we were carrying and that we took the heat on.

RICK BERKE: Charlie?

CHARLIE SPIES: Just two quick points. The *Washington Post* called that the most dishonest campaign ad of the year. I would have been mortified if we were at the RNC in 2004 and President Bush had to be up on a podium answering for ads, and that's what happened in this case. You had not only the campaign, but you actually had the president himself repudiating the ad. That does not mean, I suppose, that it wasn't effective. So his argument on effectiveness could be correct. But, at a minimum, it shows that there's a real division between super PACs because you can't coordinate with the campaign. It clearly was not part of the Obama campaign strategy when they were immediately repudiating it.

RICK BERKE: Let me ask you, Bill, just to be clear, as you go on in your political career, would you again recommend and endorse, or condone, an ad like that? Did you learn anything? Do you have any regrets or do you feel totally comfortable with that decision? [*laughter*]

BILL BURTON: I feel like I know where you stand on the issue. [*laughter*] Look, I think that anybody can be a genius in retrospect. I think that what we did had a clear impact on the race.

RICK BERKE: So no lessons learned?

BILL BURTON: I think you learn a lesson in everything you do, things that are wildly successful and things that aren't.

RICK BERKE: And what's the lesson? You would do it again?

BILL BURTON: I think it's impossible to take some hypothetical—

RICK BERKE: It's not hypothetical.

BILL BURTON: Well actually if you say "would you," I think that by definition, it's hypothetical. [*laughter*] I just think that every situation is different. Every campaign is different. I don't think Democrats will be so lucky as to run against Mitt Romney again, so I think that we'll just have to see.

••• THE BAIN ATTACKS •••

GWEN IFILL: Let me ask everybody else to respond to something else Bill talked about, which is how the Bain attacks went unanswered, for whatever reason, in the primaries. Nick?

NICK RYAN: Well actually in the primaries, I think that both Senator Santorum and Dr. Paul both attacked those attacks, said they were wrong, said it's not the direction that our party should be going. Then eventually you end up with Speaker Gingrich in the situation too where he's conflicted and having to almost walk back the attacks that his own super PAC is making as well. I think the attacks, while they were very similar, the audience that they were done to target in the general is a different audience, and attacking on something like Bain in a Republican primary didn't work. And I'm glad it didn't work.

GWEN IFILL: It didn't cause long-standing harm to your nominee?

NICK RYAN: I wouldn't say that because I think it's already there, and I think that there were some Bain attacks in 2008. And so I think what's there is there. I think the challenge is there possibly could have been a more compelling case portrayed or story given about the success that Governor Romney has had and the people that he has helped and the many jobs that have been created, and also explain some of those situations that ended badly and explain why they did, because that's life. It's not as if everything that he's ever done has turned out a winner, for him personally or for the companies that he may have invested in. I think some stories like that about not just opportunity gained but also opportunity lost would have painted a little bit different picture of Bain and of Mitt Romney.

BILL BURTON: The only thing I disagree with here is the notion that it didn't work in the primaries because Newt Gingrich, when he did it or his super PAC did it, it was the South Carolina primary which Newt Gingrich won. And then, because of pressure, he backed away from these attacks, which it was him handling the way that they did that, no doubt, but they backed away. Charlie and Carl stepped in and spent $16 million in Florida, which was no longer doing it, and that's why the tide turned. It wasn't because the Bain attacks hurt Gingrich. Gingrich won when his super PAC was using them and lost when they weren't.

GWEN IFILL: Carl? Charlie?

CARL FORTI: Look, from the super PAC standpoint, it wasn't our job to defend Mitt Romney. If Mitt Romney felt he needed to answer the Bain attacks, they were totally capable of doing it. They spent $75 million over the course of the summer, and during the time of the Bain attacks, they were still attacking President Obama. We basically get penalized for trying to do positive ads. The FEC makes it very difficult to get footage to do any at all. And so we do what we do best, and that was, over the course of the summer, we had to keep pressure on Obama and if we, the collective we, ever stepped back from doing that, that would allow him an opening that we couldn't give him because we are still working to define him. And that was our mission this summer. And to Bill's earlier point about the messaging, from the super PAC side, being all over the place, we sat down at a table like this and talked every week about what the message was going to be between all of us. And if you look at the summer, American Crossroads was run in June or July, AFP went on or one of the groups in early August, and Restore came on in later August. It was a very coordinated effort to make sure that from basically Memorial Day on, someone was on the air attacking Barack Obama.

••• THE ROLE OF THE DONORS •••

RICK BERKE: Speaking of messaging, could you all give us a sense of the role of the big donors in decision making and strategy: How much they were involved, and how often you would hear from them?

CARL FORTI: I think it's fair to say that we kept our donors informed about what we were doing, but there was really no input from the donors as to the strategy.

CHARLIE SPIES: I can think of one example where a donor said he thought we should be talking about the impact of Obama raising taxes on a specific type of small businesses. It was just a personal cause of his. In over two years, I think that's the only substantive direction that a donor has given.

GWEN IFILL: So you never looked at your Caller ID and saw Sheldon Adelson's name and said, "Oh God, he's on the phone again?"

CHARLIE SPIES: If he did call, I would be thrilled. [*laughter*]

Charlie Spies, Carl Forti, and Bill Burton discuss whether donors played a role in the super PACs' strategies.

RICK BERKE: Steve, would you say the same thing?

STEVEN LAW: Just briefly, actually one of the real challenges going into the cycle from the very beginning, which ended up being an issue where we needed to explain ourselves to donors, was as we looked at all of our focus group and polling data going into the first of the year, we realized that the people we needed to reach were independent swing voters who largely supported Obama in 2008, still liked him, didn't believe he was successfully ideological, didn't believe he was partisan, didn't believe he was a bad guy, were proud of the vote they cast in 2008, and needed some convincing to believe otherwise. And the way that was reflected in our messaging, really all the way throughout the year including into the fall, was largely with fairly gentle nuanced advertising, not aimed at character but aimed largely at his record. The kind of traditional negative campaign that the Obama campaign did and Bill Burton did, with great effect, was not available on our side to be able to effectively accomplish our mission. Just to sort of complete the point, in response to Gwen's question, a number of donors and people in kind of the larger center-right community were eager for more spirited and aggressive efforts, and I think, in the end, they were convinced that the right approach to take was the approach we took.

RICK BERKE: You guys are experts on how to calibrate this, but we always heard that the people who were giving the money, in many cases, were pushing you much more aggressively to be tougher in the advertising. You are saying that's not true; they were hands-off?

STEVEN LAW: No, no.

RICK BERKE: You seem to be saying there was some pressure.

STEVEN LAW: I wouldn't say "pressure," but we felt the need to explain why we were doing what we were doing because people who are activists, people who are on our side, there's a real desire to see something more visceral. But, from our vantage point, looking at the data—and I think, in the end, everybody understood that this was the right approach to take—it was to be more nuanced and more focused on an economic record, rather than personal attacks which our research showed would have significantly backfired or been ineffective.

GWEN IFILL: Brian Baker?

BRIAN BAKER: I would just say two quick things. In terms of donor input, I didn't see it a lot on message, but I did see it on tactics. Like, for instance, I know the donors that I worked with were very interested in seeing Restore Our Future do the Olympics ad that you did, given the governor's successful leadership of the Olympics in Salt Lake, and so I know that that was something that Restore Our Future did and it worked. On our end, another tactic that our super PAC used was something that was called the Mittzine, which was a twelve-page—I actually have a copy of it right here—

GWEN IFILL: It just so happens.

BRIAN BAKER: —insert that went into four-and-a-half million newspapers in five swing states. When it was pitched to us, I thought it was a bit goofy, but when I gave it to our principal donor, he said, "Well that's actually a great idea because the TV airwaves are so saturated." Maybe getting into print and getting into people's hands, letting them do the Mitt crossword, was a good idea. So I think that some donors did get involved in decisions like that.

RICK BERKE: Just one follow up, if I may, on the big donors and that is there are these guys out there—Adelson, the Kochs, Friess—who are very larger-than-life figures who would speak their mind, and there was a perception out there that these guys were sometimes maybe a little out there and that they were representing the Republican party in many ways. Did you all worry at all about the perception that these guys had such an outsized influence in the course of the campaign?

CHARLIE SPIES: For the record, all our Restore Our Future donors were fine people, not outsized at all. [*laughter*] Seriously, I think when you have a super PAC—and this is true whether it's presidential or whether it's House or Senate, whatever it is—but when it is dominated by one person. So—whether it was the super PAC supporting Rick Santorum that Foster Friess at one point was by far the largest donor for or the super PAC supporting Speaker Gingrich that Mr. Adelson was the exponentially largest donor for—at that point, it can get associated with the donor specifically and that becomes more of an issue. Even with Bill Burton's group, you had at one point just a few Hollywood donors and some unions that were the only people that were really giving money to the group. We were blessed to have had a long lead up time of raising money and had, in terms of the super PAC world, having five hundred donors is a broad base. I realize compared to campaigns that's not, but we had a large enough groups of donors that I don't think it was associated with any one person.

RICK BERKE: What, in your view, is the danger of having these guys with big names associated with these super PACs?

CHARLIE SPIES: I think it can become a distraction if they are not on message with what they are saying. Having said that, I think most of the political strategists would still rather have the ads and the media distraction than not.

CARL FORTI: The bottom line is that as much of a distraction Friess or whoever else wanted to be, the average voter had no idea who they were or what they were doing or their involvement. It was Axelrod who made the point earlier that, yes, I mean everyone in this room and activists on each side may know, but, and I'll use my wife as an example, she hates politics. She doesn't watch *Fox News*. She doesn't go to *POLITICO*. She doesn't read the *New York Times*. She would have no clue.

RICK BERKE: Wait, that's impossible. [*laughter*]

GWEN IFILL: I want to ask Bill to weigh in on that too. Finish Carl, but Bill, will you also talk about the fact that a few people may have had outside influence, but only insiders cared. I want to know if that happened on the Democratic side and also whether that means we're going to see a lot more of this. Start with that last piece.

CARL FORTI: I mean, look, given the impact the super PACs had on this race right now and the way the law is written, you're absolutely going to see more of it. Until the law gets changed, we are going to be here.

CHARLIE SPIES: Can I just make a very brief point on that? Carl said "the law," and just remember, this is not the Supreme Court decision; this is not about *Citizens United*. This is about the law being McCain-Feingold that was passed and pushes money away from political parties and pushes money away from candidates and forces the money into the outside groups who have an advantage of being able to take more money. So this is not a *Citizens United* phenomenon. Post McCain-Feingold, in 2004, you saw this with Progress for America, you saw the Swift Vote Veterans, and then you saw it with the George Soros groups after that. Until the McCain-Feingold law is repealed or at least modified, and you're able to get money into political parties and campaigns, you are going to have outside groups having a disproportionate influence.

GWEN IFILL: Were you surprised at all that *Citizens United* didn't have a bigger impact? Because all along people on the left especially feared the impact.

CHARLIE SPIES: I think we all thought it would have a symbolic impact and it certainly got Republican donors to feel like it was okay to give again. Because there had been a concerted effort after the 2004 elections to go after Republican donors and chill them from wanting to participate, and then you had Senator McCain, whose candidacy was based around opposition to money in politics. There wasn't a huge interest in getting involved in that. So I think *Citizens United* did have a symbolic impact, but it was not a legal impact.

BRIAN BAKER: And, Gwen, certainly we all remember the president's State of the Union shortly after *Citizens United* was handed down. And he, with the Supreme Court sitting there in the well of the House said, "We're going to have corporations buying elections, and we are going to have foreign corporations and all this foreign money." That largely didn't happen. Corporate donors were very, very small to super PACs.

GWEN IFILL: Let Bill respond before we lose that.

BILL BURTON: I think the influence question is a little misplaced in the sense that the important issue isn't whether or not a donor has a big influence on the super PAC. It's whether they have influence on the candidate. Because if you want to be Joe Ricketts and spend $10 million to talk about Jeremiah Wright, you can certainly do that, and that's not going to have the influence that would be worrisome to an American citizen who is worried about a rich person having influence on a process. Talking about Sheldon Adelson, he got a lot of time with Mitt Romney. He went with him to Israel. The first meeting that Paul Ryan did after he was picked was with Sheldon Adelson in Vegas. I think that that's the sort of thing that voters are concerned about. I mean your guys' donors must be different than ours because everybody had an idea about an ad. Maybe it's because we have such a big part of the creative community in Hollywood and New York, but no, no, we've got plenty of good ones. [*laughter*]

GWEN IFILL: Tell us. I want to hear about the crazy one.

BILL BURTON: Not crazy.

GWEN IFILL: Oh, of course not.

BRIAN BAKER: Rick will put it on the front page of the *New York Times*, if there's a real crazy one on Bill's side.

RICK BERKE: Carl's wife won't read it. [*laughter*]

BILL BURTON: Some people would want, really want us to focus on, like, wind energy or something like that. Everybody had a cause that they wanted to use. People wanted to do judges, and we just didn't have the money to do everything.

GWEN IFILL: Judges? That would get a lot of votes.

BILL BURTON: People were very motivated by it this year.

••• THE RETURN OF JEREMIAH WRIGHT? •••

RICK BERKE: Let me jump on something that Bill brought up and that's the Ricketts' ad campaign, and I'll ask you, Brian, obviously. There's the big campaign that was laid out in the papers about the effort to link Obama with Reverend Wright.[2] Can you tell us a little about that and why that, as far as our sources showed and our reporting showed, was all set to go and because of the adverse publicity was pulled?

BRIAN BAKER: I've been very clear and consistent from the very beginning that your reporting was just dead wrong. It was a proposal that was submitted to us based on an ad that was made for, and rejected by, John McCain. I remember having lunch, what, a week before I got that proposal with Carl and talking about the types of things that would work to convince Independent and swing voters why President Obama should not be reelected, and Jeremiah Wright is nowhere on that list. So I think one of the things that you'll see with super PACs is they get all kinds of ideas, all kinds of proposals. Bill just talked about them. This was merely a proposal; it was not acted on. Joe Ricketts wasn't even at the meeting where it was presented. I was, and I can tell you it was never going to be green-lighted. No ad was ever made. No dollar was

---

2.   Rev. Jeremiah Wright was Obama's former spiritual adviser whose race-related sermons made him a controversial figure in the 2008 campaign.

ever invested. So I felt like it was fairly overblown. In fact, Harvard must feel it was overblown because they didn't even put it in their timeline for this conference.

RICK BERKE: Why wasn't it going to happen, in your view? It looked like a pretty elaborate proposal. I mean it didn't look like some fly-by-night idea on a napkin.

BRIAN BAKER: Well I'm sure Fred Davis[3] would take a compliment at that. Elaborate is certainly one word for it. There's a lot of reasons why I think the Ricketts wouldn't have done it. I can tell you one, in my mind, is I don't think it would have been effective. I remember when he presented it to me. I said, "Well where's the polling data showing this will work?" "Oh, we didn't poll this." He put together some scripts based on an ad that he had made for McCain, so I think that's one reason it wouldn't have been effective. I also think it would have been divisive and it might have fired up folks for President Obama, so it might have had really an adverse impact. Not only might it not have helped Governor Romney, it really might have hurt Governor Romney. So those are really two reasons.

RICK BERKE: But this is, I think, a good example of what you all are talking about you have to deal with, or what I think you have to deal with: with some of the big donors wanting it to feel more visceral than you think is wise.

CHARLIE SPIES: Just remember, this was not a donor. This was actually a consultant that was pitching the proposal.

RICK BERKE: Right, right. That's true.

GWEN IFILL: So none of you ever considered it this year because, after 2008, there was some concern that there were some bodies left on the field and that Jeremiah Wright was one of them. There were a lot of folks that thought there could have been more made of that. It was never considered this year to bring it back up again?

CARL FORTI: Considered? Sure.

GWEN IFILL: Sure, but?

---

3. Fred Davis oversaw the proposal. He was a media consultant on the McCain campaign and had argued in favor of a Wright ad in 2008.

CARL FORTI: None of the research, the polling, had anything to indicate that that would work. As Steven pointed out earlier, we learned pretty early on that folks were going after those undecided voters. Ninety percent of them voted for Obama the last time. They liked him. They just didn't like what he was doing to the country. So anything that was attacking his character or personality was already decided in their mind. Obama had them. It was a question of, can we prove he was not doing the job and shouldn't be given another four years? And that has nothing to do with Jeremiah Wright.

••• THE ROLE OF CORPORATE MONEY •••

GWEN IFILL: We talked about individual donors. I want to talk about corporate donors because some of them we can track and we know that there were ways in which they could be convinced that it was okay to give again, as someone described it, but there was also a lot of ways we couldn't track, that weren't transparent—I think some groups call it shadow money—and I wonder the degree to which some affected decision making and drove outcomes. That is, decision making within the campaign and within the strategy that you had in mind.

STEVEN LAW: Well I would just say from our perspective that the donors who ended up supporting Crossroads did so because they believed in the team and the structure and the approach to the task. We didn't get donors saying, "You need to do this or that or talk about this issue or that issue," in part because we were very transparent about the way that we went about our decision making and why we believed that the strategies and the messages for the issues that we were using would be most effective. We just didn't encounter much of that sort of thing of saying, "Here's the issue that you ought to do that will change things."

GWEN IFILL: Was corporate money more or less important this year?

STEVEN LAW: Well for us, compared to 2010, certainly not more important.

GWEN IFILL: What do you mean?

STEVEN LAW: I mean just in terms of an absolute percentage of our receipts, it wasn't any more important in 2012 than 2010.

GWEN IFILL: Anybody else?

••• THE ROLE OF UNION MONEY •••

CHARLIE SPIES: When you say "corporate money," are you including union money?

GWEN IFILL: We can, if you like, and I'll ask Bill that question.

CHARLIE SPIES: Okay, because I think that's an important part of the discussion—the amount of union money that's being spent. I know the unions were some of Bill's largest donors.

GWEN IFILL: How big were the unions for you?

BILL BURTON: They were big. They were very important. We had more than a half-dozen unions who gave us upwards of a million dollars or more. SEIU was a critical help in us getting started and getting going and we partnered with them on what I think was one of the most important projects that we undertook. It didn't get as much press coverage, but I think it had, arguably, as big an impact on the race as anything else that we did, which was talking to voters in our Spanish language ads in Nevada, Colorado, and Florida. Even though that didn't get a lot of coverage, we watched the numbers for Romney, which were already bad, get much, much worse. And the fact that there was no positive message coming in for Romney until the end in small dribs and drabs made it impossible for recovery. Union support was no doubt important to our existence.

STEVEN LAW: To me one of the interesting tectonic shifts on the other side was the way in which organized labor, which has always been a major outside presence—when people talk about outside money, we say, "Well it's a big player that's been active with this since FDR"—it appeared to me, at least, that organized labor made a decision, either of expedience or strategy, to move from basically owning the ground game and delivering the ground game for the Democratic Party to being the source of funding for both Bill and the other Democrat super PACs. And, at least as far as I can tell, the Obama campaign itself owned the ground game, which is a change, it seems to me. In the past, organized labor delivered boots on the ground, voter turnout, and this time, they ended up being much more the bank account. I'm not saying anything disparaging about it. It just seemed to be a real shift in organized labor. It would have been good to have someone from organized labor as part of this because I think they are one of the most critical outside platforms for political spending on the Democratic side, and it seemed to be a shift.

GWEN IFILL: Was it, Bill?

BILL BURTON: Well I can't speak to what they were doing on the ground, but I do know that, as a percentage, by the raw numbers that they were able to invest in us and in other Democratic groups, it was much smaller than it has been in the past actually. While they were a very important part of what we did, there's just not as big a political bank account in some of these unions as their once was. And so the way they came in was obviously important, and we partnered on some pretty good projects, but the numbers aren't as big as they were before.

••• PRESIDENT OBAMA'S IMPACT ON FUNDRAISING •••

RICK BERKE: Could you address the president's resistance to super PACs originally and the impact that had on your fundraising ability and so forth?

BILL BURTON: Sure. It had a significant impact because Democrats generally are not for outside groups and this sort of thing being in existence. And we had to spend a good year, without the blessing of the campaign or the White House or anyone associated with it, raising money, trying to educate voters about what mean Carl Forti was going to do to the president come fall of 2012. And so it was at every single meeting we went to, one of the first things that people said was, "Well, isn't the president against these groups?" I was like, "Well, yes, obviously, but these are the rules of the game and," to paraphrase Donald Rumsfeld, "you go to the election with the rules that you have, not the rules that you wish you had."

RICK BERKE: I've heard that you were, on many occasions, nervous that the president would actually come out and publicly attack super PACs. Talk about that a little bit.

BILL BURTON: Well sure. I think that when you are at a super PAC, I can't speak for these guys, you don't really want for your principal to be against what you are doing. It makes for some tougher sledding than you might otherwise have. The irony here is that in 2008, when I was the press secretary for the Obama campaign, I was the person who had made all the statements which their colleague Collegio[4] dug up and put out the second that we announced our group. I was the person saying, "Do not set up outside groups on behalf of then-Senator Obama. If you want to help the campaign, do it through the campaign." But since, the rules had been changed. And it was a much different environment than it was in 2008. And if the president was going to remain competitive, it was going to be important to have some outside presence. Folks forget that in October of last year, the right track number was at 15 and unemployment peaked near 11 percent. Folks generally thought that President Obama was going to go the way of a lot of one-term presidents, and it didn't turn out that way. But we thought that, in order to avoid catastrophe, we needed to set up this group.

RICK BERKE: And final point on this line of questioning: You're a young-looking guy, never done this before. You are not a key kind of figure; you're not a Karl Rove kind of figure. How much did that hurt? [*laughter*]

BILL BURTON: There's a lot of ways to go with this. [*laughter*]

RICK BERKE: What was Harold Ickes's advice to you in how to do this job?

BILL BURTON: Well Harold Ickes was a huge help to us because he was the president of the board of our super PAC, and he helped to raise some money. And really, you're right: not having big pillars of the party go out and try to put this thing together was a challenge, but, after a lot of elbow grease and some smart folks with priorities figuring out who to target and when to go talk to people and how to do it, we were able to piece it together.

GWEN IFILL: Does that mean that all those people who were skeptical about it, who were slow to open their checkbooks, are now calling you on a daily basis, clapping you on the back and saying, "So what do we do next time"?

---

4.   Jonathan Collegio was a spokesman for American Crossroads.

BILL BURTON: There are a lot of folks who want to know what's next. There's no doubt that a lot of the people who invested a lot of money were happy with how it turned out and happy with the efficiency with which we spent their money and the effectiveness. And so, yes, there are people who do want to keep this effort going as long as these rules are in place. They want to make sure that, on the Democratic side, there's an apparatus to deal with what we know is going to be on the Republican side. I mean look at all these guys here, and it's just me. [*laughter*]

••• KARL ROVE'S ROLE •••

RICK BERKE: Can you explain Karl Rove's role?

STEVEN LAW: Sure. First of all, it's a tremendously important part of both its genesis and its success. Most people know this, but he and Ed Gillespie came up with the idea in about the summer of 2009. And I started to talk to them in October, and we really got it rolling in January of 2010. Karl and Ed and a few of us recognized that it was really important to not simply have an organization exist for a particular cycle for tactical use but to actually start to build enduring institutional strength on the right, the way that we saw the unions providing that for the Democrats and, at the time, MoveOn.org, which ended up not continuing. So first of all, that vision of something that was more than just a one-time, one-trick pony, but to really endure and to build. Then there were certain other parts of it that I think Karl really gets credit for. The first is encouraging us to reach out to other center-right groups and just start to try to collaborate, where we were legally permitted to do so, to share information and encourage people to pull the oars in the same direction, to the extent that we could. That was very much an idea that not only did he come up with but he initiated. The first meeting was at his house in Weaver Terrace, which is why it got to be known as the Weaver Terrace Group, long after it moved on from there. On the fundraising side, both he and Ed, and then later on Haley Barbour, were all tremendously instrumental in harvesting their Rolodexes and relationships. And then, lastly, Karl's a guy who has got tremendously good ideas and, again, not so much on the tactical side but much more kind of broad, strategic moments. And he was a tremendously useful and valuable source of ideas along the way.

RICK BERKE: Did you share his sense, in the closing days, that Romney would win?

STEVEN LAW: I did not. He and I joked that I'm from the pessimistic strain of Norwegians, and he's from the more optimistic one, so I think he's got a little Swedish blood in him, which is probably a slander from his perspective. [*laughter*] But, no, I didn't. And the reason that I didn't was that our polling, unfortunately, was fairly consistently accurate. [*laughter*] What it showed was, on the plus side, we were competitive in a great number of these battleground states and even some of the fringe states which grabbed attention near the end, but we just could never get over the lip in Virginia, Florida, even in North Carolina until the very end. And to me, as I looked at polling and as I looked at the direction of the polling, it just seemed to me that the momentum and the energy was starting to go out, or at least flatten out, on our side, and it would make it very hard.

RICK BERKE: And how would you and Carl explain his performance on Fox that Tuesday night?[5] Is he now discredited in the Republican Party? Is it going to be harder for him to raise money in the future?

STEVEN LAW: Absolutely not. No.

RICK BERKE: I mean he's been mocked worldwide.

STEVEN LAW: Well we all get our turn in the barrel and myself, as well, at different times. Not at all. I mean we've actually spent a lot of time talking to our supporters, and he has himself. First of all, I think there's a tremendous amount of regard for the fact that at least his role in this was entirely on a volunteer basis, and he gave a gigantic amount of his time to a cause that he just believed in.

RICK BERKE: Carl, how would you explain that performance on election night?

CARL FORTI: I defer to what Steven said.

GWEN IFILL: You spent a year relying heavily on, as you said, the kind of strategic vision of Karl Rove. And at the end, as you admit, he was

---

5.   On election night, Karl Rove appeared on *Fox News*, insisting that his own network was wrong in calling Ohio for President Obama.

wrong, and you were probably right. At what point during the campaign could he have also been wrong in his strategic guidance?

STEVEN LAW: Well I think you characterized something I said that I didn't say. I think the strength of Crossroads to our donors, and to really all of us, is that it isn't any one person. I mean Karl was a tremendously important factor, really in some ways the indispensable man, but he would be the first to say it doesn't just rest on his shoulders. I mean Carl Forti is probably the most experienced independent expenditure operative on the Republican side. Ed Gillespie for a long time was involved. Haley Barbour is certainly a somewhat experienced player. It was the team effort that guided our decisions, including a lot of pretty energetic discussions, arguments and disagreements about the way forward. In addition to that, I think there's a tremendous amount of value to that group discussion, and that's what ended up yielding the results and the strategy that we had. And he was a significant part of that but not the only part.

BILL BURTON: He also helped us raise money, just in fairness to Karl. He was bipartisan, and his support helped both sides. [*laughter*]

STEVEN LAW: Yeah, but you were only raising ten dollars a pop, and it really hurt his feelings. So I want you to know that.

BILL BURTON: I probably e-mailed out every one of his columns to our donors, our high-dollar list, to point out what they were saying on the Republican side and how confident Rove was. When he would go on TV bursting with confidence about Romney winning, that little clip went around every single time. Karl Rove is an enduring figure for both sides.

GWEN IFILL: It doesn't sound, Carl, like you spent a lot of time losing sleep over that though.

CARL FORTI: Not at all.

GWEN IFILL: But, and I want to get back to the earlier question, did you worry at any point as you relied on his expertise, his overall vision, that maybe you might be off at a wrong path or you might be over or underestimating the nominee's strength based on the guidance you were getting?

CARL FORTI: Most of the strategic decisions we were making were based on the research we were doing. Karl Rove didn't form an opinion and then we went and implemented it. It was the research and what we learned that dictated strategy from the beginning.

GWEN IFILL: So you, like Steve, agree that you weren't winning at the end?

CARL FORTI: I was allowing myself to become cautiously optimistic, but I mean looking back at our numbers in hindsight, the numbers we had a week out were pretty close to what actually happened.

STEVEN LAW: Look, there were a lot of people who formed that view. I mean Michael Barone, who is widely respected as one of the deans of politics by all sides, was also wrong. There were a lot of people, and one of the things that was a key factor for him and for others—and even for us when we allowed ourselves, as Carl said, to be cautiously optimistic—was the fact that Romney started picking up significant numbers of Independents. In the battleground states he started to build a lead with Independents, and he started to narrow the gender gap. And from our analysis of it, all else being equal, that gave us a sense that it might potentially be there for us to win. So there were a lot of people with a lot of different views about what might end up happening. As I said, I think my view was slightly colored by temperament, but there were a lot of people who thought that we were going to end up winning. There were a lot of people who were shocked on Election Day.

••• THE RELATIONSHIP BETWEEN THE CAMPAIGN AND THE SUPER PAC •••

RICK BERKE: Let me ask you, Charlie, if you could talk a little about the awkward dance—the legal dance, political dance—of your working to raise money and help Romney but not being part of the campaign and not crossing the line legally or politically? One example is the scene where Romney had that fundraising event in Utah, and you were in the lobby trying to get donors there, but it was his event. How do you navigate that, and can you talk a little about that?

GWEN IFILL: And were you actually grabbing the donors by their necks?

CHARLIE SPIES: If it worked. [*laughter*]

STEVEN LAW: He was tripping them actually. [*laughter*]

CHARLIE SPIES: That's probably a great example of the tension between what legally you can do and what the perception can be in the press. And so, legally, there would be no problem with my going to Romney fundraising events. You are allowed to go to any sort of public event as long as you are not getting secret strategy information. If he is doing a donor event with a hundred people, five hundred people, a thousand people, nothing he says in that is presumed to be strategic information that would constitute coordination, as you know, because they are all your sources, and anything he says probably ends up in the *New York Times*. So legally you would be okay doing that. Practically, in my personal situation, for two years I didn't go to Romney events. It was just that I wanted to be able to, when somebody filed an FEC complaint, sign the affidavit saying, "I didn't go to Romney for President events." The example you gave of a Romney donor retreat—where I think someplace in the hotel they were holding the retreat and there were lots of donors around, and I was sitting in the lobby with one of our fundraisers and saying "Hi" to folks and setting up meetings for anybody who was interested—that just seems sort of like Fundraising 101. You go where the money is, and it made perfect sense to be in the lobby.

••• IMPACT OF THE 47 PERCENT VIDEO •••

GWEN IFILL: I've been curious: you talk about the things that would leak out anyhow because he was saying this in a public event. A lot of these were not public events, and that's why the impact of the leaked 47 percent tape was so outsized because we heard Governor Romney saying things that we never heard him saying. You've all admitted that that was not helpful. The Democrats had said it was very helpful. So I'm curious whether that affected or depressed, in any way, fundraising from people who would normally write big bucks to go to events like that and now were a little but put off by it.

CHARLIE SPIES: Not for us.

GWEN IFILL: Nobody said, "Ah, you guys can't control these things. I don't want to know about it. I don't want to go."

CHARLIE SPIES: I think that was a campaign event. It certainly wasn't a Restore Our Future event.

GWEN IFILL: Yeah, yeah. I understand. But people don't make the distinction in their minds when they are asked to write checks. Did anybody get any kind of blowback from that?

BILL BURTON: I think about when it came out though, it was so far towards the end of the campaign. When an event like that happened, it was clearly a bad event for Mitt Romney. I'm sure that the panic probably drove your fundraising up, if anything.

BRIAN BAKER: Yeah and, not only that, then after that was the first debate, which we are all conferring really drove up fundraising for all of us, so that tape didn't have any impact, in terms of fundraising.

••• THE ROLE OF THE FEC •••

RICK BERKE: Let me ask—and I'm looking for some consensus among the six of you—I have a hunch, I don't know the answer, but I might be wrong: Did any of you ever worry about the FEC at all during the last two years? No? Charlie?

CARL FORTI: No.

CHARLIE SPIES: Sure. I'm a lawyer, and it's my job to do so.

RICK BERKE: But seriously?

CHARLIE SPIES: Of course. There's, right now on the commission, a three-vote block who are committed to enforcing that law as it's written. And that's not what you want them to do, and that's not what the reformers want them to do. They get pressured to be expansive in their views. But I feel comfortable knowing that the commission, as it is right now, is committed to law.

RICK BERKE: So you worried but just a little bit? Worried about what?

CARL FORTI: When you set up your groups to follow the rules, there's nothing really to worry about. People can misinterpret things, but I mean, who was it, Messina or some of the Democrat panel before this talked about how, Bill, you were fundraising slowly until they started to help you. They are allowed to help do that. They appeared at events. So when you are doing stuff legally, there's nothing to worry about.

RICK BERKE: There's a lot of money going around. You're talking about tens of millions, hundreds of millions of dollars and their role, supposedly, is as the watchdog of what you are doing.

CARL FORTI: I don't want to wind up in an orange jumpsuit, so we're not going to do anything wrong.

CHARLIE SPIES: And just to flesh that out just a little bit more—and maybe I was taking your question a little bit differently in that the core function of the FEC is to enforce the clearly written laws and the commission agrees on about 95 or 96 percent of cases—so it is unified in enforcing the laws that are clear. Now, we get requests for information from the FEC about a description on an expenditure or that sort of thing and those are the sort of things where it's clearly written and they are good at enforcing. And if you are taking in enough money and have enough donors, you are going to get questions from them.

• • • BIG MONEY IN POLITICS: GOOD OR BAD? • • •

GWEN IFILL: But I want to also talk about this whole search for some agreement on this other kind of overview question, which is—I think, Charlie, you were the one at the beginning of this conversation that talked about how everybody thought *Citizens United* and big money would corrupt the system and that in the end it didn't, and there was no scandal anyway, was the way you put it—so I wonder whether, now that we look back on this year, which turned the corner in the way that independent expenditures had an effect on this election, to what degree are we now entering a brave new world where we have a different understanding about whether big money is good or bad? Is it okay? I still get questions everywhere I go, like the question I got yesterday in Dallas about money. People are still nervous about the idea of the impact of big money, and they don't necessarily pay that much attention to who did it, who raised it, just that there's a lot of money in the system, and it can't be good. Do you, in the end, feel that we are on a good path with all this extra money?

Carl Forti, Steven Law, Bill Burton, and Nick Ryan debate whether there's too much money in political campaigns.

NICK RYAN: I think it is a good path, and I think in some ways super PACs are more of a model of transparency than campaigns are. We're filing monthly reports. When we are spending money, we are filing forty-eight-hour reports. And we are constantly telling the public and the FEC where we are spending money, how we are spending the money, who the vendor is, what the amount is, what the state is that it's being spent in, and every donor is also reported. And there's not any big lag that you have to wait, and so as the contests are happening and as you are spending the money, you are disclosing it. I'm a person that believes that you shouldn't limit speech and that if an individual wants to volunteer a thousand hours on the campaign or for a cause or a person wants to write a million-dollar check, they can express themselves in whatever way they want. And with the case of super PACs, it's all disclosed: every bit of the income and every expenditure. I think that's helped.

GWEN IFILL: Bill, healthy?

BILL BURTON: No. Ultimately, I don't think it's a good system, and it could use some reform because the spending isn't just from super

PACs, it's also from groups that don't disclose everything. That's only one piece of it though. The question of whether or not there was a problem coming out of the election, you wouldn't get necessarily by Election Day. I'm sure that you can come up with examples on the Democratic side, but on the Republican side, say Mitt Romney had been elected president, whatever happened with the investigation that the Justice Department has into Sheldon Adelson's dealings would have gotten extra scrutiny. And no matter which way it went, people would have questioned whether or not the extraordinary amount of money that he had given had played a role in the outcome of what happened there. Now, that's obviously not to say that there would have been corruption because I wouldn't imply that at all because people who make those sorts of decisions are professionals at the Justice Department. But those are the kinds of questions that get raised just because there is all this money in the system, and it's why ultimately there probably ought to be caps. Well there definitely ought to be caps on how much money people could give, and transparency is probably the best way to go about running these organizations so that people can have a clear sense. And if questions arise, people can ask them.

GWEN IFILL: But that's in an ideal world.

BILL BURTON: That's in an ideal world. But in the world we live in now, that's not the case. And there are no caps. And there are organizations—like one I run with my partner Sean Sweeney—that don't disclose every single dollar that comes in, every single dollar that goes out the door, and it's a system that needs reforming. I hope that in this next Congressional session, some of those Republican members who saw some outside money spent against them start to come to the conclusion that, yeah, maybe this is not a perfect system for how we do this thing.

RICK BERKE: Let's quickly go down the line.

STEVEN LAW: Let me just say two quick things. First of all, I think one of the most important points was made earlier by Charlie, which is that the law that we are operating under is not really *Citizens United*. It's McCain-Feingold. I often like to say that we are all the children of Fred Wertheimer.[6] This was entirely predicted at the time it was passed—that it would push money out of the parties and into other channels. The major innovation post–*Citizens United* is that people on the right started to do what was done very effectively on the left. Prior to *Citizens*

---

6. Fred Wertheimer served as president of Common Cause.

United, organized labor spent $400 million in the 2008 elections, after which point Gerald McEntee[7] said publicly, "We want payback for our investment." In this election cycle, the firefighters publicly said that they were unsure whether they were going to support President Obama again unless they got some things they wanted. And then, at some point later, they evidently got some things they wanted because they said they decided they were going to support him. I mean those are the things that strike me as a little more troubling, but nevertheless, I think the system that we operate under is a system that Congress passed, and I think it shows the folly of trying to push resources out of the parties where they can be a very effective and leveling voice, supporting both challengers and candidates.

CARL FORTI: I guess I'll just say that we are the practitioners. And to Steven's point, if the lawmakers decide there's a problem and want to try to change the law the way they did with McCain-Feingold, they can do that. But the Supreme Court is pretty clear too that people have a First Amendment right to spend their money in politics if they want to. And I don't know that Sheldon Adelson spending $20 million is any different than somebody that makes $50,000 a year writing a thousand dollar check to a candidate, from a quality of dollar standpoint, so the system is the system.

CHARLIE SPIES: And I think a lot of people would rather have you, Rick, write the column on the front page of the *New York Times* about whatever the issue is than have money in a super PAC. That has a lot more value. You have a voice of the marketplace too, and I think that's part of why there's screaming about super PACs. It's a balancing influence that puts some money into the more conservative voices, or voices that may not be heard in the mainstream media. And one other thing is it also can be anti-establishment. So I think super PACs are around. I think they are going to be a growing phenomenon in the next two election cycles. I think you'll see a lot more of them in primary elections where a smaller amount of money can have a large impact, and I also think you will see them focus on single issues. Brian's group, Ending Spending, is very effective on pushing a very narrow issue. I think you'll see more of that in the coming years—groups focused on certain ideological issues.

BILL BURTON: I have noticed that Rupert Murdoch has had a tough time getting his message out there. [*laughter*]

---

7. Gerald McEntee is the president of the American Federation of State, County, and Municipal Employees (AFSCME).

BRIAN BAKER: I would say there's two points. First, a lot of people forget that *Citizens United* helps in terms of corporations, and it helps in terms of allowing us to set up super PACs. But before *Citizens United*, people, wealthy or not, had the option to exercise their First Amendment rights in campaigns. So even without *Citizens United*, even without super PACs, I have no doubt if President Obama did his presidency the way he has so far, in terms of his fiscal policy—irresponsible fiscal policy in Mr. Ricketts' eyes—he would have still spent the $10 million or more that he spent. And the disclaimer, as opposed to saying "Paid for by the super PAC," would have said "Paid for by Joe Ricketts." I believe there was a gentleman this year who did that, the Hungarian businessman.

GWEN IFILL: With a terrible effect.

BRIAN BAKER: The law that we really should be talking about here is the First Amendment, as Carl said, so I think that's the first point. The second point is: I always come back to George Will who, I think, every year when he writes his campaign finance column, notes that we spend more money annually advertising for chewing gum than we do picking our national leaders. So I'm not so certain why, Bill, you are afraid to allow folks to exercise their First Amendment rights. Certainly our national leadership is at least as important as what gum we chew.

RICK BERKE: Before we go, what are you telling all these people that spent millions and millions and millions of dollars and the money all went down the drain? Their candidate did not win in November. What are you telling them? How are you placating them?

CHARLIE SPIES: Well two things, at least from a Restore Our Future perspective. First of all, I don't agree with your characterization that the money went down the drain.

RICK BERKE: Well if the outcome is to elect their candidate for president, and they lose, to me that's money down the drain.

CHARLIE SPIES: First of all, it's to be in a position that you can compete and win, and that means winning a primary. And second of all, it means being able to fight back against the PACs, help their effort to stay in the game over the summer when traditionally the underfunded candidate gets knocked out, and be in a position to win in the closing weeks, which I think Governor Romney certainly was. And so to come up with one metric of winning or losing—obviously that's the key but, it could have been a lot worse, I believe, without the efforts of all the groups at the table, other than Bill who wasn't helpful. [*laughter*]

RICK BERKE: When you say a lot worse, how so? How could it be worse than losing?

CHARLIE SPIES: We could have lost a lot worse and might have had a mandate. You never know. I don't think that's fair to say that money went down the drain. But, to answer your question, we made a specific effort to communicate with our donors and, no less frequently than every two weeks, probably more frequently than that, we did calls with them where we would walk through polling numbers. And we would walk through what our strategy was and tell them exactly where we saw the race going in the coming weeks, what we were doing, and how their money was being used. We also talked about the expenses and how efficient we were in the use of their resources. Because they, I think, felt vested in our strategy, in what we were doing, we did a call after the election with donors. And we did not have one donor complain about our efforts on the call. I'm not aware of a single donor complaining about our efforts.

BRIAN BAKER: And if I could just add to that, Charlie?

RICK BERKE: Final word.

BRIAN BAKER: Just real quickly, the other important thing is, I think, from the donors that we've talked to and certainly on our end, is our efforts have pushed issues to the forefront, like the fiscal cliff. And so Governor Romney unfortunately was not elected, but if we, through our efforts, force President Obama to be a more responsible president for the next four years, then hopefully some good will have come out of our efforts.

GWEN IFILL: Thank you all so much.

RICK BERKE: Thank you. [*applause*]

5

THE GENERAL ELECTION

RON BROWNSTEIN: We are Ron Brownstein from *National Journal* and Gloria Borger from CNN, and we are here to talk about the general election, essentially the postconvention period. Since the morning discussion was so engaging on the primaries and didn't get quite through

The Romney and Obama campaign teams come together for a discussion of their general election strategies.

the Republican Convention, we are going to talk about that for a few minutes at the top.

GLORIA BORGER: The Democrats talked about their convention and their critique of the Republican Convention, and so we wanted to give you guys a chance to talk a little bit about the convention and what was perceived, I think, as a lack of kind of raucous enthusiasm at that convention, and your sense of whether you achieved what you needed to achieve in setting the tone for the general.

••• THE REPUBLICAN NATIONAL CONVENTION •••

RUSS SCHRIEFER: Thanks. I think the convention was pretty successful. I think that we achieved a lot of what we wanted to do. We were hampered a bit by, ironically, a hurricane, and leading up to it the question was, "Are you going to cancel? How much are you going to cancel? Is there going to be a program?" And we had to certainly navigate our way through that. We then had to take a four-day program and make it into a three-day program and obviously, without naming names, certainly

Gloria Borger and Ron Brownstein moderate a discussion on the general election.

talked to a lot of people and managed a few egos about who was getting speaking slots and when and the amount of time that they were going to be speaking.

GLORIA BORGER: Go ahead, name some names. That's fine.

RUSS SCHRIEFER: But the goal of the convention was to start to talk about who Mitt Romney was. The first night was to lay out the problem. The second night was to talk about We Build It. The third night was to talk about the specific policies that Governor Romney would do if he was president, sort of the "day one, job one" stuff. And then the fourth night was Governor Romney and who he was. And I think that we were successful in telling a lot of those stories, stories that hadn't been told before, particularly of some of the families that Governor Romney worked with at his church. I think that Tom Stemberg[1] was incredibly effective talking about Governor Romney's experience at Bain. I think some of the women and people Governor Romney worked with as Governor of Massachusetts were particularly good. So at the end we were fine. We got a bump. We did what we needed.

RON BROWNSTEIN: Two questions. This morning, Stuart or Matt talked about how "day one, job one" was kind of the prime directive for the campaign all the way through, and we were thinking during the convention, even when you got to that in the last two days, it was less specific and detailed than I expected. It seemed in your tilt of the four days it was really much more toward the introducing of him and kind of softening his image. Was that your primary goal there?

RUSS SCHRIEFER: I think the primary goal was to introduce the governor. I think the secondary goal was to talk about what he would do, and honestly I don't think a convention is the exact time to get into it. It's not a policy debate; it's a convention. So to kind of talk about that then in very specific detail, I don't think would be the appropriate place.

GLORIA BORGER: But it was also clearly a moment to appeal to women, and maybe Neil can talk about the famous Ann Romney "I Love Women" speech and a moment to do that because you knew you had an issue. Neil?

---

1. Tom Stemberg is the founder of Staples and spoke about how Bain helped his company.

NEIL NEWHOUSE: There were a number of issues we were trying to address. I mean we had taken the pounding from the Obama campaign over the summer and, as was pointed out in one of the previous groups, it hadn't moved the ballot numbers a lot, but it had moved the image numbers. So what we were trying to do at the convention and my goal, in terms of where we wanted to move the numbers, was we were looking to move image numbers and attribute numbers. We weren't worried about the ballot test as much then as we were Mitt's fav/unfav because we knew that if we were inverted, it was going to make the fall campaign extraordinarily difficult. So when he came out of the convention, our image improved—the attributes we were looking for improved. It was a success in terms of those specific objectives we were trying to hit. You could overreach and try to do everything in a convention and end up doing nothing, and we decided we were going to limit it to some extent, become more focused. And, as I said, after the convention, when I was down to cause trouble at your convention in Charlotte, if we had wanted to hit on Mitt's vision for the future and done policy, we would have done it. That wasn't our goal.

GLORIA BORGER: By the way, we want to encourage you guys to converse with each other, should you decide to do so.

RON BROWNSTEIN: The one thing that did not go right side up after the convention in the public polling was, "cares about people like me and cares about the middle class," I believe. Even immediately after the Republican Convention, he was still facing difficult numbers on that front. You were saying earlier today, David, that the core argument you were trying to make on the business side was that even though Romney was a success, his success would not benefit people like you. So that was obviously a critical pillar of your portrait of him. Did you see the Republican Convention undoing the damage that you had done? How much had it done to, in fact, reshape his image as someone who cared about average and middle-class families?

DAVID SIMAS: On those measures, when we were looking at the empathy measures for us, we didn't see a lot of movement for Governor Romney. We did see a slight improvement in his fav/unfav, but there wasn't a lot of intensity. There wasn't a tremendous movement to the very favorable, just a lot of set in somewhat unfavorables. So we didn't see a lot of movement, and I think because the Democratic Convention came so quickly afterward that whatever kind of chance to lay into that some more was probably truncated, from at least what we saw in the data.

GLORIA BORGER: And then we have to ask you folks and anybody can pick this up, and then we can move on, about your own internal reaction to Clint Eastwood. We've already heard from these folks about that. Everybody could see the look on Ann Romney's face when we were sort of focusing in on her during that. Stuart?

STUART STEVENS: I don't know. Clint Eastwood, to his credit, has described what happened completely accurately. Personally I don't think it was a big deal. People have said, "Why didn't you show the convention film?" It's because the networks had not committed to showing it. NBC had said they would show it. The other networks hadn't, which is not slighting us. That's been their standard. I mean they did that four years ago for both convention films. They don't want to just cede time to give you ten minutes of film, eight minutes of film, so you take that primetime slot. You put it up there, and you are not going to have someone be able to carry it. A lot of people loved the film, which is great. It's really a successful film, but it wasn't an option to run that and have it shown. So originally Eastwood was going to speak the night before and then everything got truncated because of the hurricane. And, look, our voters like Clint Eastwood.

RON BROWNSTEIN: What was he supposed to achieve? Even beside the film, the woman who gave the testimonial right before about him writing the will for the teenager was so powerful and compelling. And it was also off of primetime. I remember watching him come out on stage and wondering, "Okay, well, what is he supposed to do for you?" even if he did it better than he did.

RUSS SCHRIEFER: Well first of all the woman was fantastic, but we had no idea at that point that she was going to be as good as she was, and, listen, in retrospect, if we knew she was going to be that fantastic, we probably would have rescheduled that. I mean that's just in hindsight. Listen, you have one of the biggest, most iconic Hollywood stars who has never made an appearance at a political convention willing to come in and say something on behalf of your candidate for five minutes. That's a pretty good opportunity.

STUART STEVENS: I don't really understand it, and I would be interested in what David thinks, but there was this interesting drop-off in viewership for both conventions, but mostly for the Republican Convention. I would think that knowing that Clint Eastwood was going to lead off probably drew more voters, more viewers.

RON BROWNSTEIN: We want to move on to the main event, but real quick, just for the historical record, did anybody read his speech? Did you know what he was going to do, what he was going to say?

STUART STEVENS: He was going to say what he had said at two fundraisers where he had been fantastic.

RON BROWNSTEIN: And was that what he said? Was this speech different than the fundraiser speech?

STUART STEVENS: This idea came to him as he was standing there, as he said.

GLORIA BORGER: So Russ, you are planning this whole thing and you are sitting there and suddenly Clint Eastwood comes out.

RUSS SCHRIEFER: Well I said, "Are you going to do what we talked about? Are you going to talk about what we talked about at these fundraisers?" And he looked at me and said, "Yup." [*laughter*]

GLORIA BORGER: Make my day.

RUSS SCHRIEFER: It's Clint Eastwood. You argue with him. [*laughter*]

RON BROWNSTEIN: That was the moment where you probably wish he had gone back to being the strong, silent type.

STUART STEVENS: If there were moments at the convention that weren't successful, whatever the end results of the convention, I think there were bigger forces at work. I mean it wasn't Clint Eastwood's fault that X number of people didn't watch the convention or that there was a hurricane or that there was a Democratic Convention with a lot of oomph behind it five days later.

••• THE SELECTION OF PAUL RYAN •••

RON BROWNSTEIN: One other thing is the selection of Paul Ryan. Let's posit as a given that Governor Romney thought he would be a help in governing, had a personal chemistry with him, and obviously respected him. Assuming all that, how did he rise above the other options from a political point of view?

BETH MYERS: Well this was a decision that was made a hundred percent by Governor Romney. It's something of a thankless job to be the person who selects the vice president, but this year we felt we had a great group of candidates on the Republican side. And what Mitt asked me to do in April was to put together a set of vice presidential candidates that he could consider. He didn't want us to come to the best candidate consensus. He wanted to look at dossiers on a number of candidates. And he also wanted the option to make the decision early, so he wanted all the work to be done by July 1st. He ultimately decided not to make the decision as early as July 1st, but he wanted to have that option. So between April and July we did our vetting, and the vetting also included Mitt campaigning with all the people under consideration and included all of them going on news shows. It included all of them campaigning on their own and working with our team, in addition to all the work that we did as a team back in Boston. And in the end Mitt had three criteria. One was that the person be qualified to start on day one. Two, that there must be nothing in their background that would be a distraction from the campaign and the important issues on the campaign. And three, he wanted a choice of several candidates so that he could pick not on any one issue but on a whole spectrum of issues. He was provided with that choice, and he was not concerned. I think he liked Paul for a number of reasons. He liked his youth. He liked his Midwest Wisconsin background. He really appreciated the fact that Paul took on head-on what he considered to be one of the most important issues in the country and that he took it on with courage and conviction. And Mitt was not concerned about that in the end at all. There was also something when they were campaigning together. People on the road, Stuart in particular, had commented about how, when they were together, it was more than "one plus one equals two." Mitt felt very comfortable with him, and that was his selection. It was very easy for him to make in the end, I think.

GLORIA BORGER: As part of the process, did he say, "I've narrowed it down to three people"? Did you know, Beth, when he decided?

BETH MYERS: I knew how many people that I completed vetting packages on and what I gave to him. And within that group he met with pretty much this entire group of advisors, and he asked all of our opinions. I did not share my opinion with him since I was leading the search process, but everybody else did. I didn't know until he told me who it was going to be who it was going to be.

RON BROWNSTEIN: Did this reflect at all a changing theory of the race? In September you were talking about that it's really a choice about the future, rather than a retrospective referendum. I thought on the day that you picked Paul Ryan you were kind of undermining that choice here. I mean now you are talking about very different directions for the future. The Democrats, and we'll bring them in in a second, as they said this morning, saw this as an enormous target by tying it to the Congress and so forth. When you picked Ryan, did that at all suggest that you were moving away from trying to frame this primarily as a referendum, just maybe more forward-looking?

STUART STEVENS: Look, the selection of Congressman Ryan was not a political choice in the least and was never discussed as such. It was who Governor Romney wanted to be his vice president, end of story.

GLORIA BORGER: It wasn't a political choice at all?

STUART STEVENS: It was not discussed as such.

RON BROWNSTEIN: Even if that was not a motivation, Stuart, you must have been doing a ledger of the assets and liabilities that he brought politically. What did that look like in your head, or anybody on the table?

STUART STEVENS: You mean after he was picked?

RON BROWNSTEIN: After he was picked, yeah.

STUART STEVENS: Neil, do you want to answer? [*laughter*]

RON BROWNSTEIN: Sorry, Neil.

MATT RHOADES: Dan can speak to it in a second, but it obviously was a big opportunity for us. We always felt at any point in the campaign, when we were talking about big issues, we were in a good place. And if we were talking about important issues, whether it was Medicare or spending cuts, at times the other side came after us pretty hard on it. We always felt that if we were going big, it was good for Governor Romney. So certainly the selection of Congressman Ryan was an enabler for us to go big and talk about big things. I just want to go back to what Beth said, and I think what Stuart was starting to talk about. We talked earlier on the primary panel about how each week in the primary it was a must-win. And one of our must-wins was Wisconsin. We had coordinated an endorsement with Congressman Ryan behind the scenes that he would endorse right before the Wisconsin primary. He had some fundraising commitments to the RNC that he wanted to keep. And I never went on the road. I made the decision, as campaign manager, that I was going to stay behind and be chained to my desk. But I had a regular call every day with the governor. Every day we talked at least one time. And as soon as they got out there campaigning together, it was like talking to your buddy who has just met a girl and is giddy. [*laughter*] They hit it off, and there was an immediate chemistry. The advance guys would immediately call me, and they would be like, "Oh, he's our favorite surrogate, you guys. You've got to see these guys together." It just worked. They both liked big ideas. They both liked talking about substantive issues. They both believed the country was in trouble and that they needed to do big things to fix it. And so I could see it going all the way back to the Wisconsin primary.

NEIL NEWHOUSE: Let me take a shot at this too. When I sat down and went through this thing after Paul was picked, I went through three things. Number one, he brought policy. He stood for something and it was bright lines and you knew where he stood. I thought he brought politics too. He was good politically for us. He was young. He appealed to conservatives—although we didn't need conservatives. We had conservatives locked up. But he was good in terms of politics, and I thought he added personality to the campaign. Matt talks about the two of them getting together. I watched it from the headquarters that Saturday when he was announced. And the second event of that day Paul introduced Mitt instead of Mitt introducing Paul, and I was like, "Oh, my God, these guys," I kidded Will Ritter,[2] "it's like bromance." And we made a special effort to make sure the two of them campaigned together a lot more than we would have otherwise because I thought they played off each other extraordinarily well. So I thought there were a number of different positives that he brought to the campaign.

RON BROWNSTEIN: Dan?

DAN SENOR: Building on that is that he was a remarkably disciplined surrogate. I mean the guy did over two hundred interviews in about forty days. He was doing about four to ten interviews a day, between local affiliates in the battleground states plus network stuff. When people complained, "We don't hear from Paul Ryan," it's because he wasn't

---

2. Will Ritter was the Romney campaign's advance director.

making mistakes. Trust me: if he was making a lot of mistakes, those would be going viral.

GLORIA BORGER: There was that race, the marathon.[3]

DAN SENOR: Name three. You can't name three instances. No, really. When the governor was in debate camps, so he was dark for three-and-a-half days, Paul was doing ten or twelve interviews a day. So he gave some cover for Mitt that some other picks may not have been able to. And I would just add also on the fundraising side, I was struck that we were getting donors calling the campaign wanting to build major finance events around Paul Ryan.

GLORIA BORGER: We heard a little this morning from the Obama team on their impression of Paul Ryan, but let me ask Stephanie. So he's picked Paul Ryan. There's the bromance, as Neil calls it, going on. Mitt Romney seems to have new energy. And your reaction?

STEPHANIE CUTTER: Well first let me say what Matt was referring to, the chemistry between them. We noticed that too when they were campaigning in Wisconsin during the primaries, and it's something that we picked on. And that's an important piece of picking a vice president: to make sure that there is chemistry between the principal and the VP. We were prepared for a number of different people, and, as I said this morning, the storyline was going to be the same because much of the records between the people that were being considered were the same. It was a choice between going forward or going back, and it was doubling down on a lot of the policies that crashed the economy, punished the middle class—I'm sure we've heard this ad nauseam. So when the Ryan choice was announced, obviously we had a lot of information because Ryan was a pretty public figure over the past couple of years when he really made a name for himself, and we were familiar with his policies. So we were able to articulate what that meant in terms of Governor Romney's candidacy and his agenda. And I think at the time we said, if I remember correctly, it completed the merger with the Republican Congress. We tried to tie the governor to that.

---

3.   In a radio interview before his RNC speech, Ryan falsely claimed he had completed a marathon in under three hours.

••• THE IMPACT OF THE CONVENTIONS •••

RON BROWNSTEIN: Now that we've kind of covered the backstory, let's go to what we are supposed to cover here this afternoon, which is the period from the convention to Election Day. And let me start by asking each side, and maybe, Jim and David, you could tackle this first and then a couple of folks for the Romney campaign. When both conventions are over, you are leaving Charlotte. You've left Tampa. Give me your sense of the state of the race at that point. In public polling at least, the president was ahead, but I wonder, can you talk a little bit about, in your sense, what was the choice? How was the choice defined at the end of both conventions? What was your most likely Electoral College path to victory, and what did you consider your biggest asset and your biggest liability on the morning after both conventions?

GLORIA BORGER: In other words, what work did you have to do?

DAVID AXELROD: Well we were encouraged after the conventions, I think it's fair to say. These guys got dealt a bad hand because they had to truncate a four-day convention into a three-day convention, and that

David Axelrod and Stephanie Cutter listen on as Jim Messina discusses the impact of the conventions.

created programming headaches that we didn't have. And our convention came up, and it's tremendously advantageous to have the second convention because, whatever benefit the other side derives from their convention, when you go quickly you can snuff that out. And we felt that we had done that, told the story well in our convention. Obviously President Clinton was very helpful; all the speakers were. Michelle Obama did good work for us, Castro, as our keynote speaker, and then Biden and the president. When we came out of it, we got more out of it than we ever thought we would. And we felt we were in very strong shape coming out of it. One of the things that we had discussed internally was the state of Florida and how we were going to treat Florida. We had made a decision that we were going to wait until mid-September, after the conventions, and see where we were in Florida before we fully committed. We were in. We had invested a lot in Florida, but we hadn't been, for example, in the Miami media market. And when we emerged from the conventions, not only had we gotten a little bump in our numbers, but we saw that Florida remained very competitive, despite the fact that they had their convention there, and we made the decision to go full out in Florida. So we really were very optimistic coming out of our conventions. And in terms of message, we drove the message that we went there to drive. That this was a choice. That this was about two different approaches to the economy: the top-down approach that we had seen in the last decade versus investing in the middle class and a focus on the middle class. We drove that hard during the convention. We felt that was the winning message for us, and we had amplified it. So I would say we felt very good about where we were coming out of the convention, beyond which there were ancillary benefits. The convention was very energizing for our supporters. Perhaps Teddy and others can speak to this, but money was very good coming out of the convention, and that gave us more resources than we had anticipated. As I said in the earlier session, we had kind of gambled on the front end and frontloaded our media without any guarantee that we were going to be able to make it up and be competitive on the back end.

JIM MESSINA: I think the map widened for us. I mean Wisconsin was clearly someplace that we had to pay more attention to, spend more money. The Florida decision was a big decision for us. It was a $40 million decision, and we decided right after the convention we were going to go and go hard. That was a big moment. We believed since midway through the primaries that the Midwest was always going to be where we were going to win this thing, and we came out of their convention and our convention continuing to believe that the Midwest was looking very good for us, and Ohio especially. And the other thing is, they didn't do enough to fix their Latino problem in their convention. Although I thought Rubio gave a great speech. We looked at that and said, "We are going all the way in Florida."

GLORIA BORGER: Was the Latino issue the really big piece of the Florida decision?

JIM MESSINA: And seniors and, to David's point, the middle-class stuff. We looked at this and just said there is no reason not to go now.

DAVID AXELROD: The main point though is there were a number of reasons for us to believe that we could actually win in Florida, and that it wasn't illusory. In this business, you have shiny objects out there that you chase, and you can spend a lot of money to no good purpose in the end. So you want to be careful, especially in a state the size of Florida, not to overinvest there when we knew we were going to need resources elsewhere.

GLORIA BORGER: And what about the decisions that were made on your side coming out of your convention? I mean one could argue that the Obama campaign spent a lot of money defining you over the summer, and some people say that was not responded to enough—the Bain ads being the major part of that. They got a bounce out of their convention. You did not get what they got. What were the decisions that you were making at that time, as you looked at the same playing field they were looking at, when they decide to engage in Florida? Matt?

MATT RHOADES: We obviously had some work to do on the Hispanic voter front, and we realized we needed to focus our time and energy, not nationally because it just wasn't going to be possible, unfortunately. But we put a focus on the Hispanic vote in Florida, and we shifted resources to try to improve our numbers with Hispanics in Florida. We also did the same in Nevada. We did see some movement, and Neil can speak to this, in Florida, but we definitely had issues that we inherited. And, we talked a little bit about this earlier, the long slog primary didn't help for sure. But we did make a concerted effort to move numbers, and I think we had some success in Florida. Neil can point out a few.

RON BROWNSTEIN: Before he does, let's take one minute to get a broader take from you on whether David Axelrod was right when he said the Democrats got more out of their convention than they thought they would. What was the overall state of play in your mind? I mean Rich can come in here on the Electoral College. As Jim said, it was expanding. What was your sense with your map? What was your sense of what they achieved at their convention? And then, also, what was the state of the race on the morning after both conventions?

MATT RHOADES: One thing before Rich gets to the map, with the convention comparison we obviously had some distractions at our convention that we talked about, whether it was the weather or whatnot. We had an aggressive response operation that we had down in Charlotte, and there were moments during the Democratic Convention that I was somewhat hopeful that some of the distractions that they were having at their convention, with their platform and other items, would be beneficial to us.[4] However, I was laying in bed about to go to sleep and I watched their primetime lineup of President Clinton and President Obama and it just made up for any distraction that occurred. So unfortunately there was a brief moment where we thought, "Hey, these guys are going to have to endure a little bit of what we endured," but it just didn't work out that way.

GLORIA BORGER: Did you worry about that too?

DAVID AXELROD: It's fair to say that there was a little bit of dyspepsia at that moment. I mean the truth is that the primetime lineup is pretty much everything, and this other stuff is kind of the passion of all of us who live with this moment to moment. So we were comfortable that we could overcome that. We thought we had a pretty good convention going.

RON BROWNSTEIN: So Neil, the day after both conventions, where did you think the race stood?

NEIL NEWHOUSE: Let me just address the Democratic Convention for a second because I got really tired of reading verbatim comments from voters praising the Democratic Convention for weeks afterwards. What their convention did, which we didn't expect, was we saw a change in right direction, wrong track for the country. We saw a change in economic optimism just as a result of the Democratic Convention. You just don't expect that. We didn't.

GLORIA BORGER: Bill Clinton?

---

4.   When the Democratic Party's platform was released there was controversy surrounding the fact that language mentioning God and naming Jerusalem the rightful capital of Israel had been removed. The language was ultimately put back in.

NEIL NEWHOUSE: Whatever, but it was remarkable. Of course, Democratic enthusiasm went up, but the mood of the country went up—even the economic optimism. The Michigan consumer confidence numbers go up because of the Democratic Convention because Democrats now feel obliged to say, "Yeah, the country is heading in the right direction, and the economy is getting better." And you saw that, and we were dealing with that for the first fifteen days or so of September. I mean Axe is right when he talks about their convention stepping on our convention and our growth and movement. I think we would have gained more in terms of Mitt's image, but their convention had a place right after ours and their success helped change that political environment.

••• THE TIMING OF ADVERTISING •••

JIM MARGOLIS: Can I ask one question? You guys dropped your advertising off right after your convention, which really surprised us. All of a sudden you disappeared at a point that we were kind of putting pedal to the metal here. Can you speak to that at all, Stuart?

Matt Rhoades and Jim Messina come together after a long campaign cycle.

David Axelrod and Stuart Stevens compare notes on their campaigns.

STUART STEVENS: We always had limited resource questions, and it was a finite amount of money. We went back historically and tried to look at states in which media had been run during the conventions and states in which they hadn't run during the convention to try to get the degree to which you could use television advertising during the conventions to drive a message, and we tried to calibrate really what was the delta there. It's a difficult thing to do. It's sort of junk science. But the consensus was it was really a 20 to 40 million dollar decision and that we'd rather have 20 to 40 million dollars to spend in October. It was a hard decision, but we enjoyed spending that money in October.

GLORIA BORGER: So that brings a larger question, which is spending the money early, as you guys did over the summer, versus spending the money late. Well who was right?

STUART STEVENS: It cost us $135 million, we were talking about this earlier, to win the nomination. The president got it for free, so he gets a $135 million advantage right there. And I go back to this: The day Mitt Romney announced in June of 2011, he had, I don't know, about 25 percent or so support of the Republican Party, that's it. The day that the president of the United States announced, he had, I don't know, close to 50 percent of the support of the country, so, you know, 47 to 48 percent. So over the course of that process, we had to win the Republican nomination and then go about the business of getting the majority of the country. The president's task was very different. He had to grow his vote share, if at all, very marginally. And he had more money to accomplish that goal and the leverage of the White House, and, having done a reelect in '04, that's better. [*laughter*]

RON BROWNSTEIN: In fairness though, you also had four, six, seven months of blanket coverage of a race in which you were getting a tremendous platform to make a case to the country.

STUART STEVENS: Please, please.

RON BROWNSTEIN: Well no, no. I'm not saying it's comparable, but it existed. I'm wondering if you felt that, at the end of that process, say late spring, you were in a stronger position than you were the fall before?

STUART STEVENS: I'll just ask that. In February and March and April of 2008 did you guys feel you were being a gift by the primary?

GLORIA BORGER: Well Jim, can you talk about the early money?

JIM MESSINA: Well we had a theory which is different. Our theory was, at the end, ubiquitous spending. I mean the last two weeks of the campaign were at, what, Margolis, about 6,000 to 8,000 points in all of our markets? We just didn't think at that point TV mattered, and we thought it was way more important that we get a deeper view. The other thing, coming out of the conventions our research showed that 75 to 80 percent of all voters had already made up their minds. We just thought that spending earlier was a very important moment because that number in June was 60, 65, 70, and so we banked basically our entire campaign on spending money in June. We moved $65 million out of October and September and put it into June and July.

DAVID AXELROD: I would say this. First of all, I think we probably got a better deal on our primaries in 2008 than you got in 2012. We didn't have this sort of hammer in time, ideological thing to deal with so much in our primary. So I don't think that to say that they had sort of this blank slate on which to paint is not really true. But there's no doubt that we took advantage of that period in between, after your primary, when that ended, and to the convention to fill in some blanks that you didn't have the opportunity to do. And that was important in terms of framing the race.

STUART STEVENS: We spent all the money we had, and we spent money that we didn't have and went and borrowed money. So it wasn't like we were making a decision not to spend any money. We spent it all. And the only question was, once we got money kicked in from the general, whether or not we spent money on the Democratic Convention that week. So it wasn't like we had X amount of money and we were holding it back.

GLORIA BORGER: But they spent the summer hitting you on Bain.

STUART STEVENS: We spent all the money that we had. They had a lot more money.

NEIL NEWHOUSE: It goes back to the independent expenditure conversation that happened a couple of hours ago, which is, it depends on when you have the money in the campaign. You can have all the money in the world, but if you don't have it at the right times, you can handcuff the ability of the campaign to respond.

RON BROWNSTEIN: Let's get from Rich one more point about where things stood in everybody's mind in early September. Jim Messina said they felt the battlefield expanding, the Electoral College map. When you are sitting there after both conventions, what seemed to you the most likely pathway to 270 Electoral College votes? And what were some of the states that seemed most in play for you and then those that seemed most difficult?

RICH BEESON: Well I knew once they decided not to play in Indiana that we had them on the run. [*laughter*] It was just a matter of time at that point. But no, I mean our path, it always had to include Florida. We had to take North Carolina back. Then you got into Virginia, Ohio, then across New Hampshire, Wisconsin, Colorado, Iowa, Nevada. So it was an amalgamation in there. And Jim is exactly right: coming out of the convention, it was just a low number of persuadables. Obviously the path that they took was entirely correct. Ours was to go after Independents, high-propensity, low-support voters that we could move our way and turn out. That was the approach we took with all the volunteer voter contacts and with all of the paid voter contacts. Ultimately we moved some numbers there.

RON BROWNSTEIN: And at that point then, the nine states that we kind of ended up focusing on, at that point, those were what you were looking at?

RICH BEESON: Yes, yes sir. But at the end, going into Pennsylvania was not a snap decision. We had offices. We had sixty-five staff on the ground there, twenty-six offices all the way through. We didn't know what turnout could be generated in the Philly market. We knew as you got further west our turnout would increase, and, as you saw on election night, the numbers closed as the night wore on.

RON BROWNSTEIN: We'll come back to Pennsylvania later.

DAVID AXELROD: Can I just say one thing? Forget about who is right and who is wrong and so on—the election is over. But there is a clinical question to be asked, especially in this age of super PACs, which is, how much is every media dollar worth? How impactful is it as you moved forward in the campaign? So in the last six weeks of the campaign, when coverage is so intense, when debates are so important, how much impact does this media really have? Neil, you may have a sense of this and, David, you may from our own stuff. I think that's an open question and one that people are going to have to look at as they plan future presidential races because I have this feeling that media is very effective before the conventions, and it is decreasingly effective after the conventions.

GLORIA BORGER: You think the negative ads cancel each other out?

DAVID AXELROD: Look, people understand that what we do in some ways, maybe in every way, is propaganda. This is not objective truth. So they are more apt to believe what they can see with their own eyes. They can see debates with their own eyes. They watch the news. They see wall-to-wall coverage. I think that, at the end of the day, moderates the impact of paid media.

MATT RHOADES: I think that's an interesting point, and we talked a little bit about super PACs in the Republican primary. During the primary the super PACs were good for Mitt Romney and bad for Mitt Romney. But after going through a primary and a general election campaign, and this is by no means a slight to the super PACs, they were just much more effective in a primary because there wasn't as much saturation on TV. They were just able to break through more. I don't know if they had a numbing effect because in many of these states our primary went so far out, many of the target states were exposed to super PAC ads. Maybe there is a sense by voters who were watching TV to kind of tune out ads that aren't Obama ads or Romney ads. I can't quite explain that, but it's definitely something that people are going to have to really look at as they plot out their strategies in 2016.

STUART STEVENS: I think it's a very interesting question, but the thing is no one has the nerve to pull off their television. If we really believe that, we go dark, and what we're talking about is sort of equal force. The only time that we had equal force with the Obama campaign was toward the end on television, and so I think they do, at that point, begin to cancel each other out. But I think had you gone dark in a state, you would have been crushed.

DAVID AXELROD: As you heard Jim say, and Margolis can speak to this, the spending was, on both sides, like nothing we've ever seen before, which is part of the question in this sort of super PAC age. I mean every one of us was in a battleground state at one time or other. Matt, even you got to New Hampshire. You tried to escape it by staying chained to your desk, but you probably got some of the New Hampshire volume. I don't know that we fully comprehend the impact of all of that.

JIM MARGOLIS: That was going to be my point exactly. There's a point of diminishing return somewhere and probably, before the end of this conversation, you are going to say, "What are your regrets?" And my regrets are what we collectively did to the poor people of Ohio and all these other states. [*laughter*] One point I would make is we weren't looking at you as Romney and Obama; we were looking at you as Romney and allies and Obama and allies. And when we were getting up to 7,000 points collectively on your side, and we were kind of hanging in there at 5,000, and a couple of places we were at 6,000 points, for those of you who weren't focused on gross rating points every day, this is just beyond any comprehension.

NEIL NEWHOUSE: Jim, in our morning meetings—and Matt can attest to this—we had 10:00 a.m. meetings every morning, and we would once in a while say, "Okay, let's take a snapshot of Columbus on any one given day on how many ads they see on each channel from you and your allies and us and our allies," and it just got off the page.

STUART STEVENS: Let me just make one point. I mean for us it was very frustrating that the only message we could have any impact on whatsoever or control at all was what we were doing. It was frustrating to see people say, "Well you know, Romney versus Obama, they've got this parity and stuff," and we're going, like, "No. We don't have parity because we don't have anything to do with these, and it's not what we would be saying half the time." So you look at it, you know, red/blue, but the amount of money, when you compare it, that we were able to spend versus the Obama campaign, that had more efficiency in it.

RON BROWNSTEIN: Let's talk about how the race moves forward now in September.

••• ROMNEY: A DIFFERENT KIND OF GENERAL ELECTION CANDIDATE? •••

GLORIA BORGER: I want to talk about Mitt Romney going on *Meet the Press* on September 9th, which was the first time, I think, that we may have seen a little change in Mitt Romney. He talked about keeping parts of Obamacare. I'm sure you might recall that appearance. So let me ask, whoever wants to take this in the Obama campaign, what was your reaction to that moment when there seemed to be, I don't know if it's a different Romney, you guys would have to characterize it.

DAVID AXELROD: I definitely would characterize it that way. Well all I would say is this: we paid a lot of attention to what Governor Romney was saying. We were aware of subtle nuances of change. More than anything, what we were aware of, and this accelerated as the debates approached, was that his performance improved dramatically over the course of that month. That might have been a clue to us before that first debate.

GLORIA BORGER: In September you are saying?

DAVID AXELROD: In September, yeah.

GLORIA BORGER: What were the discussions going on? That he is a better candidate? What did you see?

DAVID AXELROD: Well I mean, David, you were probably showing some of this footage to voters, but I mean he very clearly was more relaxed. He was more connecting, and his rhetoric was a broader, more inclusive rhetoric. That was very, very clear to us.

DAVID SIMAS: To David's point, what we began to hear in mid-September, which we had never heard before, was people referring to Governor Romney as relatable. The one thing that we understood is that we held this card on middle-class values that we did not believe, based on what we had seen in his record, that he could attain. And so it was the humanizing of him. And, you know, he was much more crisp in his presentation. And we were looking at the same voters—Obama voters in 2008, Independents, undecided, that is the universe. As soon as they start saying, "Huh, that's a different guy than what I have learned," then that becomes the moment where we all paid a lot more attention.

••• COURTING THE HISPANIC VOTE •••

RON BROWNSTEIN: Matt, Mitt Romney went on Univision and struck a different tone than in the primaries. His tone was much more welcoming for Hispanics. What did you think was realistic to achieve at that point with Hispanic voters? There was one report, that was renounced, that you were hoping to get to 38 percent as an internal goal. What did you think you could do, and how were you trying to do it as you moved into September?

GLORIA BORGER: Was that an internal goal?

RON BROWNSTEIN: There was a report of it. Go ahead.

GLORIA BORGER: Was there an internal goal? Let's ask that.

RICH BEESON: That was a Florida activist that had said it much earlier in the year and said our goal was to get that number. That was not the number we talked about.

RON BROWNSTEIN: Was there a number you talked about?

RICH BEESON: No, not nationally.

RON BROWNSTEIN: Not nationally?

RICH BEESON: Not nationwide.

RON BROWNSTEIN: Not nationwide?

RICH BEESON: In Florida we broke it down to the Cuban community in the south, the I-4 Corridor with the Puerto Ricans, and the I-4 Corridor in Nevada. It wasn't a national number. It was where do we need to be in these specific states?

RON BROWNSTEIN: What did you think was achievable with Hispanic voters after the conversation in the primary in the states that you cared about, which were presumably Florida, Colorado, and Nevada?

MATT RHOADES: Well obviously we thought we could do well enough with the Hispanic community to win Florida, and we knew we had certain vote goals that Rich just outlined. So we put a premium and an effort on that. We also thought we could potentially move numbers in Nevada. I don't think we were successful at that, but this is also a time where we used some of our über-surrogates: some of our rock stars in the Republican Party, including Senator Rubio and Governor Martinez from New Mexico. And we tried to flood the zone in many parts of the country with these surrogates. And we were much more aggressive with our TV buys in the Hispanic media markets in those two states, and so we were making a push to gas it.

GLORIA BORGER: Was there ever a point at which you thought about changing on self-deportation, which became a very big topic of conversation? Was that ever considered?

STUART STEVENS: No.

GLORIA BORGER: Okay.

STUART STEVENS: The Obama campaign can speak to this, but clearly one would think that the timing of the waiver on the Dream Act,[5] whatever the technical term is, was raised because it raised the profile of the issue, and that was the sort of thing you can do as president. I felt it was very smartly played. That is an example of the advantage you have, that incumbents have.

RON BROWNSTEIN: David, you said this morning that the governor made Faustian bargains during the Republican primaries. Was immigration one of those that you were specifically thinking of?

---

5. In June 2012 President Obama signed an executive order for the Deferred Action for Childhood Arrivals Process, which allows certain people who would qualify under the DREAM Act to be granted deferred action and obtain work permission.

DAVID AXELROD: Well yes. I felt like they had a short-term strategic imperative, which was to get by Rick Perry, and I thought that there were reverberations from some of that positioning throughout. I don't think it was the only thing but it was definitely important from a tonal kind of standpoint, and it was hard to get out from under that.

RON BROWNSTEIN: So David, you are seeing Romney doing better, relating?

••• THE 47 PERCENT VIDEO •••

DAVID AXELROD: Let me just say this one thing in the middle of it. I know you get giddy when we talk about demographics [*laughter*]—

RON BROWNSTEIN: I'm waiting.

DAVID AXELROD: But, and I'm sure you guys are going to get to this, there was one big sort of event in the midst of this, which was this tape. And so that was on the negative side of the ledger for these guys, even as he was making progress.

GLORIA BORGER: So let's start. Talk about the infamous 47 percent. First of all, let me ask you guys, did you have any idea this was coming out?

RON BROWNSTEIN: Same question over here, did you know this existed? Were any of you there? Had any of you seen it? Had any of you heard him say anything like it on another occasion?

STUART STEVENS: I was there.

RON BROWNSTEIN: You were there? And?

STUART STEVENS: I think I was actually out of the room. [*laughter*]

GLORIA BORGER: That's a good story, you're sticking to it.

STUART STEVENS: But I was at the event.

RON BROWNSTEIN: So when it appeared, was this kind of like a bolt from the blue, or was this something that you had heard him say? Had you thought about how you would respond to it, or was it just a complete surprise? Gail maybe?

GAIL GITCHO: No, I don't think I have anything to add to what Stuart had said. We were surprised to see it too.

GLORIA BORGER: Let's talk about the reaction. Go ahead, Matt.

MATT RHOADES: Let me talk a little bit about the 47 percent. We didn't know it existed. I wasn't there. Maybe Stuart was there. Obviously, unfortunately, campaigns are long, laborious processes at times, and there's many a fundraiser. And the governor was very good the second go around, as a candidate, to make less of these kind of mistakes, but nobody is perfect. And so this occurred, and I think that David is right, having worked for Governor Romney for two times, two different campaigns, he could be somewhat streaky. He starts to get hot, and he is a candidate that can put it out of the park. Some candidates can't. He can go into a debate, and he can win a debate. He can give a good speech. I think often times his political skills are underestimated, but there are things that he can do. He can put it out of the park, and he was starting to get his mojo. And then this event happened, and it's unfortunate. But one thing I would like to talk about, before we get into the response of it all, was, as the governor was getting hot, everything coming out of the convention, our campaign was not. There's often in-fighting stories, and I know that you guys went through some of them as well. And they are often not always based in reality, but they were starting to exist. I think it's a moment that speaks to the gov's character because he pushed through and plowed through. I remember speaking to him, and there was a lot of negativity about our campaign as a whole but he's a person that takes personal responsibility about it, and he would say to me, "You didn't say 47 percent, Matt. Stuart didn't say 47 percent. I did." And obviously it was not a high moment for our campaign, but I think it speaks a lot to who Mitt Romney is. And I also like to think it speaks a lot to who this campaign team is that we were able to make a run and come back from that. Because there were periods during that time where people, and many people in this room, said that we had no chance. We never allowed ourselves to believe that, and the governor never allowed himself to believe that either.

GLORIA BORGER: But what does the governor do when this occurs? You are all figuring out how to do the damage control, and we could ask Gail about that because that didn't go that smoothly either, but we can talk about that. Take us inside your room, your headquarters, and how the governor dealt with it—as you said, "taking responsibility"—but Gail, how you dealt with it. Because at first it took him a few days to say "I'm for 100 percent of the people."

GAIL GITCHO: Well actually the reaction was pretty immediate because we had seen the video. We had learned about it at the same time everybody else did and wanted to verify it, of course. We had some trouble verifying exactly where the video had come from, and it appeared to be cut up. So there was a process there where we wanted to see what came before and what came after and if there was some kind of context that it was being taken out of. But the governor did respond that evening. If you remember, he was in Arizona for a finance event and stepped outside the event, and he did make a response.

RON BROWNSTEIN: But just to interrupt though, the initial response was not to renounce it, right? The initial response did not renounce the comments.

GAIL GITCHO: No, it did not. And, as you said, in the next couple of days we did make a point to emphasize that the governor is for 100 percent.

RON BROWNSTEIN: Can you talk a little bit about the process from your initial reaction to getting to that point? What happened?

GAIL GITCHO: Well we wanted to provide a statement and some of kind of an explanation immediately, which is why we had the governor go out and do that at the fundraiser. And it was something that he wanted to do. He wanted to address it because he saw the clip and we read him the transcript. And then the next couple of days, it was one of those things that we both have experienced in the campaign that just doesn't go away. It was there for three or four days as the first question, the second question, the third question that we were getting.

RON BROWNSTEIN: Dan, can I bring you in here before we get in the Obama folks because, although he hadn't phrased it the same way, this was pretty much a staple of Paul Ryan's major economic speech—the idea that we were reaching a dangerous tipping point in the history of the country where a majority of the country would be dependent on government benefits. It was in his big AEI speech, his big Heritage speeches. This was something he said quite often, and I'm really wondering, as Mitt Romney was moving away from these comments, did the renunciation create any concern for Paul Ryan, who had made a similar argument for years?

DAN SENOR: It's a different argument. I don't want to get into it, but I think one of the problems with the 47 percent comment is it sounded like this was a pundit. So it sounded almost too analytical. So it wasn't just that the language was offensive to a lot of people, but it didn't sound like a president; it sounded like an analyst.

GLORIA BORGER: What's wrong with analysts?

DAN SENOR: Paul obviously had the same reaction we did to it, but he didn't feel that Mitt was moving away from some sort of economic philosophy that he had advocated.

GLORIA BORGER: Let me ask Neil, and then we'll go to the Obama folks: what happened to your internal numbers when you saw this, when the 47 percent became—as Gail points out—a three-day story, a four-day story?

RICH BEESON: We got bitter and started clinging to our guns. [*laughter*]

NEIL NEWHOUSE: We first saw it in the verbatims coming back. It was almost immediate. It had the effect of washing out the convention bump. But you saw it in the verbatims, and you saw the numbers. And the ballot test began to edge up hard a little bit, so this was a difficult time. It was a challenging time for us.

RON BROWNSTEIN: David, what was the effect of this on the race, particularly given the portrait that you are trying to paint? And then maybe Teddy can come in and talk a little bit about the effect in terms of activating the online community.

DAVID SIMAS: So first, on the qualitative side, we picked up within twenty-four hours. There were a couple of lines. The one that stuck out the most, and Neil probably heard it in the verbatims, was, "I don't have to be concerned with those people." And what we started hearing in the focus groups a lot was this kind of recognition of, "This is the story that I was hearing about this guy during the summer." So in some ways it was affirming or reaffirming the narrative. In the quantitative, in the polling, what we saw in both our aggregate battleground level polls and then within states, was probably about an increase of about 2 percent on the margin. When we took a look at who those folks were, it was interesting that people were not moving towards Obama. There was a peeling off from Governor Romney to undecided. And all of our analysis at that time, when we looked at who those people were, based on support scores that analytics was doing, was these voters are going to go back to Governor Romney at some point. So we always looked at the fact that we had gone from a three-and-a-half point lead to maybe four-and-a-half to five as, in realistic terms, kind of a temporary piece to this. But it was Republican-leaning Independents that we saw—white males, especially on the younger side—who weren't necessarily open to the president but were once again undecided. And so that was kind of the immediate research perspective that we saw.

STEPHANIE CUTTER: I know everybody in this room didn't believe us at the time, but we were saying, very publicly, that as this 2 percent moved away from Romney, that it wasn't necessarily ours, and the race was much closer than people thought at the time. And going into that debate, we did face a problem—coming out of the 47 percent and the conventions—of expectations. We didn't believe we were that far ahead. We thought the race was very close.

GLORIA BORGER: But this helped you?

STEPHANIE CUTTER: It certainly helped us, in terms of an overall narrative.

RON BROWNSTEIN: And so was this a galvanizing event for your organization and your base?

TEDDY GOFF: I think obviously it was galvanizing, but there's a degree to which, and I'm sure Zac will sympathize, the political purposes and the motivational purposes are sometimes aligned against each other. And to the extent that our people perceived that we were becoming the clear favorite in the race, that's not helpful. And that cost us money, and that cost us volunteers. So I think that it certainly helped burnish some of our folks' opinion of Governor Romney, but it wasn't helpful for us at all. I suspect you saw the same.

JEREMY BIRD: Yeah. I mean it wasn't as helpful in the sense that some of our folks did get a little bit, not necessarily complacent, but there was less urgency to come into the office the next morning when you feel like you are up by 7—and in a couple of states up by 4—as opposed to being a very close race. Although I do think that it was harder online than on the ground because of the way that we built our field program and the relationships that we had with folks, and that we treated every state differently. I don't think it ever really set in with our volunteers and certainly our staff, probably because of Jim and Axe's leadership and how they would talk about, "Do not let high polls at any time get you up or low polls get you down, because this race is going to be tight."

GLORIA BORGER: Well let me ask Zac about this. Did you see it, and was this demoralizing? These things can demoralize campaigns. You feel like you are kind of in a trough. Did you see that?

ZAC MOFFATT: I think, again, your core group—that's what is online— has the ultimate ability to scale and be flexible. You have people who kind of rally to the flag and come together. I think the challenge is it gives people opportunity, who didn't like you in the first place, internally—and I don't mean internally in the campaign but on the Republican side—to start to take shots and that makes it very difficult.

GLORIA BORGER: And that happened?

ZAC MOFFATT: That happens, and that makes it very difficult because that dominates the conversations on Twitter. It really kind of seeds conversations that spin out to these larger narratives that you are dealing with. It also gave us kind of the bigger catapult out of the first debate, which allowed us to make up almost all the ground that we had lost. You almost could see it. After that first debate, it was like you're on air for thirty-six hours. I mean everything was so simple because all this pent up energy just waiting to move from a campaign to a cause, and that was kind of the signal going off, I think, throughout.

GLORIA BORGER: So Matt, you wanted to talk about the digging out, and you talked about the piling on first, not only from the Democrats but also from Republicans. Peggy Noonan called the campaign the "rolling calamity," if I recall, and there was piling on and despair in the Republican Party. Ann Romney, you could see her frustration in her interviews. When people were talking to her, she said, "You go run a campaign and see how tough it is."

MATT RHOADES: Let's dig out of this. It's getting depressing. [*laughter*] First off, we had all staff meetings going back to the very day when it was a very tiny, small room. And whether the campaign staff listened to me or not, I can't speak to that, but we always warned everybody on our campaign that there was going to be highs and lows. Never get too high when things are going well; never get too low when things aren't going well. This obviously was the epitome of low during the course of the campaign. However, when you are on a campaign, you have to fight back, and you have to put a plan together, and you have to execute on it. So what we did is, we put together a basic, simple, five-point plan that we knew we had to execute on if we had any chance of coming back. That's how the governor solves problems. He gets people together. We had an opportunity late in September where the gov was back in Boston, we gathered some of our brightest minds together, and we laid out the plan and got people's input.

GLORIA BORGER: Which was?

MATT RHOADES: The first step of the plan was pretty simple: it was to have a good first debate. The second point of the plan was to really gin up our surrogate load because, to Zac's point, it was popular at the time to pile on the governor. So we had our loyal, best surrogates—whether it was folks like Governor John Sununu, who is sitting over there, whether it was Senator Marco Rubio, Governor Bob McDonell, Senator Kelly Ayotte, Governor Nikki Haley, or Senator Rob Portman. They went out in heavy doses and went out as surrogates and as people to speak to the governor's character all over the country. Third, and this goes to what I talked about before, whenever we went big it was good for Mitt Romney. So we knew we had to give some big speeches. We decided we needed to give three big speeches. Our goal was to give a big speech on national security. Our goal was to give another big speech on jobs and economy and expand on what the gov was going to do to turn around the economy. And third was to talk about deficits and entitlement reform. We felt if we were talking about big topics, big issues, it would force the media to talk about policy and ideas. Fourth, we knew coming out of the debates that we would have to take a look at potentially shifting resources to different target states, and we can talk about that a little bit later. And finally, we knew we needed to freshen up our events because—to the point that David made, or maybe it was Neil—some people at that moment thought that that moment in time was not very presidential. It was one of the tips that I got and what I heard often. And, again, I was at the campaign headquarters not at the events, so you're watching these events on TV. We had the gov up there walking around the stage before big, huge rallies, and he was always screaming. So when you watched the nightly news, you would have the president of the United States, who you guys had behind a podium with some notes, not a teleprompter, and we had the gov walking around at a rally feeling like he needed to get everyone—all the 5,000 people there—all riled up. It was a simple change, but it was important because it's all about the pictures. So we had, from that point on, the gov stand behind a podium and stick more to notes. So that was a five-point plan we felt that we could execute on and, even if it didn't work, it gave our campaign something to focus on and something to execute on.

GLORIA BORGER: So this was how long after the 47 percent? This sort of took a week or what was it?

MATT RHOADES: It was days after the 47 percent comment.

••• THE DENVER DEBATE •••

RON BROWNSTEIN: So as both Matt and David have suggested, the next big event in the campaign obviously is the first debate.

MATT RHOADES: Thank goodness. Let's start talking about that. [*laughter*]

RON BROWNSTEIN: Let me start by asking each side how they prepared for this debate and what goals you identified. What were you, above all, trying to achieve in this debate? We heard this morning that Governor

Rich Beeson, Zac Moffat, and Dan Senor listen to the Obama campaign's reaction to the first debate in Denver.

Romney wanted more and more preparation on debate time in the spring. Was it that way in the fall as well? How did you prepare? What were you trying to achieve at that first debate?

BETH MYERS: Well Mitt indeed wanted a lot of preparation. I think the words that he used at one point were, he wanted this to be "the Manhattan Project of our campaign."

GLORIA BORGER: When did he say that? Early on?

BETH MYERS: Oh, in the springtime. I looked at my notes. We had our first debate prep in June. We had, going to exactly what David said, anticipated in advance that in October there would be wall-to-wall coverage, that people would want to see it on the line. And we knew that there was a good chance that whatever was happening in the campaign, that we'd need a winning jolt. Mitt was very aware of that, and he wanted to make this a big project. The way he does that is he prepares. We planned to do three things with him: policy sessions, strategy sessions, and mock debates. We started the policy sessions in June. We would go about preparing deep dives that were different from the policy he'd seen in the primary. They had all of our policy, all of President Obama's policy, quotes from President Obama, quotes from Mitt Romney, and then what we called factoids and nuggets, which was just sort of interesting things about that topic that might get Mitt thinking about how he would want to answer this, how he would want to handle this. We would look at his schedule to see when we were going to take a cross-country trip. I would want our policy shop to deliver those things before the trip so that we could use this time to study because he always complained, as I'm sure President Obama did, that he didn't have enough time to look at the stuff that we prepared. We started, as I said, in June. We had a series of policy and strategy meetings, in June, July, and August.

RON BROWNSTEIN: Define what you mean by "strategy." Debate strategy?

BETH MYERS: Yeah. Those were led mostly by Stuart. The policy briefings were pretty much led by Lanhee Chen.[6] Stuart would lead the strategy meetings. The policy was a very small group: Lanhee and Stuart, me, sometimes Dan if we were doing foreign policy. And when we did the strategy, we expanded the group a little bit. And we had the

---

6. Lanhee Chen was the Romney campaign's policy director.

team here and some of our colleagues sitting over there, a larger group, and we would talk about, how do we want to approach this? We would bandy ideas about how do we attack President Obama's positions. Then the mock debates, of course, were somewhat different. We recruited Senator Portman to play President Obama, and he did it with aplomb and pretty much came loaded for bear every time. We didn't do any mock debates before the convention. His head wasn't in that game. But starting during the Dem Convention, we had what we called "debate camp" up in a house in Vermont, and we did five mock debates in three days. And then, for fun, at night we did white-board sessions. So it was a pretty intense time, and, all told, we did sixteen mock debates.

GLORIA BORGER: How was he? I mean, because he had spent a year debating.

BETH MYERS: Yeah. I mean that's an interesting point. We looked at that very different. The debates in the primary were really like candidate forums. They were nothing like what we did in preparing for our debates with President Obama. And what we also did before each debate, we created a series of goals. We'd synthesize, and then Stuart and I would meet with a couple other people at times and come up with a list of goals for each debate, and each of them were different. Stuart's mantra was always, "Mitt's got to stay loose. He's got to be relaxed. He's got to be comfortable." And the way he gets relaxed and loose and comfortable is being prepared. So we really knew we needed to prepare him and make him comfortable. It was a lot of time.

RON BROWNSTEIN: Stuart, was there a goal beyond the case that you were trying to make against President Obama or the case you were making for your own agenda? Was there kind of a portrait of the governor that you wanted to emerge from this, especially about him personally? Why was it important for him to be loose? What were you trying to convey about him through this, and how did that fit into your strategies you were preparing?

STUART STEVENS: That's a good question. I think everybody that spends time with the governor—and some people in this room spent a lot of time with the governor—and I think the reporters saw, I think it probably happens with every campaign, well, if only you could see the real Mitt Romney. He's very funny and very positive. He's someone who people are drawn to, and we wanted to capture some of that, a sense of bigness. He's a big guy. And part of the process in that primary debates, when you have eight or nine people up there, it seems to reduce you in stature. And so, as David has spoken to, there is something about standing on stage as a president that automatically benefits the challenger, and you wanted to like this person. It's tricky because most times the person who is most aggressive in a debate wins. So it has to be a balance, and you kind of never know what will happen.

GLORIA BORGER: And Romney had had problems with his favorable/unfavorable ratings, so that was always an issue you guys were thinking about.

BETH MYERS: One other thing. On every issue, one of the things that was also very different from the primary is that we were very focused on finding an attack—a place to attack President Obama on every issue. We didn't do that in the primary but in the general election, that's what we did so that when Mitt came on that stage at the first debate, he was loaded for bear on every issue.

RON BROWNSTEIN: Let's talk about the president's sixteen mock debates now, David. [*laughter*]

DAVID AXELROD: I just got an e-mail from Messina, saying, "Call me when the debate discussion is over." [*laughter*]

RON BROWNSTEIN: What were your goals going in?

DAVID AXELROD: Well our goal? Simas mentioned that we had this inflated lead, and we wanted to erase that in one night, bring expectations down. I would say we were rather effective. [*laughter*] I always had circled on the calendar this date as a potential problem for us just because of history. History has been very clear on this. Very rarely does a president escape this first debate.

GLORIA BORGER: Did you tell him that?

DAVID AXELROD: Yeah, and by the way, he had voluminous materials that are probably not unlike the ones you prepared, and he would read them also on cross-country flights. And I really believe actually we gave him too much material, which also I think is a mistake that's been repeated in history over time. You can overprepare in that regard. But yeah, we had that discussion, and I talked to Mark McKinnon about the Bush debates in 2004. Stuart, you may have been around for that. Mark said exactly what we experienced. Presidents, first of all, no one has been in their grill like that for four years, right? We had twenty-eight primary debates, I think—most of them with then-Senator Clinton, who was quite a sparring partner. And then-Senator Obama was sort of in game shape by the time we got to these debates, so it was a simpler task. To be honest with you, Senator McCain was not the debater that Mitt Romney is. And we had respect for Romney as a debater, even though you're quite right, Beth, that the primary debates were much different. They were much different. Particularly since we got down to one-on-one debates. You never had one-on-one debates. But primarily, even in that setting, when he needed to do something—you guys had your backs against the wall in Florida, and he executed—every single time he had to execute, he did. We also studied the debates with Ted Kennedy back in 1994. I mean it was clear that he was going to be prepared, that he'd have a strategy, and that he would execute on that strategy. So presidents aren't used to this, and there is sort of a why do I have to do this attitude, even if it's not articulated. I mean the president showed up for all the prep, read everything we asked him to read. But in a sense, it's almost as if he showed up for a discussion, and they showed up for a debate, which is largely a performance. You've got allotments of time on given subjects, and you need to know what you are going to say. I would venture to say that these guys knew, when they heard the questions, what Governor Romney was going to say in answer to those questions. And that's how you know that you are well prepared.

GLORIA BORGER: And you didn't?

DAVID AXELROD: In that first debate, I would say we didn't. I put this on us. I mean we learned a lot from the first one.

RON BROWNSTEIN: What were the strategic goals going into the debate?

DAVID AXELROD: The strategic goal was to burnish our message—you know, the über-economic message of middle-class economics versus top-down economics.

RON BROWNSTEIN: And yet, as you say that, he did not repeat at the debate the most common attacks that you had been making on Romney. Was there any explicit desire to be above the fray? Was there a feeling that if you really engaged with Romney, it would somehow be diminishing as a president?

DAVID AXELROD: Well there was a concern that engaging in the wrong way could be diminishing. Angry exchanges are not helpful exchanges. So there was a concern on that, and I think those discussions probably were counterproductive. We have a superb debate team. Ron Klain is as good as there is. But I think we made adjustments between the first and second debate based on our experience.

GLORIA BORGER: To Stuart's point though, just by appearing on the stage with the president, Mitt Romney becomes elevated.

DAVID AXELROD: Absolutely.

GLORIA BORGER: Did you have a sense that you could disqualify him in any way from that characterization in the first debate? Was that part of your goal?

DAVID AXELROD: Well I think that part of that, you just have to concede. Just the act of standing on that stage, it's an elevating deal. Now the two guys are on an equal plane. Yeah, we obviously had a strategy for engaging on elements of these issues where we felt he had vulnerability and where we felt we had strength, but I do think we were a little phobic about engagement. We gave that instruction to the president, and I think that was not helpful.

GLORIA BORGER: What's the instruction?

DAVID AXELROD: Well don't get into a brawl.

RON BROWNSTEIN: So our two leading characters are about to step onto the stage in Denver.

GLORIA BORGER: Frank, do you want to talk to us a little bit, just tee up the debates?[7] We know that the debate commission spent a long time thinking about the format of these, and this year was different from previous years. Less involvement by the campaign?

FRANK FAHRENKOPF: No involvement by the campaign.

GLORIA BORGER: And tell us why.

FRANK FAHRENKOPF: Well we've been at this now for twenty-five years, and we really have trouble getting candidates to debate. I mean the debates for many years were nothing more than, in our view, glorified press conferences where we had rules that said a question would be

---

7. Frank Fahrenkopf is cochairman of the Commission on Presidential Debates.

aimed at a particular participant, they would have two minutes to respond, the opponent would have one minute to respond to them and then thirty seconds to have a counterpresentation. And then we were to move on to another subject. So really, at the behest of former Senator Jack Danforth of Missouri, who has been a member of the Commission for many, many years, we sat down early in 2012, as we do between every cycle, to determine how could we improve the debate process and how could we actually get the candidates to debate? You may remember that in 2008—I don't remember what the question was, but—Senator McCain answered the question, was looking at Jim Lehrer and Jim Lehrer said, "Senator, tell him," pointing to Senator Obama. And Senator McCain did not look at Senator Obama and wouldn't reply. So the Commission spent a couple of days figuring out how we could make these debates more like debates and with the ability to drill down on subject matter. And that's when we came up with the concept of dividing the first and last debate into these six pods of fifteen minutes long. To be candid, I think we did a disservice to Jim Lehrer on the first debate. I don't think the Commission did its job in explaining the change that was going to take place in the debate. Jim took a lot of hits afterwards. Why did they let them go so long? Our basic instruction to Jim was—and to Bob Schieffer on the last one—if they are debating, let them debate. Don't interrupt. Let them go at each other. Now, some people said, "Well he should have interrupted and maybe moved to another subject," but we felt the first and last debates accomplished our purpose and that there was real debate between the candidates on the issues that were important. We think that the same took place in the other two debates.

The only changes that we made that were requested by the campaigns is that we wanted to do all the debates with the candidates seated at a table. We did a lot of study over twenty-five years, and we think that the nature and tenor of discourse changes when you are seated at a table, rather than standing behind a podium. And Bob Bauer, who was representing the president, and Ben Ginsberg, who was representing the governor's campaign, said we would like to do one with the podium. So we said, "Fine. We're not going to argue about those things around the edges, so long as the basic guts of the debates are not tampered with." And we think it was the most successful series of debates that we've had since we've been in existence.

RON BROWNSTEIN: It was certainly among the greatest effect on a race that we have seen from a single debate. So let's start. Let's go to Denver. And I think in many ways the question people may be most wondering in this campaign was, what happened to the president at the first debate? What explained that performance? To what extent was it an outcome of the goals and preparation going in? What happened?

DAVID AXELROD: I thought we covered this. [*laughter*] I mean what happened was he showed up for a discussion, and Governor Romney showed up very well prepared to deliver the kind of performance the debates require. Governor Romney did some, in our view, significant repositioning in the debate, and that was a little jarring to the president. But, by and large, he showed up for a discussion.

GLORIA BORGER: What do you mean by repositioning?

DAVID AXELROD: What do you think I mean?

GLORIA BORGER: Well you tell me. [*laughter*]

DAVID AXELROD: I mean, you know, the first answer, the "I don't have a $5 trillion tax plan" and very, I thought, effectively, sort of looking at the president as if he were nuts. "A $5 trillion tax plan? What are you talking about?" You asked me why, and I think it's a combination of things. I think it is incumbent disease for that first debate. I actually think and, Frank, you may remember this, after the first debate, Ronald Reagan lost maybe ten points against Walter Mondale. Ronald Reagan was a pretty fair debater. So this isn't a new effect. We had hoped to counter it, but sometimes you just need to take the punch in order to focus in the way that you need to focus.

GLORIA BORGER: He didn't bring up the 47 percent. He didn't bring up Bain Capital, the tax returns?

[*Editor's Note*: At this point in our program there was a citywide power outage in Cambridge, Massachusetts. The remainder of this session was recorded by staff and participants with smartphones. You will notice that we could not identify with 100 percent certainty a few of the participants who made comments that are included in this transcript.]

DAVID AXELROD: As I said, I take some responsibility. I'm happy to take all of it. But we had a strategy of limited engagement that we took to an illogical extreme.

RON BROWNSTEIN: So you explicitly decided not to raise Bain?

Observers take notes by the light of their computer screens during a citywide power outage.

DAVID AXELROD: What we assumed was that these guys having practiced for as long and as hard as they had, had an answer prepared. And we just felt like we were going to lead into something that might not be productive.

RON BROWNSTEIN: So you did not want to give them the opportunity to respond to either the 47 percent or Bain, and that's why you didn't raise them?

DAVID AXELROD: Yeah, because we felt that it would lead to sort of vituperative exchange.

GLORIA BORGER: Even taxes?

DAVID AXELROD: Well on taxes, there were a lot of opportunities to which we could have responded. When Governor Romney said, "I didn't know about that tax break for companies that moved jobs to overseas. I may need better accountants." With all due respect, I don't think that's the thing he needs.

GLORIA BORGER: Right, exactly.

DAVID AXELROD: So there were answers that we could have given, but they would have been more personal in nature. And if there was a preparation problem, it was on that strategic level.

GLORIA BORGER: So let's ask the Romney camp, which was sort of in the trough there. Beth, you had been so involved in the preparation here. Describe watching this.

BETH MYERS: We were feeling good. The first five minutes, ten minutes, twenty minutes went by, and I kept getting nervous that it couldn't keep going on, that we'd have a really good first half and bad second half. But there's a couple of pictures of me hugging Stuart enthusiastically, and we felt very good backstage. One of our goals in the first debate was to make this a conversation—the first of a three-part conversation. So even while our debate was going well that night, we were very cognizant that we had two more conversations. So we were happy that it went well for us. It got us back in the game. I think if it had gone differently, it would have been a very different race in October.

RON BROWNSTEIN: Was there a sense of that in the campaign, that this was an absolutely must moment? In fact, there was a lot of press commentary going in, that if the president had a good debate, he could almost win the race.

MATT RHOADES: We talked about it more as the response to the 47 percent. Our first goal was to have a good debate.

GLORIA BORGER: Could you tell from your interactions with the governor how much more pressure he felt because of the 47 percent going into this first debate? Did he talk about it when you had your meeting after the 47 percent problem, predebate?

MATT RHOADES: He's always been a candidate that does better when things are on the line and there's more pressure. This is why he excelled during the primary process when it was a must-win situation. When it's on the line, he is very good. As the campaign manager, I don't like that, but he performs at a higher level. He's like a quarterback that has three bad quarters, and then all of a sudden you hit the two minute drill and he knows how to throw the touchdown pass. So obviously there was a tremendous amount of pressure on him, but I never felt that that would impact his ability to do what he needed to do in the first debate because he had a track record of doing it.

RON BROWNSTEIN: Coming out of the debate, what was his reaction?

MATT RHOADES: I was chained to my desk.

BETH MYERS: He was very happy. I think he knew coming off the debate that it had gone well. I'm not sure he had a sense of how well it had gone, but I think he got a sense as he walked backstage and saw us all very happy.

STUART STEVENS: He went to an event in Virginia the next day with Ed Gillespie.[8] Ed's not here today, but he was invaluable. He was a tremendous asset, a brilliant, wonderful guy. And we were driving to this event, and there was this massive traffic jam on the interstate. We thought that there had been an accident or something. We came to realize it was people coming to this event. They had, after the debate, you know, you have these things ticketed, and it had exploded in the number of people who were planning to come to this event. The traffic jam went fifteen miles to get to this event in the middle of nowhere in Virginia.

RON BROWNSTEIN: The famous story after the debate was no Democrats in the spin room for quite a while after that first debate.

GLORIA BORGER: Long conference calls.

RON BROWNSTEIN: What was going on?

DAVID AXELROD: At every debate we always started a conference call about fifteen minutes before the end of the debate so that we weren't having longtime conference calls after the debate.

GLORIA BORGER: Jim Messina said that Mitt Romney could have won the presidency after that debate, that he had a sense. Could you guys talk about that?

DAVID AXELROD: Since he's not here, I'm going to disagree with him. Here's what happened, and David, you can speak to this as was referenced earlier: I think what he did was, in one night, he got back those

---

8. Ed Gillespie was a senior advisor to the Romney campaign.

Republican-leaning Independents. I think he improved enthusiasm among his base. I think the race snapped back to where it was essentially before the conventions. That was my impression. But as I said earlier, in our own data we were never trailing in the race. Look, the president obviously didn't perform well in that debate. On substance, he performed a little better than the performance elements of it. What we saw in our own data was his numbers really didn't suffer, but Romney's numbers definitely improved. And so, no, I didn't feel that way. The thing that it did do, Zac talked earlier about after the 47 percent tape, all the helpful advice that these guys were getting from members of their own party, this was our turn in the barrel. Everybody was very generous with their advice for us. [*laughter*]

GLORIA BORGER: And what was the president's reaction? We heard about Mitt Romney after the 47 percent mistake. Can you tell us a little bit about the president's reaction to his own performance?

DAVID AXELROD: Well just as Governor Romney didn't know how well he had done, I don't think the president knew that it was as negative as it turned out to be. I was in the spin room. By the time I talked to him, he had read some of the coverage and said, "Consensus seems to be we didn't have a very good night." And I didn't try and disabuse him of that.

RON BROWNSTEIN: So you have several days of campaigning in between, but the next big event is the vice presidential debate.

DAVID AXELROD: Well actually, the next big event was the next event we had, which was the next day. And it was absolutely essential that he come out tough and energetic in that event and he did.

RON BROWNSTEIN: Maybe we should talk for a minute about that kind of period immediately after the debate. You said you believed you were still ahead. To what degree did you believe the debate did in fact restart the race? What did you have to do differently after the debate than you did the morning before the debate? Were your imperatives any different after the debate than they were before?

DAVID SIMAS: What we saw after twenty-four hours was a consolidation back to Governor Romney. It accelerated in the second twenty-four-hour period. So at this point we were looking to see where the floor is from us. What we saw is, by the third day, as David said, the race had settled back to preconvention levels. When we analyzed who it was that moved, it was precisely those voters from our perspective who had peeled off during the 47, so that's on the quantitative side. The qualitative was really interesting and it set the dynamic for the second and third debate. In terms of Governor Romney, we heard voters saying, "You know what, he looked presidential. He didn't seem like the guy either that we saw or heard in the 47 percent video or that we had seen over the summer. I will give him another look." Undecided voters and this is what we were hearing them say: "Not that I am sold, but I am once again open to giving him review." When it came to the discussion on the president, as Axe said, people were chalking it up to basically having a bad day. Now, that made the imperative of not having a second bad day that much more important. So in the qualitative, it opened up the door for Governor Romney. It corrected with a whole bunch of voters the problem that he had. And to the point that Stuart made about the Virginia rally, for the first time we saw his very favorable numbers among the Republicans rivaling numbers that we had seen in 2008.

GLORIA BORGER: So Neil, were you seeing the same thing?

RON BROWNSTEIN: Do you agree that the debate only affected Mitt Romney's image positively and that it had no negative effect on the president's?

NEIL NEWHOUSE: No, I don't. Let me back up for a second. Actually very close to what the Obama team is saying, these voters saw Mitt Romney, and they watched the debate. They're impressed. I would kind of off-handedly say that they didn't see him outsource a single job; he didn't close down a single business; he didn't lay off a single worker. And the image that had been portrayed of him, painted of him, had begun to kind of wash away a little bit. So then, in all the verbatim comments we got after that, 47 percent kind of went away. Now, it didn't go away completely, but it went away from the verbatims. Keep in mind this was the longest period of time between the first presidential debate and the second presidential debate since 1988: thirteen days. The entire verbatim comments over the next two weeks were all about the debate. And it was all good for us. It gave us perceived momentum. Not just that our numbers were moving—there was initial movement but it didn't really continue to move significantly—but we began to see some erosion and some softening of Obama support. The information flow numbers, everything, began to kind of trend our way a little bit so that you got a sense there was wind at our back.

RON BROWNSTEIN: How did it affect the president's image?

NEIL NEWHOUSE: It actually didn't affect his image all that much, maybe a point. But it didn't do much to the president's image. He came down just a little on the ballot. It's more of what it did for Mitt Romney.

••• THE VICE PRESIDENTIAL DEBATE •••

GLORIA BORGER: So, Dan, now we're trying to move along to the vice presidential debate. Obviously some pressure on Joe Biden, but also some pressure on the junior partner.

DAN SENOR: Yeah, the primary question for us was readiness. We weren't going to win this thing on the vice presidential debate. It could do real damage if we didn't pass the readiness test. That was where we were most vulnerable, more vulnerable than anything going into the debate. And you watch a lot of these Biden debates over the years, as I've watched one or two of them when I've come home. A day off the campaign, my wife would say, "It's very nice of you to be home, but did you have to bring Joe Biden?" [*laughter*] We would watch hours and hours of tape. If you go back over, like, two decades—during the lead up to the debate, this sounded like spin, setting expectations—but the truth is he does whatever he needs to do in just every debate he does. And actually Ryan, the only debate he watched of Biden was the 2008 Palin debate. He said, "Look how respectful he is." And you know, he did exactly what he needed to do in that debate. And our sense was he was going to have a much different approach to dealing with Ryan. So Ted Olson, who played Biden for the vast majority of our mock sessions, he played crazy Uncle Joe. I mean, screaming, yelling, interrupting. He didn't do the laughing, but he did about as close to it. It wasn't like Senate Judiciary Committee Joe Biden. We watched a lot of that too and that was very, you know, focused and prosecutorial. Olson did mostly sort of the crazy uncle. I remember Russ and I were talking the day before the debate, "You know, it's great that he has done the crazy uncle, but what if he shows up very serious and just sort of prosecutes?" Turns out he was even more of the crazy uncle than Ted Olson had done in the mock sessions. The challenge for Paul was that he can't get drawn into that. I mean it's one thing for someone like Joe Biden, with his experience and his stature, to do that and he can get away with it, but a forty-two-year-old congressman can't get away with that. And so if Biden had gotten into that zone, there is no way you're going to win just trying to engage him back and forth. If Biden is doing the constant interruptions, just sort of walk in and almost operate like you're doing an interview with Martha Raddatz and just go one-on-one and hold your own and pass the readiness test. The other challenge in all this was that, you know, he's not the only VP nominee who has had to do this but, he also had to be able to defend his own record, the Ryan record. And he hadn't had a real tough congressional campaign debate since his first run in 1998. He had to be able to defend his own record. He had to defend the Romney record. There was a lot of stuff he had to defend— Bain Capital and Massachusetts—and obviously prosecute the case against Obama and Biden.

RON BROWNSTEIN: Stephanie, one of the reactions to the first debate you would hear, as a journalist interviewing voters, would be, "The president didn't seem to have any energy or passion or drive to defend his agenda or seem to have any energy or passion or drive for what he was going to do his second term." As Dan was saying, Biden gave you plenty of passion and energy. Was he encouraged to simply be forceful above all, to respond to that kind of sense that the president seemed without those qualities?

STEPHANIE CUTTER: Axe can answer this better than I can, but I don't think there was any big alteration to the preparation of the vice president. A lot of that was just the vice president. We were pleased with that debate because there was criticism that the president hadn't forcefully defended everything he'd accomplished or looked like he wanted to fight for the job. Obviously the vice president swung the other way. But in terms of his preparation, I don't think there was a big strategic change.

DAVID AXELROD: I would say that we felt that there was a little bit more of an imperative to be aggressive and to aggressively both defend and go on the offense. Let me just say one thing parenthetically about Denver though, and then I'll get back to this. And Bird, you may want to talk about this: One of the counterintuitive impacts of the Denver debate was that the complacency that people felt about the election disappeared, this notion that Teddy had seen that somehow this thing was done. That went away overnight, and we had a huge bump in volunteer activity after that debate. So that was the upside of the downside.

••• THE SECOND DEBATE •••

RON BROWNSTEIN: That imperative you talked about for Biden certainly carried over to the second debate for the president, where his tone was very different. So what was your calculation then? I mean, you said going into the first debate you were worried about basically seeming unpresidential by mixing it up too much. That concern seemed to have pretty much evaporated by the time he got on the second stage.

DAN SENOR: Can I ask one question? It's a question that I've had for a long time, the laughing thing.

GLORIA BORGER: Yeah, that's what I wanted to ask.

DAN SENOR: Because we were watching it, we were like, is this the plan? We didn't know if it was sort of Biden being Biden or was this actually like, in mock sessions, the laughing was part of the planned performance.

DAVID AXELROD: Well there was some of that in the prep. I think he maybe was a little more amused than he expected to be. [*laughter*]

GLORIA BORGER: Can I just ask one more question about that? This can be on the president and the vice presidential debate—the split screen, which magnifies every facial expression. It seemed to me that both Mitt Romney had sort of a practiced pose and the president tried to find his in the first debate.

DAVID AXELROD: Romney handled it perfectly. He was well prepared for it. The president we prepared for it. But, you know, obviously the split screen worked against us in that debate, and these guys were pretty artful about using that tape after, for good reason. So, you know, we were even more rigorous in preparing for the subsequent debates. Now, the second debate was a Town Hall debate, so it's somewhat different. But we spent a lot more time on the whole reaction shot thing and the notion that you are going to be on camera all the time.

STUART STEVENS: I think one of the difficulties that the Obama campaign had in that first debate is the sort of blood lust on the part of his supporters—that they wanted the president to go out and bash Mitt Romney. I think they were smart. I think that would have been a mistake for the president of the United States.

RON BROWNSTEIN: But he did echo a lot more of that language in the second debate. He was much tougher in the second debate. He raised more of the economic arguments. I remember there was one answer about the auto industry where he managed to get in Bain very quickly. He got in Planned Parenthood repeatedly before he was asked. So obviously you made a very different calculation by the time of that second debate. Talk about that.

DAVID AXELROD: Well to Stuart's point, it was still modulated.

RON BROWNSTEIN: Well there was no physical violence. [*laughter*]

DAVID AXELROD: Although there were moments.

RON BROWNSTEIN: But you did tone it up quite a bit.

DAVID AXELROD: First of all, let me say the Town Hall formats were useful to us because it was something that he felt comfortable with. There were other people who you could speak to. You know, you could move around. It was more difficult in certain ways, the choreography, but it was also greater opportunity. But basically, as I said earlier, he came to the first debate treating it as some sort of discussion, and the second debate he focused much more on, "If this comes up, these are the points I want to make. If this comes up, these are the points I want to make." A lot of the language that he used in that debate was language that emerged from him during the course of those prepping, you know, one question after another.

GLORIA BORGER: Let me ask Matt and Beth this, and Neil can chime in. So we get through the next two debates, and how did you feel in terms of the playing field? The consensus, I think, was the president did very well in the second and the third debates. Mitt Romney held his own. How did you feel, with the debates over, heading into the next part of the election? Did you feel you had sort of stabilized? Did you feel you had stopped the bleeding?

MATT RHOADES: Definitely. There was a sense that we had, you know—I don't know if the word is "stabilized" or "picked up a little bit of momentum"—but obviously we were on a positive information flow trajectory, and that's what Neil was talking about. And so we, as a campaign, went back to the plan that we had laid out and started to execute on the various points of it.

••• THE FOREIGN POLICY DEBATE •••

RON BROWNSTEIN: Maybe just to clarify one point on that for you. In that third debate, Mitt Romney was the opposite of the first. He was extremely nonconfrontational to the point of not repeating again many of the criticisms that he had earlier made of the president's foreign policy. What were you hoping to achieve in that debate? Did you think basically you were ahead and all you had to do was get through it? Or, why was he taking a less confrontational pose in that third debate?

BETH MYERS: Stuart, do you want to take that? We gave that a lot of thought in our strategy, and actually he was executing on strategy.

STUART STEVENS: Look, 70 percent of the public cared about foreign policy, our polling showed. That was really a test of, are you comfortable with this person's demeanor as president? It was not to prosecute the president on foreign policy. It was to get people to, if Mitt Romney were my president, would I be comfortable with this person? What's his judgment? How does he go about making a decision? It was clear that they were going to attempt to paint a picture of him as being someone who was bellicose. And it was not a Foreign Service exam.

GLORIA BORGER: But there were Republicans who criticized you guys for not attacking—

STUART STEVENS: You can say that about any moment, about any attack. [*laughter*]

GLORIA BORGER: But particularly in the foreign policy debate, on Benghazi.

STUART STEVENS: It was a moment where we agreed completely with the problems the president had with Benghazi. This was not a Sunday show. The goal of the debate was a different moment and a different risk and a different opportunity.

RON BROWNSTEIN: The goal of the debate was to improve perceptions about the governor on foreign policy, not to diminish them about the president.

STUART STEVENS: You wanted to see someone who is going to be a strong leader, and he came across as such—someone who you're comfortable with their judgment when they are sitting in the Oval Office.

NEIL NEWHOUSE: The bigger picture is we came out of the debates much stronger than we went into the debates. And that's really a critical point, in terms of image, in terms of favorability, in terms of ballot. And in the battleground states across the country, we were doing much better. And we felt we were in a pretty good position coming out of those debates. We did what we wanted to do. Mitt delivered. As Matt was saying, in big moments, he came through. He delivered. And he delivered in those debates.

DAVID AXELROD: Let me just say one thing about this because it's really interesting to me. People don't get to be the nominee of their party, and get through this process, by accident. And that's a quality that these guys are describing that you have to have if you're going to get there. And both of these guys had it. We prepped differently for the second debate. Obviously there was a lot of tension around the second debate. The president said to David Plouffe and myself going into the second debate, "We prepped well, and I feel good. We're going to have a good night." And we left and I said to Plouffe, "You know, you don't get to be president by accident. You get to be President because at those big-money times, you come through." And I think you're hearing this on the other side as well. You know, you have to have that quality, and both of them were called under the course of these debates to show that quality where each of us, to some degree, had our backs against the wall, and the candidates performed.

••• THE PATH TO 270 •••

RON BROWNSTEIN: So we're out of the debates. We're now into the reality of somebody's got to get 270 Electoral College votes. There is a sense frequently argued by the Obama campaign that they have many more pathways to get to 270. They have a Rust Belt path. They have a Sun Belt path. Rich, let me start with you. As you get down to mid-October, to what extent did you feel that you needed to, in effect, thread the needle to get to 270? How much was available to you and, as Matt alluded to before, where were you starting to think that you might have to shift away from in order to concentrate your resources?

RICH BEESON: Getting back to Axe's favorite subject, after that first debate, it's almost a distinction without a difference—and Jeremy probably saw this as well in some cases—we went from people wanting to beat President Obama to people who wanted to elect Governor Romney. Our victory centers filled up. Our phones filled up. Our doors filled up. That first debate really kicked it off. We saw numbers slide pretty dramatically on the volunteer side. As far as the path, we always conceded that they had a wider path to 270 than we did. It was just a matter of there were certain states that we needed to win, and then we could pick from one of several. But as you looked, Nevada was always going to be a tough sled for us. But as it turned out, since President Obama didn't take public financing in 2008, this was the first time both campaigns were being able to run without public financing. So it didn't become a resource issue.

RON BROWNSTEIN: When you're two, three weeks out, did you sit down and say, "Okay this is our most likely path," and, if so, can you share what that was?

GLORIA BORGER: We all heard the three, two, one plan early on.[9]

RON BROWNSTEIN: What were you looking at, at that point? As you point out, Nevada was looking tough. What was looking to you like the way you were going to get there, and did it have to run through Ohio?

RICH BEESON: Well, I mean, it didn't have to, but it made it a heck of a lot easier. Inside we called it "climbing the back side of Everest," if we didn't have Ohio. But again, it was always Florida, North Carolina, Virginia, and Ohio, and then you pick from the buffet of New Hampshire, Wisconsin. I knew Wisconsin, being a same-day registration state, was going to be tough. We saw what they did on same-day registration in New Hampshire. It was epic, as the kids say these days. And I always liked Colorado. I liked our absentee early vote numbers. The path was always those states and then picking something else.

MEMBER OF THE ROMNEY TEAM: We never once considered that Ohio was not part of our plan.

GLORIA BORGER: So you never thought you could really do it without Ohio?

---

9. In May 2012 Karl Rove wrote that Romney can get to 270 electoral votes with a "3-2-1" strategy, that was 3 = Indiana, North Carolina, Virginia (states Obama flipped that have historically gone Republican), 2 = Ohio and Florida, and 1 = one more state from the following: Colorado, Nevada, New Mexico, Michigan, Pennsylvania, Wisconsin, or New Hampshire.

STUART STEVENS: We always thought we had a good shot, which we did. It was very close.

••• GETTING OUT THE VOTE •••

GLORIA BORGER: Rich, let me ask you this. We talked earlier in the day about Get Out the Vote and the extensive amount of money and effort that the Obama campaign put into that early on while you guys were fighting a primary for a year. How often did you run into them and their extraordinary effort and say, "You know what, we may be outgunned here in Ohio"?

RICH BEESON: That's the key point. And that's where I want to make sure we give them credit. We didn't see them out on the doors and the places where we were. Because we were out there knocking on Independents and the low-propensity, high-support type folks that we could get. We weren't seeing them out on the doors, and I couldn't figure it out. All we ever heard was how many staff and how many offices they had. And yet, in Neil's polling and our internal stuff, we saw that the

Obama's senior staff reflect on what worked—and what didn't—in the general election.

number of contacts were roughly equal. And so they were talking to different people. We were concentrating, you know, we said if we could win Independents in Ohio, we're going to win Ohio. And they took a different route. That's why it was so perplexing to me that all of the intel that we got from the field, we'd see them occasionally out on the doors but not in the same places.

RON BROWNSTEIN Jeremy, will you talk about what was going on, mid-to-late October now, in these battleground states? What's happening on the ground?

JEREMY BIRD: Sure. Well you know, at this point we had been on the ground for a year plus in a place like Ohio. And look, when reporters ask, "Have you seen the other side on the ground?," no, you never see the other side on the ground. And that's not because we weren't talking to Independents in Ohio and knocking on their doors. We had multiple paths to the states. At this point, registration is over in most states except for the same-day registration states. So we had two things to do at that point: turn out our folks, especially in places with early vote which we had a huge emphasis on, and then get the remaining persuadables. And there were obviously very few left. I think we were doing what we needed to do and you saw Rick Wiley[10] tweet about 7,000 doors being knocked on the weekend before the election, maybe it was the week before, I can't remember exactly. That day, we knocked on 370,000 doors in Ohio. And we had more time to do it. We had more resources. We had a ton of organizers on the ground who had been out for a long time recruiting these volunteers. We had a big head start and a lot of time and a lot of money while these guys were in the primary. And so we were building and we were executing at that point. There were a very small number of persuadable voters we still needed to talk to multiple times, and then the rest was all about GOTV and early vote. That's what we were focused on.

GLORIA BORGER: Can I ask an Ohio-specific question to the Romney team, which is the Jeep ad which became so controversial about outsourcing to China?[11]

---

10. Rick Wiley was the RNC's political director.
11. In October 2012 Romney ran an ad in Ohio arguing that he would be better for the auto industry than Obama. The announcer says, "Obama took GM and Chrysler into bankruptcy and sold Chrysler to Italians who are going to build Jeeps in China. Mitt Romney will fight for every American job."

STUART STEVENS: I'll speak to that. Look, we think that ad helped us and the numbers back us up. I know that there's two ways to look at this. One is it brought up the subject, which is a difficult subject for Romney. The other is it provided people the information that reassured them and reduced the impact to the advertising that had been against Romney. But if you look in those markets, we did better in those markets for having run that.

RON BROWNSTEIN: Jim, what was your interpretation of the effect of that ad?

JIM MARGOLIS: I think we have a different interpretation. [*laughter*]

DAVID AXELROD: No, we have the same. We think it helped us too. [*laughter*]

JIM MARGOLIS: I think our view was that it reinforced very clearly the kind of message that was critical in Ohio in terms of auto and what the president's record had been, and that this was something that—both in the earned media and our ability to come back in paid media and have that be part of the closing conversation—it was something that was very helpful to us. I wanted to ask one question though. One of the things we had to do was sort of put aside some money in case you all went to any number of different states that we ultimately could push over and go into some of the other states, like Florida, at the end. Did you ever consider going earlier to, whether it was a Pennsylvania or Minnesota or some of the other states, in a more concerted way, or was the decision really one that you just sort of reserved to the end?

MEMBER OF THE ROMNEY TEAM: We reserved that decision to the end. Many of us believed, you know, Pennsylvania was similar to what our strategy was in Iowa, to always keep our options open. And it just seemed that traditionally Republicans had chased shiny objects, in this case being Pennsylvania. So we were always of the mindset that we would make the decision late. If we had resources and it looked like, you know, we could "rush the net,"—is what we said inside the campaign at the end—we would take a stab at it and try to make a final expansion.

RON BROWNSTEIN: Was the decision to go into Pennsylvania at all a reflection that you concluded you were not going to win in Ohio?

MEMBER OF THE ROMNEY TEAM: No, no, no. In Pennsylvania, 96 percent of the vote was on Election Day. So we weren't in the same early absentee hold as we were in some of these other places.

NEIL NEWHOUSE: We had seen data after data in this state, polling down by 3 percent in the state; nobody was playing there. Our super PAC buddies are getting interested. They're going on the air there. It looked like, with maybe a week, week-and-a-half to go, it might be a state that we could kind of steal.

RUSS SCHRIEFER: And to go to a point that these guys made earlier, you couldn't buy any more time. You couldn't buy any more time in Ohio. You couldn't buy any more time in Florida. I mean, it was just maxing out. So we weren't taking away any resources away from any other state; we just had the resources and were able to ship them into other states.

RON BROWNSTEIN: By saying "rush the net," I wondered whether you chose not to go into these states earlier, in part, because they would have then responded by kind of pulverizing you with the same attacks they were using in Ohio and Wisconsin. Was Pennsylvania and Minnesota attractive at all because that had not happened there?

MEMBER OF THE ROMNEY TEAM: It was relative virgin territory.

MEMBER OF THE ROMNEY TEAM: There was a freshness to it. I mean there was some logic there.

GLORIA BORGER: I have to ask one question to both campaigns. For those of us who covered them, it was like living in alternate universes at the end of the campaign. Neil, your late polling was showing you up in a bunch of states. They were saying, "There is no way. This is crazy." So I want to know, and I'll go to Neil first on this, did you think you were going to win on Election Day?

NEIL NEWHOUSE: I'm always kind of a pessimist on campaigns, but I was cautiously optimistic. Here is what we saw in the data that's really interesting. You've got to give credit to the Obama campaign for kind of undercutting it. We saw, throughout the last few weeks of the campaign, an intensity advantage, a campaign interest advantage, and an enthusiasm advantage for Republicans who were for Mitt Romney. The higher interest voters were voting for Romney—voters who were more enthusiastic, all these different measures—just the same as we saw four years ago on behalf of President Obama who was running against John

McCain. We thought that that had the potential to tilt the partisan make-up of the electorate a couple of points in our direction. So instead of being a minus six or minus seven in terms of Democratic versus Republican, it would be minus three. And so we weren't surprised at the racial composition, the ethnic composition of the electorate. We were surprised at the partisan composition.

RON BROWNSTEIN: The two are related, aren't they?

NEIL NEWHOUSE: They are related. But then you look at the real hidden story here from our side—because when you lose you nitpick the numbers as you go through this stuff—the number of white men who didn't vote in this election compared to white women compared to four years ago is extraordinary. I mean, it's something like 286,000 white men who voted in '08 in Ohio didn't vote in '12. And in Florida something like 400,000. And these white men were replaced by white women. We were taking a group where we won by 27 points and replacing them with a group that he won by 12 or 14.

JEREMY BIRD: I have a question. So 30 million people voted early. You can ask people in polling where they are going to go, but there was data already on 30 million people who had voted. I know, Rich, we had some back-and-forth memos, but take all that aside because we were talking to the media on that. Did you really think that in those early vote numbers that that was reflected? Because those numbers on our end were the most encouraging thing we had to show that the electorate was going to look more like 2008. I'm just wondering, did you think maybe that was just too small of a piece or still in some states it wasn't enough?

RICH BEESON: It's what we chalked up to you having the time to do that, being able to build that infrastructure and do that. But in a very small space of Election Day, that was going to be a little bit different story. We looked at our Election Day numbers in Florida, Ohio, Colorado, I mean, the margins were there. So yeah, we were always polling the people who had already voted, knew what we would go into Election Day with, what the deficit would be.

• • • AN OCTOBER SURPRISE? HURRICANE SANDY • • •

STUART STEVENS: One other thing. We hadn't talked about it this morning but the impact of the storm.

GLORIA BORGER: Sandy. [12]

STUART STEVENS: Every race that I've ever been involved in where we beat an incumbent, we always controlled the dialogue at the end of the race. You had to put an incumbent under pressure at the end of a race. It's like an NBA game in the last minute. And we saw ourselves in a position, like an NBA game, there at the end, where we could win. I think the impact of the storm was we lost control of the race and the ability to control the race. The ball went out of our hands. We didn't have any big sweeping rallies. We were just sitting in our hotel rooms watching the television.

NEIL NEWHOUSE: Well, you know, I think that the storm did for Obama kind of what the debate did for us. It showed Mitt, in our case, in a different light, and the storm reminded voters of Obama the president that they kind of liked.

DAVID AXELROD: There is no doubt the storm sort of froze the race in the sense that coverage was dominated by the storm. You turn on the news and, instead of the election, you saw the storm. But I think I also would say that we didn't perceive a big change in the numbers. It simply froze the race in the position where we were. So I don't think the storm was determinative, but it was certainly helpful in a sense that it froze the race in an advantageous position for us. But we had banked a lot of vote early as well, and that was good.

I just wanted to say that this is a big, brawling, messy process sometimes and maddening sometimes, but I think every single person on both sides of the table—Beth and I were talking about this—appreciate the fact that it is an enormous privilege to be in a position to compete for the presidency and to work for someone that we care about, our respective candidates. So I just want to say, on behalf of the Obama team, that we respect you guys as opponents, and we respect you also as colleagues in this great pursuit. We should never lose sight of the fact that, no matter how hard we compete, that we all are ultimately lucky for living in a country where we can have that competition and where all of us can have an opportunity to participate in it. So I just want to tip my hat to our colleagues across the table. [*applause*]

TREY GRAYSON: I want to thank everybody for coming and echo what David said. For the journalists and the folks who work these campaigns,

---

12. Hurricane Sandy hit the East Coast during the week before Election Day.

Beth Myers and David Axelrod talk about the privilege of working on a presidential campaign.

you're the inspiration for the students that we're hoping will encourage them to follow in your footsteps. It is why this country is a great place to live. So thanks to all, whatever role you play. It does seem fitting that an election that was marred by storms and hurricanes ends in a conversation with a citywide power outage. We're worried that at some point the generator is going to run out of fuel, so we're cutting this conference off early to get everybody out safely. So thank you to everybody. Thank you to Gloria and Ron. Thank you to our moderators and everybody for putting this together.

2012 CAMPAIGN TIMELINE

••• 2010 •••

January 22	Governor Mitt Romney wins New Hampshire Straw Poll.
October 1	Rahm Emanuel announces that he will resign as White House chief of staff.
November 2	2010 midterm election—Republicans pick up sixty-three House seats, six Senate seats, and six governors.
November 4	New Jersey Governor Christie says nothing "short of suicide" will stop questions about him running.
November 17	Governor Sarah Palin confirms she is talking to her family about running for president.

••• 2011 •••

January 5	Robert Gibbs announces he will step down as White House press secretary the following month to become an outside advisor to the administration.
January 12	Herman Cain forms exploratory committee.
January 28	Rep. Mike Pence announces he won't run for president.

Dan Balz and Harvard student Sam Adams created a timeline of key events of the cycle.

January 28	David Axelrod leaves his post as White House senior adviser in order to focus on running the reelection strategy.
February 3	Rep. Paul Ryan announces Republican budget with $35 billion in cuts.
February 10	Donald Trump attends CPAC.
February 12	Congressman Ron Paul wins CPAC Straw Poll.
February 22	South Dakota Senator Thune declines to run.
February 24	U.S. Justice Department announces it won't enforce the Defense of Marriage Act.
March 3	Congressman Newt Gingrich forms informal exploratory committee.
March 3	Buddy Roemer forms exploratory committee.
March 21	Tim Pawlenty announces exploratory committee.
March 24	Congresswoman Michele Bachmann expected to form a presidential exploratory committee.

March 28	Obama delivers foreign policy address responding to critics on Libya intervention.
April 4	Obama files papers with FEC and announces reelection campaign.
April 5	Congresswoman Debbie Wasserman Schultz named new DNC chairwoman.
April 5	Republicans hold Wisconsin Supreme Court seat in high-profile election.
April 7	House passes GOP short-term government funding extension; Obama pledges veto.
April 8	Deal to avoid government shutdown reached; one-week extension passes both houses.
April 11	Romney announces exploratory committee.
April 13	Rick Santorum forms exploratory committee.
April 13	Obama lays out his plan to cut the national debt by $4 trillion over twelve years.
April 14	Haley Barbour goes to New Hampshire for the first time.
April 21	Gary Johnson announces he will run for president.
April 25	Haley Barbour announces he won't run for president.
April 26	Congressman Ron Paul forms exploratory committee.
April 27	White House releases President Obama's long-form birth certificate.
May 1	Obama announces that Osama bin Laden has been killed.
May 3	Governor Jon Huntsman forms H Pac as precursor to presidential run.
May 5	Republican primary debate held in Greenville, South Carolina (Fox).
May 9	Gingrich announces presidential run via Facebook and Twitter.
May 11	Gingrich officially announces presidential run on Fox News.
May 12	Romney gives speech on health care, saying solutions should be tried at state level.

May 13	Ron Paul officially announces presidential run on *Good Morning America*.
May 14	Mike Huckabee announces he won't run for president.
May 16	Romney announces $10.25 million raised in connection with Vegas event.
May 16	Donald Trump announces he won't seek the Republican nomination for president.
May 17	Gingrich reported to have line of credit at Tiffany's of up to $500,000.
May 19	Palin says she has "fire in my belly" to run for president.
May 21	Cain officially announces for president.
May 22	Pawlenty announces for president in a web video.
May 22	Indiana Gov. Mitch Daniels announces he won't run for president.
May 22	Gingrich explains Tiffany's line of credit, saying he's not in debt.
May 23	Pawlenty announces candidacy in Iowa.
May 24	Governor Rick Perry says he is thinking about running.
May 24	Democrat Kathy Hochul wins special election in conservative upstate New York district.
May 29	Palin launches nationwide bus tour at Rolling Thunder.
May 31	Christie criticized for taking helicopter to son's baseball game.
May 31	Palin dines with Donald Trump in New York City.
June 2	Romney officially announces candidacy.
June 6	Santorum officially announces candidacy.
June 9	Gingrich campaign's senior staff members quit.
June 9	Romney announces he will skip Iowa's Ames Straw Poll.
June 10	Palin's e-mails from her time as governor are released.

June 13	Republican primary debate in Manchester, New Hampshire (CNN/Union Leader/WMUR)
June 13	Bachmann announces she will run at CNN New Hampshire debate.
June 16	Pawlenty acknowledges mistake in not attacking Romney on health care at debate.
June 16	Romney jokes that he is "also unemployed."
June 16	Republican Leadership Conference begins in New Orleans.
June 17	White House communications director, Dan Pfeiffer, gets a chilly reception at Netroots Nation.
June 18	Perry speaks at Republican Leadership Conference.
June 18	Paul wins Republican Leadership Conference Straw Poll.
June 21	Huntsman officially announces his candidacy.
June 21	Huntsman rollout is criticized as campaign misspells candidate's name on press passes and stage set up poorly.
June 21	Gingrich discovered to have second line of credit at Tiffany's of up to $1 million.
June 21	Huntsman campaign manager, Susie Wiles, resigns.
June 21	Gingrich campaign staff departures continue with two top fundraisers leaving.
June 22	Obama gives speech on Afghanistan, announcing 33,000 troops to come home by end of 2012.
June 23	Three former Romney advisers launch super PAC to support his presidential bid.
June 24	Crossroads announces $20 million summer ad campaign.
June 24	New York becomes biggest state to pass gay marriage bill.
June 25	First Des Moines Register poll: Romney 23, Bachmann 22, Cain 10, Gingrich 7, Paul 7, Pawlenty 6, Santorum 4, Huntsman 2.
June 25	Palin announces she will attend the Iowa premiere of *The Undefeated*, a feature film about her.

June 26	Chris Wallace asks Michele Bachmann in an interview if she is a "flake."
June 27	Bachmann officially announces her candidacy in her birthplace of Waterloo, Iowa, incorrectly claiming it was the birthplace of John Wayne.
June 27	Former Illinois Governor Rod Blagojevich found guilty on seventeen corruption counts.
June 29	Obama holds a press conference on the debt limit debate.
June 29	Priorities USA, Obama's super PAC, airs Medicare ads.
June 30	White House announces a Twitter town hall.
July 1	Minnesota government shuts down over budget stalemate; Pawlenty seeks to take advantage.
July 5	Pro-Romney super PAC says it raised $12 million in its first fundraising quarter.
July 6	Pawlenty adviser Vin Weber apologizes for saying Bachmann had "sex appeal."
July 6	Romney announces $18.25 million raised in 2Q.
July 6	Gingrich announces $2 million raised in 2Q, with more debt than cash on hand.
July 10	Republican primary debate in Las Vegas, Nev. (Daily Caller/ATR)
July 10	Palin featured in *Newsweek* cover story.
July 12	Ron Paul says he won't run for reelection to House seat.
July 13	Obama team announces $86 million raised—$47 million for OFA, $38 million for DNC through joint committee.
July 14	John McCain compares Bachmann to Senator Obama.
July 14	Palin PAC announces $1.6 million raised in first half of 2011.
July 15	2Q reports filed—Obama $47 million ($38 million OFA), Romney $18.25 million, Pawlenty $4.5 million, Paul $4.5 million, Bachmann $4.2 million, Huntsman

$4.1 million, Cain $2.5 million, Gingrich $2.1 million, Palin PAC $1.6 million, Santorum $582,000.

July 20	Bachmann releases letter from Congressional physician that says her migraines are not a problem.
July 21	Roemer officially announces his candidacy.
July 22	Obama announces he has been "left at the altar" by Boehner on debt limit deal.
July 23	Ames Straw Poll ballot set; Perry and Palin aren't on ballot, but write-in option available.
July 29	Top four Democratic super PACs announce $10 million raised in first six months of 2011.
July 31	Obama announces deal reached on debt limit.
August 5	U.S. credit rating downgraded by S&P from AAA to AA+.
August 6	Perry holds "The Response: A Day of Prayer" in Houston.
August 7	Bachmann featured in unflattering photo on cover of *Newsweek* for article titled "Queen of Rage."
August 9	Democrats take two seats from Republicans in $40 million Wisconsin State Senate recall campaign but fail to reclaim majority.
August 10	Palin announces she will attend Iowa State Fair.
August 10	*Huffington Post* investigation documents how Bachmann sought stimulus funds.
August 11	Republican primary debate in Ames, Iowa (Fox).
August 11	Perry aide confirms he will run.
August 11	Romney at the Iowa State Fair says that "corporations are people."
August 13	Ames Straw Poll—Bachmann 4823, Paul 4671, Pawlenty 2293, Santorum 1657, Cain 1456, Perry 718, Romney 567, Gingrich 385, Huntsman 69.
August 13	Perry officially announces his candidacy.
August 14	Pawlenty drops out on ABC's *This Week*, citing Ames Straw Poll finish.
August 16	Bachmann says that it's Elvis's birthday on the anniversary of his death.

August 17	Bachmann super PAC formed.
August 17	Christie dismisses report that he conducted focus groups for a presidential run.
August 18	Huntsman announces he believes in global warming and evolution.
August 18	Obama leaves for a ten-day Martha's Vineyard vacation amidst Republican criticism for leaving D.C.
August 19	Palin releases Iowa-themed video.
August 21	Karl Rove says he thinks Palin will run for president.
August 22	Paul Ryan announces he won't run for president.
August 23	Palin suggests she won't announce whether she is running until September 3.
August 24	Romney announces he will skip Sen. Jim DeMint's South Carolina candidates' forum.
August 24	Romney aide Eric Fehrnstrom admits to authoring fake Twitter account related to Massachusetts U.S. Senate race.
August 26	Governor George Pataki announces he won't run for president.
August 27	Hurricane Irene hits North Carolina, Virginia, D.C., Maryland, and Delaware; Obama cuts vacation short.
August 30	Romney announces he will attend Tea Party Express rally and DeMint forum.
September 3	Palin addresses Iowa tea party rally.
September 7	Republican primary debate held in Simi Valley, California (Reagan Library/NBC/*POLITICO*).
September 12	Republican primary debate held in Tampa, Florida (CNN/Tea Party Express).
September 14	Perry speaks at Liberty University.
September 22	Republican primary debate in Orlando, Florida (Fox).
September 24	Cain wins Florida Republican Party Straw Poll in Orlando.
October 4	Christie announces he will not run for president.
October 5	Palin announces she will not run for president.
October 11	Republican primary debate held in Hanover, New Hampshire (Washington Post/Bloomberg).

October 18	Republican primary debate held in Las Vegas, Nevada (CNN/Western States Leadership Conference).
October 20	Gaddafi is captured and killed.
October 24	Cain ad featuring his campaign manager leads to fundraising boon.
November 1	Republican candidates' forum held in Pella, Iowa.
November 1	Four women accuse Herman Cain of sexual harassment during his days as head of National Restaurant Association.
November 9	Perry forgets the third federal agency he would eliminate.
November 21	Deficit reduction "supercommittee" announces that it is close to failure.
November 21	Romney admits that as a rebellious teen he once tasted beer and smoked a cigarette.
November 22	Gingrich advocates a "humane" immigration policy in which we only deport those who are new and unrooted in America.
November 27	New Hampshire's Manchester Union Leader endorses Gingrich in the primary.
November 28	A woman comes out and claims to have had a thirteen-year-long affair with Herman Cain; Cain campaign denies allegation.
November 29	Cain tells top aides he is "reassessing" his campaign.
November 29	Perry accepts the endorsement of controversial Arizona sheriff Joe Arpaio in Amherst, New Hampshire.
November 29	Perry encourages those citizens "that will be 21 by Nov. 12" to support him.
November 30	New Hampshire State Senate President Peter Bragdon endorses Romney.
December 1	After Britain withdraws its diplomats to Iran as a result of Iranian dissidents storming its Tehran embassy, Bachmann announces that if elected she would close our embassy in Iran; the U.S. has no embassy in Iran.

December 3	Cain suspends his presidential campaign.
December 6	Romney declines invitation to Trump-moderated debate.
December 7	Former Illinois Governor Rod Blagojevich is sentenced to fourteen years in prison.
December 7	Gingrich announces that, if elected, he will name John Bolton as his secretary of state.
December 10	Republican primary debate held in Iowa (ABC).
December 10	During a heated exchange with Perry during a Republican debate, Romney attempts to bet $10,000 that he didn't support an individual health care mandate.
December 10	Gingrich refers to Palestinians as an "invented people."
December 13	Because he is unwilling to rule out the possibility of running as an Independent, Donald Trump withdraws plans to moderate a GOP debate.
December 17	Des Moines Register endorses Romney in the primary.
December 27	The Virginia GOP announces that only Romney and Paul had collected the required 10,000 signatures to get on the state's primary ballot; Gingrich accuses fraud and compares the announcement to Pearl Harbor, while Romney asserts it is more akin to Lucille Ball at the chocolate factory.
December 28	Iowa State Senator and Bachmann Iowa Chairman Kent Sorenson switches his support to Ron Paul.
December 31	Gingrich, Santorum, Bachmann, and Huntsman join Perry's lawsuit to be included on the Virginia ballot.

••• 2012 •••

January 3	Romney declared winner of the Iowa caucus, beating Santorum by eight votes. Paul: 21 percent; Gingrich: 13 percent; Perry: 10 percent; Bachmann: 5 percent.
January 4	After initially announcing he would semi-suspend his campaign to reevaluate after his fifth-place Iowa

finish, Perry tweets "And the next leg of the marathon is the Palmetto State. . . . Here we come South Carolina!!!" along with a picture of a thumbs-up candidate.

January 4	Bachmann announces she will drop out of the race.
January 7	The five remaining candidates square off in back-to-back debates Saturday night and Sunday morning in New Hampshire.
January 9	White House Chief of Staff William Daley announces he will resign from his post, to be replaced by OMB director Jack Lew.
January 10	Romney wins the New Hampshire primary with 39.3 percent. Paul: 22.9 percent, Huntsman: 16.9 percent, Gingrich: 9.4 percent, Santorum: 9.4 percent
January 12	Republican primary debate held in Des Moines, Iowa (Des Moines Register/PBS/YouTube).
January 15	Huntsman drops out of the race, endorsing Romney.
January 16	First of two Republican South Carolina debates held in Myrtle Beach.
January 17	More than one million signatures are filed to force a recall election of Wisconsin Governor Scott Walker.
January 17	A federal appeals court in Virginia rules against the candidates (Perry, Santorum, Newt, and, irrelevantly, Huntsman) who failed to acquire enough signatures to get on the state's primary ballot.
January 17	After being pushed regarding if/when he would release his tax returns, Romney announces that he pays around the low tax rate of 15 percent, largely as a result of his capital gains income. He also states that he will likely release the documents in April—after the primary season.
January 17	Palin announces that if she could vote in the South Carolina primary, she would vote for Gingrich.
January 18	The Obama administration formally rejects the Keystone XL pipeline project.
January 18	President Obama releases his first ad of the campaign cycle in six states on his record on energy.

January 19	Republican primary debate held in Charleston, South Carolina (CNN/Republicans Leadership Conference).
January 19	Perry, stating that he sees no viable path to the nomination, ends his campaign and endorses Gingrich.
January 19	A *Nightline* interview with Gingrich's second wife, Marianne, is released, along with her allegations that he had pursued an "open marriage" while they were together.
January 19	CNN holds Republican primary debate. Moderator John King's first question is about the open marriage that Gingrich allegedly requested from his second wife. Gingrich responds: "I am appalled that you would begin a presidential debate on a topic like this. The story is false. Every personal friend that I had at that point knows that the story was false. To take an ex-wife and make it two days before the primary a significant question in a presidential campaign is as close to despicable as anything I can imagine."
January 19	ABC News announces that Romney has up to $30 million of money invested in Bain Capital funds located in Cayman Island accounts.
January 19	A recount of the Iowa caucus reveals that Rick Santorum beat Mitt Romney by 34 votes.
January 19	Republican primary debate in South Carolina. Gingrich announces in the opening moments of the debate that he released his 2010 tax returns to the public.
January 21	Gingrich wins South Carolina primary with 40.4 percent. Romney: 27.9 percent, Santorum: 17.0 percent, Paul: 13.0 percent, Cain: 1.0 percent.
January 23	Republican primary debate in Florida.
January 23	Ron Paul's Endorse Liberty super PAC announces it will spend $1.4 million on radio and TV advertising in Florida.
January 24	Romney releases his last two years of tax returns.

January 24	The Romney campaign announces a reward of $1.6 million to anyone who can release Gingrich's Freddie Mac contract.
January 25	President Obama gives his State of the Union address. Indiana Governor Mitch Daniels delivers the rebuttal.
January 25	Gingrich denies any hypocrisy in his infidelities occurring at the same time as the Clinton impeachment process.
January 25	Gingrich elaborates on his plan to establish an American colony on the moon, which could apply for statehood after reaching 13,000 members.
January 26	Second Florida Republican primary debate held in Jacksonville.
January 27	Mike Huckabee objects to a Gingrich ad targeting Romney that quotes him as saying, "If a man's dishonest to get a job, he'll be dishonest on the job," saying the quote was taken out of context.
January 28	Cain endorses Gingrich at a rally in West Palm Beach, Florida.
January 30	Republican primary debate held in Sioux City, Iowa (Fox).
January 31	Romney wins the Florida primary with 46 percent of the vote, acquiring the state's fifty delegates in the winner-take-all contest.
January 31	Fourth quarter fundraising numbers released: Obama raised $40 million (plus $20 million for DNC), Romney $24.3 million, Paul $13.3 million, Gingrich $9.8 million, Perry $2.9 million, Santorum $920,000.
February 2	Donald Trump endorses Romney for president.
February 4	Romney wins Nevada caucuses with 50 percent.
February 7	Santorum wins the three primaries in Minnesota, Missouri, and Colorado.
February 7	A Ninth Circuit court rules that California's Prop. 8, which banned gay marriage, is unconstitutional.
February 7	The Obama administration announces a new rule mandating that all faith-based employers provide free contraception coverage.

February 11	Romney announced winner of Maine caucuses.
February 11	Romney wins the CPAC straw poll with 38 percent of the vote.
February 13	*National Review* calls on Gingrich to drop out of the race in favor of Rick Santorum.
February 13	Obama releases a new budget that increases taxes on the wealthiest Americans in favor of infrastructure investment.
February 15	Michigan Governor Rick Snyder endorses Romney.
February 16	During a congressional hearing on contraception and religious freedom, Rep. Darrell Issa bans a female Georgetown Law student named Sandra Fluke from testifying.
February 17	Obama announces raising $29.1 million in January.
February 17	Casino magnate Sheldon Adelson donates an additional $10 million to Gingrich's super PAC.
February 22	Republican primary debate in Mesa, Arizona.
February 22	Obama offers to cut the top corporate tax rate from 35 percent to 28 percent.
February 26	Romney attends the Daytona 500, and when asked how closely he follows the sport, says he doesn't follow it super closely but has friends who are team owners.
February 28	Romney wins Michigan and Arizona primaries.
March 1	The Senate defeated the Blunt Amendment, which would have allowed employers to refuse to provide coverage for contraception.
March 1	Rush Limbaugh calls Sandra Fluke, the law student who tried to testify in favor of insurance-provided birth control, a "slut."
March 3	Romney wins the Washington State caucuses.
March 3	President Obama calls Sandra Fluke to offer moral support.
March 5	Republican primary debate held in South Carolina (Fox).
March 6	Super Tuesday: Romney wins Ohio, Virginia, Vermont, Massachusetts, Idaho, Alaska; Santorum

	wins Tennessee, Oklahoma, North Dakota; Gingrich wins Georgia.
March 7	Romney campaign announces that it raised $11.5 million during the month of February.
March 10	Santorum wins the Kansas caucus.
March 13	Santorum wins the Mississippi and Alabama primaries; Romney wins Hawaii caucus.
March 18	Romney wins Puerto Rico.
March 20	Romney wins the Illinois primary.
March 23	President Obama makes comments about the killing of Trayvon Martin: "When I think about this boy, I think about my own kids. And I think every parent in America should be able to understand why it is absolutely imperative that we investigate every aspect of this and that everybody pull together. But my main message is to the parents of Trayvon Martin. You know, if I had a son, he'd look like Trayvon."
March 23	Gingrich asserts that Obama's comments on the Trayvon Martin case are "disgraceful" due to his perceived racial bias in the remarks.
March 24	Santorum wins the Louisiana primary.
March 28	Gingrich announces a large scale-down of his day-to-day campaigning schedule and says he will lay off a third of his staff, instead orienting toward a "big-choice convention" strategy.
March 29	The House approves the Ryan budget on a 235 to 193 vote that fell along party lines.
April 3	Romney wins Maryland, D.C., and Wisconsin primaries.
April 10	Rick Santorum drops out of the presidential race, making the announcement that he is suspending his campaign in Gettysburg, Pennsylvania.
April 13	Democratic operative Hilary Rosen sparks a controversy when she suggests that Ann Romney is not a valid spokesperson for women because she "never worked a day in her life."
April 24	Romney wins Connecticut, Delaware, New York, Pennsylvania, and Rhode Island primaries.

May 1	Gingrich releases a video on his website "thanking his supporters," setting the stage for a campaign suspension.
May 2	Gingrich announces in Arlington, Virginia, that he is suspending his campaign.
May 5	Vice President Biden states on *Meet the Press* that he is "absolutely comfortable" with the idea of gay marriage.
May 7	Santorum endorses Romney in the thirteenth paragraph of a late-night campaign e-mail, after meeting with Romney in Pittsburgh a few days before.
May 8	Romney wins the Indiana, North Carolina, and West Virginia primaries.
May 9	President Obama announces that his views on gay marriage have evolved to the point that he "just concluded that for me personally it is important for me to go ahead and affirm that I think same-sex couples should be able to get married."
May 14	Paul announces that he will not be spending any more resources in states that have not yet voted, but he will retain his delegates and keep trying to amass more.
May 15	Romney wins Nebraska and Oregon primaries.
May 30	By winning the Texas primary, Romney secures the 1,144 delegates necessary to win the party's nomination on the first ballot.
June 6	Wisconsin Governor Scott Walker defeats a recall initiative to stay in office.
June 7	Romney outraises Obama in the month of May, the first time this has happened; Romney acquired $76.8 million to Obama's $60 million.
June 8	President Obama, while speaking on the state of the economy in a press conference, says that "the private sector is doing fine" and that the real problem lies within state and local government.
June 17	Obama administration announces that it will stop the deportation of illegal immigrants brought to the country as children.

June 25	The Supreme Court strikes down much of Arizona immigration law SB 1070 and reaffirms its *Citizens United* decision by striking down an old Montana law that limits campaign contributions.
June 28	The Supreme Court issues a ruling on Obamacare, allowing the individual mandate to stand under Congress's constitutional taxation power.
July 8	Obama deputy campaign manager, Stephanie Cutter, says that since Romney claims to have left Bain in 1999 but was still in charge on SEC papers until 2002, Romney either lied to the SEC or to the American people.
July 9	President Obama announced that he will seek to extend Bush tax cuts only for those making less than $250,000.
July 11	Marco Rubio slams Obama for his comments that Venezuela dictator Hugo Chavez does not pose a serious threat to national security.
July 11	American Crossroads releases a new ad campaign trying to reframe the "War on Women" as one waged by Obama through the lack of relative increases in economic recovery among women.
July 13	Romney defends his Bain tenure narrative in a CNN interview: "I was the owner of the entity that was filing this information, but I had no role whatsoever in the management of Bain Capital after 1999. I left in February of 1999. There's nothing wrong with being associated with Bain Capital, of course."
July 19	A gunman kills 12 and injured dozens more at a midnight screening of *The Dark Knight Rises* in Aurora, Colorado. Obama travels the next morning to Aurora, and both campaigns suspend their TV advertising in the state.
July 30	The DNC announces that it will include gay marriage as a plank in the official party platform for the first time.
August 1	Romney returns from a three-country foreign trip. In London, Romney questioned the city's readiness to host the Olympics right on the eve of the opening

ceremonies; in Israel, he suggested that cultural differences could explain the economic disparity between the Israelis and Palestinians and stated that as president he would relocate the U.S. embassy to Jerusalem should Israel ask; in Poland, an aide told reporters to "kiss his ass" for asking questions during a visit.

August 1   Sen. Reid and Speaker Boehner agree to a six-month extension on government funding, postponing any action to after the election.

August 2   Sen. Reid asserts in an interview that he had a credible source who claimed that Romney didn't pay any taxes for a full ten years. RNC Chair Reince Priebus lashes back, calling Reid a "dirty liar."

August 5   Romney raised $101.3 million in the month of July.

August 11   Rep. Paul Ryan is announced as Romney's vice presidential candidate, at a campaign event in Norfolk, Virginia.

August 13   Paul Ryan announces that he will release only two years of tax returns.

August 14   Vice President Biden tells a largely black audience in southern Virginia that, as a result of Romney/Ryan's re-deregulation of the financial industry, "they're going to put y'all back in chains." The Romney campaign accused Obama of running a "campaign of hate." Biden later clarified that he meant to say "unshackled" rather than "unchained."

August 19   GOP nominee for Missouri Senate seat Rep. Todd Akin says in an interview that in the event of a "legitimate rape," a woman rarely gets impregnated.

August 24   Hurricane Isaac threatens Tampa in advance of the RNC convention, leading organizers to cancel the first day of programming.

August 27   Republican National Convention begins in Tampa, Florida.

August 28   Ann Romney speaks at the convention.

August 29   Supporters of Rep. Ron Paul walk out of the convention floor after the former candidate was

	denied a speaking slot when he refused to endorse Romney.
August 29	Vice presidential nominee Paul Ryan speaks at the convention.
August 30	Romney delivers his acceptance speech at the convention.
August 30	Clint Eastwood delivers a speech at the RNC in which he conducts a one-sided argument with a chair that presumably holds an invisible Obama.
September 3	Democratic National Convention begins in Charlotte, North Carolina.
September 4	San Antonio Mayor Julian Castro gives the keynote address at the convention. First Lady Michelle Obama speaks.
September 5	The Obama campaign moves the president's acceptance speech from the Bank of America stadium into the Time Warner Cable arena, citing weather concerns. Critics allege that the downsizing showed shrinking enthusiasm for Obama.
September 5	Following criticism, the DNC platform is changed to include God and affirm Jerusalem as the capital of Israel.
September 5	President Bill Clinton speaks at the convention.
September 6	Obama delivers his acceptance speech at the DNC.
September 12	The U.S. ambassador to Libya, Christopher Stevens, is murdered in an attack on the embassy in Benghazi.
September 15	A judge in Wisconsin strikes down Gov. Scott Walker's law that bans collective bargaining rights.
September 17	Chief Romney strategist Stuart Stevens announces that the campaign will take a strategic pivot, reframing the campaign as "status quo vs. change" as opposed to merely a referendum on the Obama years.
September 18	A video emerges of Romney speaking at a private fundraiser for large donors in which he declares 47 percent of Americans to be dependent on public support and therefore unwilling to vote for him.

September 19   A video is leaked of President Obama's comments made in 1998 about the "redistribution" of wealth in America.

September 21   Romney's campaign releases his 2011 tax returns.

September 27   George Soros agrees to contribute $1 million to Priorities USA Action, an Obama super PAC. Priorities reports $10.1 million in August fundraising, surpassing for the first time Romney's Restore Our Future.

October 2   American Crossroads releases a $16 million one-week ad buy in Senate and presidential contests in Colorado, Florida, Iowa, North Carolina, New Hampshire, Nevada, Ohio, and Virginia.

October 3   First presidential debate held in Denver, Colorado; moderated by Jim Lehrer.

October 6   Obama campaign raises $181 million in September.

October 11   Vice presidential debate held; moderated by Martha Raddatz.

October 17   Second presidential debate with town-hall format held; moderated by Candy Crowley.

October 23   Third and final presidential debate held; on foreign policy and moderated by Bob Schieffer.

October 23   Indiana Senate candidate Richard Mourdock, when asked about abortion in the case of rape or incest, says: "I think even when life begins in that horrible situation of rape, that's something God intended to happen."

October 28   Hurricane Sandy hits the Eastern Seaboard.

November 1   New York City Mayor Michael Bloomberg endorses Obama on the basis of his position on global climate change, on which he blames the hurricane that flooded much of his city.

November 2   Report released that economy added 171,000 jobs in October, exceeding predictions of 125,000, despite the unemployment rate increasing to 7.9 percent

November 6   President Obama wins reelection.

INDEX

Abramson, Jill, 2
Adams, Sam, 236
Adelson, Sheldon, 115, 155, 157, 172, 173
ads. *See* advertising
advertising (ads): impact of, 195–196;
    timing of, 191–197; wars, 131–136,
    149. *See also* super PACs; *specific ads*
advertising strategy: Axelrod on, 135; Goff
    on, 134; Margolis on, 132, 133, 134;
    Obama campaign strategy and,
    131–136; Simas on, 136
Amash, Justin, 10
American Crossroads, 143, 152
Americans Elect, 30n21
Anzalone, John, 136
Audacity to Win (Plouffe), 13
Axelrod, David, 45, 46, 116, 148, 187, 192,
    233; on ad impacts, 195, 196; on ads
    and timing, 193; on advertising
    strategy, 135; on Bain attacks, 115,
    117; Brownstein to, 199, 211; on
    cancer ad, 119; on Democratic
    Convention, 124, 126, 188, 189, 190;
    on Denver debate, 214, 215, 216, 217,
    218; on foreign policy debate, 225; on
    47 percent video, 200; on general
    elections, 197; on Hispanic voters, 200;
    on Huntsman, 115; on Hurricane
    Sandy, 232; Karl to, 111; on impact of conventions,
    187; Karl to, 111; on Obama campaign
    defining, 111, 112; on Obama

campaign strategy, 110; on polling,
    137, 139; on potential opponents, 114;
    on presidential debate goals, 210, 211,
    212; on Republican Convention, 125,
    126, 187; on Republican Party, 110;
    Romano to, 111; on Romney
    campaign, 111, 121; to Romney
    campaign, 232; on Town Hall debate,
    222, 223; on VEEP selection, 121; on
    vice presidential debate, 221, 222

Bachmann, Michele, 9, 24, 26n19, 82n11;
    at Black Hawk County Republican
    Party's Lincoln Day dinner, 24n18; as
    female candidate, 80–82; health
    problems, 80–82; Pawlenty and, 59, 60
Bachmann campaign: in Iowa, 7, 26, 80;
    Romney and, 27; Santorum campaign
    and, 33; strategies early in, 24–27. *See
    also* Nahigian, Keith; *specific team
    members*
Bain attacks (Bain Capital), 98n18, 99,
    149, 151–152; Axelrod on, 115, 117;
    Burton on, 152; Cutter on, 116;
    Gingrich campaign and, 97, 98, 98–99;
    Haley on, 98, 99; Messina on, 117;
    Obama campaign and, 115–118; Paul
    and, 151; Perry and, 99; Republican
    Party and, 117; research and, 117–118;
    Ryan, N., on, 151; Santorum and, 151